81516

ORGANIZING FOR PEACE

A ~~Cass Canfield~~ BOOK

ORGANIZING FOR PEACE

*A Personal History of the Founding
of the United Nations*

CLARK M. EICHELBERGER

1817

HARPER & ROW, PUBLISHERS

NEW YORK, HAGERSTOWN, SAN FRANCISCO
LONDON

FIRST EDITION

Designed by Sidney Feinberg

Library of Congress Cataloging in Publication Data

Eichelberger, Clark Mell, date
   Organizing for peace.
   (A Cass Canfield book)
   Includes index.
   1. United Nations. I. Title.
JX1977.E38 1977   341.23   76–5127
ISBN 0–06–011114–3

77 78 79 80 10 9 8 7 6 5 4 3 2 1

To Rose

Contents

vii

Foreword

Ever since a handful of discontented colonists improvised the Committees of Correspondence, Americans have sought through collective effort to mobilize opinion in support of a wide variety of public policies and actions. Today—after two centuries—what are awkwardly known as "Non-Governmental Organizations" have become an integral part of the complex machinery of American democracy.

Important as are such groups in the formulation of United States domestic policy, they have a special significance in shaping our relations with other nations. Domestic politics largely reflect the play and interplay of well-defined economic and political interests but our foreign political policies normally lack a special interest constituency.

There are, of course, exceptions. United States policy toward the Middle East responds to the well-orchestrated pressures of citizens passionately dedicated to Israel, while Greek-American organizations imprint their views on our relations with Turkey and Cyprus. Lately, an insistence on a somewhat factitious ethnicity threatens to distort and circumscribe United States policy toward southern Africa.

Ethnic influences are, however, narrowly aimed at a particular country or countries. Only rarely is there spontaneous

American support for United States initiatives that are world-wide rather than regional in focus. It is here that Non-Governmental Organizations play a unique role. Our country—and the world—have greatly profited from the devoted efforts of a handful of citizens who have tried untiringly to spread the word that our nation dare not refuse an active involvement in world affairs.

Clark Eichelberger has been in the first rank of these Americans. He is, in a sense, the Dean of the corps. Influenced by his experience as a soldier in the First World War, he has ever since been a fervent advocate of the principle that national rivalries must be subordinated to an overriding international discipline. Eichelberger saw the First World War as resulting largely from the failure of the European nations to apply lessons learned from cooperation in the nineteenth century. What was essential was to extend the Concert of Europe through an organization not confined merely to a half-dozen powers committed to the defense of the dynastic principle but through an institution that would include all nations—an institution dedicated to the maintenance of world peace in accordance with an agreed body of principles.

With this as his central objective, Eichelberger quite naturally committed himself to the movement to support and establish the League of Nations. Working outside official circles he soon became a friend and counselor not merely of pro-League Americans but of the Europeans who emerged as international civil servants of the new League bureaucracy.

For Eichelberger the recalcitrance of a willful clique of Senate leaders in rejecting the League covenant was a tragedy of the first magnitude. He saw—and saw quite rightly—that America's surly refusal to participate in the effort to create a rational international system would, sooner or later, ease the way toward another holocaust. He seems to have perceived what many others ignored—that the European powers had never effectively made peace after 1918. With the persistence of old rivalries and parochial ambitions and without the strong hand of an ascendant United States to help enforce an essential world discipline, all they had achieved was a respite after exhaustion only to be followed in two decades by the second phase of what Dean Acheson used to call the "European Civil War."

It is one of the tragic wonders of history that American politicians of the twenties believed—because they wanted to believe —that America could sit comfortably on its mountain while the tigers fought, smugly admonishing each side to repeal the law of tooth and fang. Yet, fortunately, such stupidity was not unanimous. Many private citizens, including Clark Eichelberger, were aware of the forces and counterforces loose in the world. And it was with growing desperation that they watched the repeated efforts of the members of the League of Nations, denied help from America, to resolve the petty quarrels that national leaders seemed unable to contain.

Eichelberger detected with increasing alarm the accumulating portents of a gathering storm as variant forms of fascism appeared both in the Far East and West. As the world's economic structure collapsed into chaos, evil took to the road all over the world. Japan invaded Manchuria in 1931; Mussolini attacked Ethiopia in 1935; the Spanish Civil War broke out in 1936; Japan invaded China proper in 1937; Hitler seized Austria and the Sudetenland in 1938. Meanwhile America watched with a kind of detached fascination.

Aware as he had long been that our own values could never survive if the other major nations of the world fell victim to tyranny, Clark Eichelberger automatically undertook to try to alert his fellow citizens to the realities of the world scene. As a driving force in such organizations as the Committee to Defend America by Aiding the Allies (the William Allen White Committee) he sought to persuade Americans of the urgent need to help the Western democracies halt the onrush of Hitler's armies while there was still time.

Americans under fifty who read this book today will no doubt detect an unreal quality in the struggle between the so-called America Firsters and the interventionists. In view of what later occurred it seems incredible that otherwise rational Americans could have regarded themselves as unconcerned spectators while Hitler imposed his obscenities on the whole face of the West.

Yet, as a young lawyer in Chicago—the heartland of American isolationism—I felt far from confident that America would face the reality of its own predicament before it was too late for our force and power to redress the European balance. Though I recall that period of frustration and uncertainty as a protracted nightmare, it is an episode overlooked or forgotten by most Americans. Clark Eichelberger has done our country a service by recreating in this book the intensity of the argument that marked those dramatic days. What few remember is that the outcome was never really clear until one of those curious aberrations of history happened—those spectacular interventions of the unexpected that our ancestors used to hail as miracles—when Hitler, out of pettish arrogance and incredible stupidity, resolved America's dilemma by declaring war on us immediately after Pearl Harbor. Without that unifying act, our country would almost certainly have wasted priceless energy in a divisive debate, instead of concentrating first on defeating the Nazis in Europe, then turning our energies against Japan.

With America deeply involved in a struggle which, in Eichelberger's view, it was bound to win, he quite naturally concentrated his energies on assuring that history did not ignorantly repeat itself. Having, by the blindness of its leaders, renounced any role in the building of an international structure after the First World War, America dared not, as Eichelberger saw it, walk blindly into the same cul-de-sac a second time. Applying his knowledge of the League experience, he thus undertook to assist in the preparatory work to launch a new effort at international peace-keeping. This time the country's leaders did not fail him.

Obviously, few in the 1930s or even the early 1940s could have foreseen the advent of the Cold War and the fundamental conflict between two competing systems that so seriously hobbled the work of the United Nations Security Council. Yet, in spite of this major constraint, the UN has been able, with help and support mobilized by such earnest citizens as Clark Eichelberger, to carry through a number of essential tasks, not the least of which has been to assist roughly a third of the world's population to make the perilous passage from colonial dependence to some form of juridical independence. It has placed the mark of legitimacy on the new nations and given the new leaders a place in the sun they could otherwise never have found.

It has been a long road from the fragmented world of the 1920s to our present-day system under which the key nation-states practice among themselves a modest measure of cooperation. It is a far from perfect world structure yet, with all its imperfections, this earth would be more dangerous had Clark Eichelberger and similarly dedicated Americans not given tireless support to collective efforts to improve international understanding. This book should be read then not merely as a memoir but as documentation of the efficacy of that unique type of American institution: the Non-Governmental Organization. Such organizations have now been highly developed with sophisticated techniques to improve their effectiveness. In today's troubled world they play an essential role in providing a constituency for foreign policies not focused merely on short-term national advantages but on a more spacious future.

—GEORGE BALL

ORGANIZING FOR PEACE

1

The United States Rejects the League of Nations

President Woodrow Wilson was received with great acclaim on his arrival in Europe to participate in writing the Treaty of Versailles in December 1918. No foreign statesman was ever received as Wilson was throughout all of Europe, said Lord Robert Cecil, "not only for himself but because he embodied the passionate aspiration of the world for peace."[1] Yet a year and a half later, the League of Nations Covenant was finally rejected by the United States Senate.

The world was to undergo twenty-five years of doubt and turmoil, minor wars, and a world war before it again could try to realize the ideas of the League of Nations Covenant, in the form of the United Nations Charter. However, during those twenty-five years, constant and untiring work was being done on behalf of American participation in a world organization. Indeed, United States involvement in the United Nations can be traced to those early efforts, in which I participated.

My purpose in this book is to follow the development of American attitudes and policies from the isolationism that kept us out of the League of Nations in 1920 to our entrance into the

1. Robert Cecil, *The Way of Peace* (London: P. Allen & Co., Ltd., 1928), p. 235.

United Nations in 1945. This is not intended to be an autobiography, but rather a presentation of the events of this crucial period through the eyes of one who took part.

I have been asked frequently how my interest in the League of Nations arose. I can give no answer, for it seems to me now that I always believed in the idea. If I write from the standpoint of the Midwest, it is because my origin is there. I was born in Freeport, Illinois, and raised in the tradition of the Lincoln-Douglas debates. I was a student at Northwestern University and left there to enlist in the army during the First World War.

While I was in the army in France, my conviction grew that only a League of Nations capable of preventing wars was worthy of all the sacrifices of the war. After the armistice, newspapers reached our company telling that Woodrow Wilson and the other members of the United States delegation were at the Versailles Conference. News was carried about the fourteen points, and about the opposition to Wilson's program. The information was thin—it was unfortunate that our government did not get out more about what was going on and what Wilson planned. Nevertheless, many of us were inspired to believe that there would be a League of Nations, and that on it the peace of the world would depend. A few of us would sit around the mess hall in the evening and talk about the hope of a League of Nations. Sometimes I was called upon to lead the discussion.

Thus, my belief in the League of Nations was a conviction with me in the army; it was a conviction with me during the bitter turmoil when the League was defeated in the Senate; it was a conviction with me when I went to Geneva in 1923 to study the League and work for the League of Nations Non-Partisan Association afterwards.

How could the tragedy of 1920—the rejection of the League by the U.S. Senate—have occurred? The answer to that question lies in the confusion in public opinion and the political bitterness in the United States during the two years 1919 to 1920. Many of the soldiers of the American Expeditionary Force came back from Europe with a "never again" attitude. Many of the civilian population were equally disillusioned. Their reasons went back to their roots in American soil.

In that crucial year of 1919 I was on a slow troopship carrying soldiers home from France. An army recruiting officer appeared before the members of our company to tell us of the benefits of reenlisting. The attitude of my comrades was frank, negative, and profane. They had seen enough of the Old World, and they never wanted to see it again. Although many of them were from the East—in the United States in 1919 there were millions of people who had never been west of the Alleghenies —their longing for the United States was often expressed in the language of the pioneer. Their wish was to lose themselves in the prairies and the mountains of the West, to "go back" to a frontier that was fast vanishing. Subconsciously they thought in terms of the early pioneers as later described by the "sage of Emporia" William Allen White, editor of the Emporia (Kansas) *Gazette:*

They were free men, these American westerners, free bodies, free spirits. No king could tax them. They did not have to bear arms for any tyrant. They could worship God as they pleased. They could establish their own form of government without let or hindrance. They had the right of trial by jury and carried with them the writ of habeas corpus. . . . These western pioneers of the eighteenth and nineteenth centuries, the children of the Colonialists . . . fought not only for freedom —they had that—but for security. The civilization which the pioneers of the nineteenth century set up out beyond the Alleghenies on across the land was unique. . . . There in this West of ours, for the first time on earth, a free people worked at their own political and social salvation.[2]

2. William Allen White, *The Changing West* (New York: The Macmillan Company, 1939), pp. 7–8.

These qualities made the frontiersmen—and, by extension, a good many who were not pioneers—proud and gave them an attitude of moral superiority. Thus, even as early as 1821, a Spanish diplomat had lashed out at the United States for acting as though it were "superior to the rest of mankind." Its leaders, he said, regarded their country as "the only establishment on earth founded on a grand and solid basis" and "the only country embellished with wisdom." Their arrogance sprang from the feeling of freedom and opportunity of the pioneer combined with a feeling of social and cultural inferiority.

By the time I returned from Europe, the political fight was on as to whether or not the Senate should ratify the Versailles Treaty, including the League of Nations Covenant. President Wilson's illness prevented him from leading the struggle. One wonders what the result might have been if the President could have campaigned for the League of Nations in a series of "fireside chats"—but there was no radio. And there was no air conditioning. In that very hot weather of late summer 1919 the failing President embarked on a special train, to promote the League throughout the western part of the country. It was an arduous trip, and he became seriously ill. Nothing is more pathetic than the description of the President's train, with blinds drawn, returning to Washington, D.C.

The Senate voted twice on the League of Nations Covenant in 1919, the first time with reservations attached, the second time without. One could say that it was defeated by its supporters. Massachusetts Senator Henry Cabot Lodge, Republican floor leader and chairman of the Senate Foreign Relations Committee, and his followers were opposed to ratification of the Treaty with the Covenant unless some fifteen reservations or amendments were attached to it. The President, however, could see no compromise. When the first vote was about to be taken, on November 17, Senator Gilbert Hitchcock of Nebraska, the Democratic minority leader, went to the White House to ask the stricken President what should be done. The

President replied that there could be no amendments, no reservations. Anything but complete acceptance would constitute nullification. Hitchcock returned to the Senate and delivered the President's message.

Gene Smith says in *When the Cheering Stopped,* "the question of whether the Senate should approve the Treaty with the Lodge reservations was put to a vote. It was defeated by those men who complied with the President's instructions. Then the Senate voted on the Treaty as it was brought back from Paris. It was defeated by Senator Lodge's followers."[3]

Paradoxically there is overwhelming evidence that the American people favored entrance of the United States into the League of Nations in 1919. Some of the League's opponents recognized this. When Senator Lodge asked Senator James E. Watson of Indiana to lead in organizing the Senate against the League, Watson replied, "Senator, I don't see how we are ever going to defeat this proposition. It appears to me that eighty per cent of the people are for it. Fully that percentage of the preachers are right now advocating it, churches are very largely favoring it, all the people who have been burdened and oppressed by this awful tragedy of war and who imagine this opens a way to world peace, are for it, and I don't see how it is possible to defeat it." Lodge retorted, ". . . I do not propose to try to beat it by direct frontal attack, but by the indirect method of reservations."[4]

In March 1920 the Treaty with the Lodge reservations was again presented to the Senate. Wilson again urged that Democrats vote against it. On March 19, the Senate voted 57–37 in favor of ratification, failing by only 6 votes to obtain the necessary two-thirds majority. It was the end.

Frank Walters, former Deputy Secretary-General of the

3. Gene Smith, *When the Cheering Stopped* (New York: William Morrow and Co., 1964), p. 120.

4. James E. Watson, *As I Knew Them* (Indianapolis, Ind.: Bobbs-Merrill Co., 1936), p. 190.

League of Nations, describes the defeat of the League in the following words:

It was a bitter and dramatic story; perhaps no historical event of modern times contains more of the tragic grandeur of Aeschylean drama.[5]

For those who had hailed Wilson in Europe, the final rejection of the Covenant was a shattering experience. The reservations had serious drawbacks which, interpreted literally, could scarcely have been accepted by the other nations. But interpreted in good spirit they might have been palatable. One may speculate whether, with the United States in, the League of Nations might not have been able to tie the world together, and whether the tragedy of the Second World War might not then have been avoided.

The period between the final rejection of the Covenant on March 19, 1920, and the presidential election in November 1920 was a most confusing one politically. Thirty-one prominent Republicans, led by Nicholas Murray Butler, Charles Evans Hughes, Elihu Root, and others, issued a manifesto to the effect that a vote for Harding and Coolidge was the surest way to get the United States into a "league to preserve peace." However, there seems to have been some political confusion and hypocrisy in this statement. For there is no evidence that Harding would have been concerned with a "league to preserve peace," nor is there evidence that the European nations would have been willing to scrap the League of Nations, to which they were committed, for a new American initiative.

In November 1920 Warren G. Harding and Calvin Coolidge were elected President and Vice President of the United States by a considerable majority over James Cox and Franklin D. Roosevelt. In a post-election statement in Boston, Vice President-elect Coolidge denied that the League of Nations had been a major issue in the campaign:

5. Frank P. Walters. *A History of the League of Nations*, Vol. I (New York: Oxford University Press, 1952), p. 69.

I doubt if any particular mandate was given at the last election on the question of the League of Nations and if that was the preponderant issue. In the South, where there was decided opposition to the League, they voted the Democratic ticket. And as far as the League of Nations was concerned in the North, the vote was with equal and even greater preponderance in favor of the Republican ticket. Of course, many men voted thus who were in favor of the League. With them it became simply a question of supporting the Republican or the Democratic Party. So you can't say that there was a preponderance of votes against the League of Nations.[6]

Nevertheless, the myth soon developed that the overwhelming vote that elected Harding and Coolidge had been a "solemn referendum" of the American people against the League of Nations.

If the American public seemed to be in favor of this country joining the League of Nations in 1919 and 1920, why did isolationism arise not long after? I suppose, in part, the answer is simply that the original enthusiastic support for the League had withered with the passage of time. And, as the uncertainties of the postwar world became more evident, with increasing unemployment, some began to doubt that the possible benefits of joining the League were worth the risks of becoming "entangled." Indifference, then, left the field to the isolationists, whose propaganda could not help but affect public opinion.

With my Midwest background, I had a chance to see more intimately the many faces of isolationism in the Midwest, which, while somewhat distinctive, were probably not too different from those found in other parts of the country.

There were, of course, those embittered isolationists who hated almost everything European. Their voice was clearly reflected in the Chicago *Tribune,* the most influential newspaper in the Midwest at the time, owned and edited by Colonel Robert R. McCormick. It was well edited and well made up, but it

6. Statement of November 23, 1920, quoted in *The New York Times,* December 10, 1923.

was a source of poison as far as international relations were concerned, and for many other liberal causes as well. In addition, the nation-wide chain of Hearst newspapers was violently opposed to the League. In the Midwest, these were balanced in excellence but unfortunately not in influence by the Chicago *Daily News*, which at one time was said to have as fine a group of foreign correspondents as any American newspaper. The dean of its staff abroad was Paul Scott Mowrer, and its Paris office was a mecca for many serious-minded visitors.

Another face of isolationism might be said to be the attitude of many people who had come from the Old World, and who did not want to see their new country become involved in the problems of the old. Two such groups of Americans were especially anti-League—one, the Irish Americans, because of their anti-British feeling, the other, the German Americans, many of whom had opposed American entrance into the war.

A particularly Midwestern group of isolationists was otherwise noted for its progressive and liberal views. Concerned with improving the social order, many of its members were afraid that if this country participated in solving the problems of the Old World, attention would be diverted from the social revolution at home. Thus, idealism became confused with isolationism.

Isolationism also came from resentment over the necessity for adjusting our economic point of view to the world situation. The United States had been a debtor country at the beginning of the First World War. European capital had played a large part in developing the Midwest and West—legend has it that the Chicago and Northwestern Railroad runs left-handed because it was built by British capital and Dutch engineers. When war broke out in Europe, the British and French had had to liquidate their investments to provide money for the purchase of materials from this country, with the result that the United States came out of the war as a great creditor nation. Americans failed to understand or refused to understand that a creditor nation could not maintain a high tariff and expect other nations to pay their debts to it. They resented the inability of others to repay war debts. When someone tried to explain to Calvin Coolidge why it was impossible for the Europeans to do so in the face of high American tariffs, he replied, "They hired the money, didn't they?"

The Midwest area, however, like other parts of the country, was full of contrasts. Another branch of the McCormick family —the Harvester McCormicks—supported the League of Nations. In fact, Mrs. Anita McCormick Blaine, a Democrat, along with Congressman Morton D. Hull, a Republican from what was then known as the "Silk Stocking District" of Chicago, gave substantially in later years to finance the establishment of the national League of Nations Non-Partisan Association, with particular emphasis on the work in the Chicago area. So, in spite of the anti-League mentality, the early twenties saw glimmers of light. Although the United States had shied away from any form of political commitment to the League, certain individuals started rallying to continue the fight for American participation in organizing the peace. The churchmen whom Senator Watson had cited to Senator Lodge as a reason why the League of Nations could not be killed in the Senate continued their support. Many organizations—religious groups, women's groups, fraternal, business, and labor organizations—supported the League of Nations. As the years went on those organizations multiplied; their programs became more vigorous.

In 1923 George W. Wickersham, former Attorney General in the Taft administration, joined forces with John H. Clarke, a Democrat, who resigned from the United States Supreme Court so the two of them could take the iniative in organizing the League of Nations Non-Partisan Association. Its aims were (1) adherence of the United States to the Permanent Court of International Justice, and (2) an increase in the existing cooperation between the United States and the humanitarian, health, and technical work of the League of Nations. The Association's ultimate goal was "membership of the United States in the League of Nations on such terms as the then-existing Administration shall deem wise."[7]

In the latter part of the nineteenth and the early part of the twentieth centuries, the American people were developing a sense of oneness. The rush to the frontier had quieted down. Most of the railroads had been built. The schools and the churches taught pretty much the same things from New York to California. There were a large number of small-town colleges and teachers' training schools, many of them called "normal" schools, and there was a growing demand for ideas from the outside world.

To satisfy this demand, the Chautauqua, one of the most interesting phenomena in American life, arose almost overnight. It began at Chautauqua Lake, New York, where some people owned summer cottages. Under the inspiration of Bishop Vincent of the Methodist Church, a summer program of lectures, opera, and popular entertainment was given. Then the idea developed that the Chautauqua should take to the road, and for a few years there were thousands of communities that had Chautauqua programs.

The Chautauqua organization was something as follows: A Chautauqua Bureau might have several circuits. Some circuits covered the summer months; others, however, ran for as long as forty weeks, beginning in Florida and ending in the Southwest. A tentman, a superintendent, and a young person to develop programs among the young people stayed in each community for the five days or week or whatever was the length of

7. At almost the same time, the League of Nations Union was founded in the United Kingdom. However, the British Union had easy sailing because Britain had no postwar isolationist mood, and such was the case with most of the League of Nations Associations that sprang up in other countries.

the program. Each day there was usually a morning program for young people, and a lecture, popular concert, or dramatic presentation of some kind in the afternoon and evening. The concert companies and lecturers moved daily. In thousands of communities, the people became guarantors of the next year's Chautauqua, all feeling that it was worth running the risk of having to pay part of a deficit so that their communities could have some of the programs that only a Chautauqua could bring them.

The Chautauqua was influential in the struggle for the creation of a League of Nations with American membership. Ruhl Bartlett in his book, *The League to Enforce Peace*, says: "Through the influence of Louis J. Alber, general manager of the Coit Alber Chautauqua System, the league's program was presented to 3,878 Chautauqua audiences attended by an estimated number of 4,000,000 people."[8]

The Chautauqua Bureau for which I was speaking was anxious that a different theme be developed by the speakers each year, but the management gave up in my case. They said that no matter how much they remonstrated with me, my speech always wound up with the League of Nations. The Chautauqua provided me with the opportunity to speak in every state of the Union about the economic and social programs which the League of Nations had developed. It gave me the belief that one could discuss very difficult subjects with any audience providing the material was presented in plain English and the speaker used the pronoun "we" instead of "you." In other words, one was not to preach to an audience, but let its members feel that the speaker and the audience shared a common experience.

At a particular moment in our country's history, the Chautauqua was an important factor in contributing to the unity of the land. But with the coming of the radio, the mobility that good

8. Ruhl J. Bartlett, *The League to Enforce Peace* (Chapel Hill, N.C.: University of North Carolina Press, 1944), p. 89.

roads made possible, and the growth of the cities, eventually people felt that it was not necessary to maintain a Chautauqua in their communities, and, except for its parent body at Chautauqua Lake, it disappeared as suddenly as it had arisen.

CHAPTER

2

First Steps Toward Cooperation
with the League

My first direct contact with the League of Nations was at the close of my Chautauqua lecture tour in the fall of 1923. I was anxious to see the League, about which I was saying so much in speeches, and wrote to Arthur Sweetser, receiving a cordial invitation to Geneva some days later.

Sweetser had been a newspaperman during the war. He then joined the staff of the League of Nations, where he was assistant in charge of the Information Section until 1934. After that he became director attached to principal officers of the Secretariat. There were few other Americans with the League in the early days. Raymond Fosdick, who was named Assistant Secretary-General, resigned when the Senate rejected the League of Nations Covenant. But Sweetser stayed on. He was a rugged person with a sense of humor and considerable tolerance. It was not easy to be a member of the League of Nations staff when seemingly the entire United States had turned against the League. Later, however, as the American attitude changed, life became much easier for him.

My brother, J. Herbert Eichelberger, accompanied me to Geneva. We landed on Christmas Eve, 1923. The ground was covered with snow. It was a custom of the Swiss to have lights on the bridge that connected one part of Geneva with the other, and there were various booths selling food on the bridge as well. The many lights reflecting in the water made the scene a fairyland. It was a bright welcome to the city.

The next morning we could scarcely wait to visit the site of the League of Nations, even though everything was closed for the holiday. Two of the buildings housing the League of Nations were to be on the lakefront. One, a very large structure, had been the Hôtel National. It housed the Secretariat and various committees, and later an addition was made to it for the League of Nations Council. We were moved by a plaque on the wall of its grounds, which read, in English translation, "To the memory of Woodrow Wilson, founder of the League of Nations." Further down, near the Secretariat, was the plot on which the International Labor Organization (ILO) was to be built.

The Assembly met in the Salle de la Réformation, a comparatively small hall attached to the Hôtel Victoria, a short walk across the bridge from the other buildings. Several times in the next few years I was to stay at the Victoria to assure quick access to the Assembly Hall. It was in this sparse building that some of the greatest speeches of the League of Nations were given, but it soon was outgrown. For a few years thereafter the Assembly met in a building about one-half mile away, called the Bâtiment Électoral. In 1936 the Assembly was able to move into the Palais des Nations, which was the League of Nations' new home.

After that first Geneva visit, when Sweetser introduced me to a number of statesmen and early Secretariat people, I returned to the United States more anxious than ever to work for the success of the League of Nations. Not only did I continue my lectures; I also began to work through the League of Nations Non-Partisan Association, which was by then expanding and organizing additional chapters throughout the country. Whenever I was in New York I visited the Association office and occasionally made speeches for it, usually on a volunteer basis but with my expenses paid.

One September afternoon in 1924, I arrived at Association headquarters and was greeted with enthusiasm by Miss Mary W. Fry, head of the Speakers Department, who had been trying to reach me by telephone. She was very anxious that I deliver an address at a Latin American Trade Conference that was to be held in Atlanta—the speakers included Don Benjamin Cohen, who later became an official of the United Nations. I would have to leave for Atlanta that night. I wanted to accept immediately, but it happened that I had what might be called a "previous engagement" the next day—I was going to be married. My fiancée, Rosa Kohler of Baltimore, and I had finished our tour on the Chautauqua, and had come to New York to get married quickly, then to go to Chicago, where I had signed up for some courses at the University of Chicago.

I went back to Rose's hotel and explained the situation to her: that of course I couldn't go to Atlanta, that of course it would never do to put off our marriage. Rose, however, knew perfectly well how much I wanted to make the speech, that this would be my only chance to give this particular address, while we could get married any day. So in the end, at Rose's urging, I made the speech, and the wedding was put off until my return.

Following the Senate's rejection of the League of Nations, the United States government seemed bent upon humiliating the international organization in every possible way. Some officials actually acted as if they were afraid to have anything to do with it. For a period of approximately six months, communications from the League of Nations were not acknowledged by any department of the United States government. Pinkney Tuck, then American consul in Geneva, called on the Secretary-General of the League to tell him that unofficially and orally he was instructed to say that the State Department had received its registered mail from Geneva, but inasmuch as the American government did not recognize the existence of the League, it would not reply.

When the American consul in Geneva wanted a document, Arthur Sweetser would meet him on a bench along the lakefront and hand it to him. Officials of the government were afraid that should an American official enter the League of Nations building, the newspapers would call attention to it. One time an American consular official did enter the League of Nations building, to present statistics from the United States for inclusion in the League's *Monthly Bulletin of Statistics*. The piece of paper which he deposited on an official's desk was not marked in any way as to its origin or its contents.

Another example of our government's refusal to be associated with the League occurred when the Secretary-General's invitations to make nominations for judges to the Permanent Court of International Justice were not forwarded by the Department of State to the members of the American panel of the Permanent Court of Arbitration as requested. The Secretary-General, receiving no replies from the group, cabled the four members direct, following which Elihu Root, one of the panel, contacted the State Department. The original invitations were then forwarded in time for the panel to meet and make their nominations. They agreed that the State Department should be informed, as a matter of courtesy. But the Secretary of State, Charles Evans Hughes, raised objections to the procedure. As a result the group cabled Geneva declining to make nominations, stating they could not exercise this function "under a treaty to which the United States is not party." This technical objection, however, was not raised later when a vacancy occurred in the Court. In July 1923 the panel met, made its nomination, and saw its candidate elected to the Court. And subsequently, in 1928, Hughes himself was nominated by the panel; the nomination was forwarded, following the prescribed procedure; and he was elected to the Court.

When the committee to organize the International Labor Organization convened in Washington in 1919, as provided in its constitution, it found the political situation hostile. Even though William B. Wilson, Secretary of Labor, presided over the group, it was denounced by Senator L. Y. Sherman of Illinois as containing "a number of Socialists and also a number of those who go beyond Socialism—radicals, alien firebrands but a few degrees removed from those who believe in Soviet principles." Incensed, the delegates threatened to move elsewhere unless assured that Senator Sherman's remarks were not representative of the Senate.

In the Chicago *Daily News* of September 5, 1921, Paul Scott Mowrer wrote:

> Rightly or wrongly everybody here is convinced that the aim of the present American Administration is to wreck the League, if possible, by refusing to cooperate therewith in even the most laudable humanitarian tentatives. The result is that the League is merely strengthened in its determination to preserve its own existence.

This American obstructionist mood, much more a mood of the government than of the people, could not last, for shortly after the rejection of the Covenant the parade of Americans to Geneva began. I have already spoken of the presence of my friends the Sweetsers in Geneva. Other Americans who had official positions in the League during the twenties included Howard Huston, who held an important technical post as chief of Internal Service; Huntington Gilchrist, who served from 1920 to 1924 as chief of the Department of Administrative Commissions, and from 1924 to 1928 as assistant director of the Mandates Section, which prepared the way for the United Nations trusteeship system; Dr. Frank G. Boudreau, member of the Health Section and later its director; Florence Wilson, chief librarian, and her assistant, Alice C. Bartlett; and Benjamin Gerig, formerly of the University of Illinois, who was to join the Information Section of the Secretariat in 1930.

During the fall of 1927 I made one of my visits to the national office of the League of Nations Non-Partisan Association. A rather casual conversation with the director led to a decision that was to affect my entire future. I was asked if I would be interested in being the director of the Chicago office of the Association. Without any hesitation I replied yes. The board of directors of the Chicago office accepted me and I became the director of what was later to be called the Association's Midwest office. I was getting more and more deeply involved in the international situation, and with a group of people who were trying to use international organization to avoid war. My enthusiasm in this work never faltered—I was doing exactly what I'd always wanted to do.

In my new work in the Chicago office, I soon discovered that while the national office had a house organ, the *League of Nations News,* greater coverage was necessary. It would be valuable to present news of the League of Nations, pertinent international news, editorials, and book reviews. I decided that we needed our own publication. A former newspaperman who had lectured on the Chautauqua platform with us for several years, J. William Terry, helped work out the plans for the new *League of Nations Chronicle.* Mrs. Eichelberger was to write reviews of books dealing with international affairs under her maiden name, Rosa Kohler. Albin E. Johnson, a freelance correspondent in Geneva agreed to be the correspondent of the Association's Midwest office.

The following dispatch, which appeared in the *Chronicle* under Johnson's name in November 1928, shows that changes had occurred since the early days in the attitude of the United States toward participation in the League:

The past ten months have been among the least spectacular in the history of the League, yet during that period the United States, besides taking the lead in Outlawry of War through the Kellogg Pact, and furnishing a judge on the bench of the Permanent Court of International Justice—Charles Evans Hughes, an ex-secretary of state in an anti-League administration—has played a role in every activity of the Geneva organization.

Pursuing the official records one finds Washington's mark in Disarmament, Economics, Health, Social, Intellectual cooperation, Financial and Judicial questions which have come before the League. The State Department has sent to the League's Treaty Registration department at least four treaties; military, naval and air statistics have been submitted for incorporation in the League's Official Armaments Yearbook; official reports on opium and narcotic drugs, on illegitimate children, on film censorship and official state department communications in reference to transit and communications and trade treaties have come from Washington. And in addition the American Minister to Switzerland has signed two treaties negotiated exclusively under the auspices of the League.

At the present moment, with elections just over, four official or unofficial representatives or delegations are representing Washington in commissions sitting in the League Secretariat. Headed by Prof. Thomas Adams, of Yale University, four Treasury Department officials are cooperating with delegates from twenty-eight countries, members of the League and Soviet Russia on Double Taxation and kindred problems. Lucius Eastman, president of the New York Merchants' Association, with the approval of Washington is participating in the sessions of the League's Permanent Economic Committee which is seeking to eliminate trade barriers and restrictions; Prof. Charles Lyons, personal representative of Herbert Hoover as head of the Department of Commerce, is in Geneva for his weekly conference with League Financial, Trade and Economic officials and arranging for the participation of an American delegation in the November International Statistical Conference; Dr. Alice Hamilton of Harvard, as substitute of Surgeon General Cumming, U.S. Army, is working with the League Health Committee in its contemplated crusade against disease-bearing mosquitoes.

In Disarmament work the last American delegation consisted of an ambassador, Hugh Gibson from Brussels, a minister, Hugh Wilson from

Berne, an admiral, Andrew Long of the Navy Department, and several state, navy and war department officials. Minister Wilson participated in the subsequent Special League Commission for the supervision of private manufacture of arms as well and a responsible delegation from Washington is scheduled to take part in the final drafting of the League's General Disarmament Treaty early in 1929.

In economic endeavors besides signing two League Treaties during the year, an American Delegation headed by Minister Hugh Wilson, with four assistants and experts played an important part in the drafting of the conventions for Abolition of Import and Export Restrictions and the State Department complained formally to the League against the number and extent of exceptions made by various countries, as a result of which many "reservations" were withdrawn. Unofficially, yet with the full sanction of the State Department, four prominent Americans took part in the sessions of the League's Economic Consultative Committee. They were Dr. Alonzo T. Taylor of Leland Stanford University; Prof. Asher Hobson, American delegate to the International Institute of Agriculture at Rome; Prof. W. H. Willetts, of the University of Pennsylvania; and Roland Boyden of the International Chamber of Commerce.

At the Financial Commission meetings were found such well-known Americans as Jeremiah Smith, Jr., of Boston, Roland Boyden of the Reparations Commission, M. Jay of Morgan and Co., Royal Tyler, Boston, who is administering Hungary's financial affairs for the League, and Charles B. Eddy of New York, who administers the League's Greek Refugee loans.

Health and Social questions, as heretofore, drew heavily from American sources. The Rockefeller Foundation still contributes largely to the support of the scientific and investigative work of this department and no less than ten American doctors appeared in Commissions. Dr. C. A. Winslow, director of the Health Section of Yale, Dr. Hamilton of Harvard and Surgeon General Cumming headed the list. . . .

On the Codification of International Law Committee, George W. Wickersham, ex-attorney general of the United States, played a leading role, while Major Bascom Johnson and L. W. Carris of New York continued their cooperation in Child Welfare and Prevention of Child

Blindness work by the Social Section. T. B. Kittridge represented the American Red Cross.

Last, but by no means least, is the part Americans are taking in the Intellectual Cooperation work of the League. The American Educational Council made a grant of $5,000 for an international enquiry in regard to exchanges of professors and students while Dr. Stephan Duggan, director of the International Educational Institute, Stuart Chapin, of Minnesota University, Prof. C. Vibert and others took part in various committees and Commissions.

What were the reasons for this radical change in the United States attitude in the years between 1920 and 1928? Bad conscience, for one. Millions of people and government officials wished the League of Nations to succeed. The League was doing things in which the United States could not help but be very much interested. It was dealing with important economic, social, and health matters in which this country felt it should participate. The United States did not want to be left out in the cold. So long as technical cooperation did not seem to bring the United States nearer the League's political problems, all well and good.

The number of Americans in Geneva on various missions continued to increase. Some were there more or less on their own; some represented national organizations; some served on technical bodies with the permission of the government; others, such as those at the Disarmament Conference, were there representing the United States government.

On June 3, 1930, Prentiss Gilbert was appointed diplomatic representative of the United States at Geneva. According to an article which appeared in the *League of Nations Chronicle* of June 1930,

Mr. Gilbert, who has been assistant chief of the Division of Western European Affairs at the State Department . . . will have the title of American Consul. This is because Geneva is not the capital of Switzerland and only a Consular office may be maintained there. The position, however, will be one having to do almost entirely with liaison between the United States Government and the League of Nations. This is made clear by the appointment of so experienced a diplomat as Mr. Gilbert. . . .

The few American members on the Secretariat staff, in addition to their official duties, played a unique role. They welcomed and made to feel at home the increasing number of Americans who were coming to Geneva, including some in an official capacity. These Americans came rather modestly at first but finally, some of them, more openly as delegates of the United States government.

Part of Arthur Sweetser's role was to receive Americans and to deal with the American press. The Sweetsers lived in a châlet on the outskirts of Geneva. Nothing was more beautiful than the various shades of blue in the valley viewed from their house at sunset—a peaceful setting that sometimes made their guests linger late into the evening. A number of Americans and non-Americans who had things to talk over were invited to the Sweetsers' receptions. The conversation was warm and expansive, the atmosphere relaxed, and time was frequently forgotten. On one occasion, I wrote in the November 1928 issue of the *Chronicle:*

A group of Americans standing on the porch of Arthur Sweetser's home on the outskirts of Geneva and looking across to Voltaire's home remarked the fact that from the day of the French philosopher to the present, with the exception of a few brief lapses, Geneva had been unusually tolerant toward foreigners.

This impression was undoubtedly emphasized by the fact that in this group were Charles Clayton Morrison [editor, *Christian Century*], Frederick J. Libby, Raymond T. Rich [World Peace Foundation], James G. McDonald [Foreign Policy Association], and some representatives of the League of Nations Non-Partisan Association, including the Midwest Secretary. Coming from a country that has refused to join the League, these men were much in evidence on all occasions. Some of them made speeches, and at least one of these speeches was very critical of the League. When an American asked a resident of Geneva if he did not think it strange that representatives of these American peace organizations should be making speeches there, the Genevan shrugged and said he thought it a good thing. Geneva, he said, had always been the home of free speech, and the value of the League was not so much in the treaties it produced as in the drawing of divergent minds to think in one place on world problems.

So it is that Americans may go to Geneva and without presumption speak frankly about a League which their country refuses to support. The tolerance of the League staff and of the delegates who attend the League meetings is one of the happiest signs in the world today.

Quite a few years later—in 1937—friends in the Secretariat prepared a comprehensive report on American activity in the League of Nations' economic and financial work. The report stated that there were three types of participation by Americans:

American participation in the financial and economic work of the League has probably been more extensive than in any other branch. While obviously there have been and still are great gaps in it, nevertheless, the total volume has been considerable.

This applies equally to official participation by United States Government representatives and to non-official participation by private individuals or organizations. All three types of participation have shown similar characteristics.

The development of this participation has been progressive during the years. It was at first cautious and restricted, particularly on the part of the Government. With the years, however, it has strengthened and confirmed itself until today it is open and confident.

But it has great weaknesses. Most important of all, the United States is not represented in either the Assembly or the Council, which usually initiate, approve and execute this work. It does not, therefore, have a full voice either at the start, in setting activities under way, or at the conclusion, in deciding as to their future. Similarly, the United States is always somewhat in the position of a guest, not a member . . . and pays only a small share of the expenses.

While the United States might pay something toward the expenses of a conference, it usually contributed nothing toward the planning that led to the conference or the future results. Unofficially, however, many Americans contributed time or money to the League. According to a report issued by the Secretariat in 1930, Americans, officially and unofficially, were by that time supporting League activities in the amount of $250,000 a year.

The report estimated that contributions from the United States amounted to one-twentieth of the League's expenses. A substantial part of the money came from the Chicago area, as a dispatch appearing in the July 1929 issue of the *Chronicle* reveals:

Chicagoans have been appearing prominently in the League news. Gifts and property transactions totalling several hundred thousand dollars for the benefit of the League have been forthcoming from James J. Forstall, Julius Rosenwald, Mrs. Emmons Blaine, Mrs. William G. Hibbard and Mrs. Robert Gregory. All but one of these are members of the board of the Chicago Office of the League of Nations Association.

James J. Forstall, a lawyer of Chicago and member of the Executive Committee of the Chicago Office . . . has purchased a magnificent estate of twelve acres on which is located a sixteen-room mansion overlooking Lake Geneva. The property, which is now the home of Sir Eric Drummond, Secretary-General of the League, is of particular importance to the League because it adjoins Ariana Park on which are to be erected the new League buildings. . . .

In addition to purchasing the property for the League, Mr. Forstall has defrayed the expense incurred in procuring the services of Edmund Weigele, a New York consulting engineer who gave the building committee of the League advice on mechanical equipment . . . for its new buildings. . . .

Another large property purchase made last week was that of the Widemann Institute, the buildings of which were bought for $220,000 by the American Foundation for the International School at Geneva. The school was founded several years ago largely through the efforts of Arthur Sweetser . . . and it was he who made this purchase possible.

The Institute is meant as a "contribution of American culture to international education." In addition to Mrs. Emmons Blaine, Mrs. William G. Hibbard, Mrs. Robert Gregory and Mr. and Mrs. James J. Forstall . . . Julius Rosenwald, John D. Rockefeller, Jr., and Thomas W. Lamont also contributed.

Looking ahead a few years to when the new League of Nations buildings were to be put up, Forstall, as well as other Americans, was afraid that speculators might purchase property in the vicinity, property that should be used by the expanding organization. When, for financial reasons, Mr. Forstall was not able to carry through his commitments to the League, the Rockefellers helped out, Raymond Fosdick making arrangements with them to underwrite Forstall's obligations.[1]

The Rockefeller family and Rockefeller agencies stood above all others in their financial contributions to many of the League's activities. The largest of such gifts was $2 million to build the League of Nations Library, which is used even today as the library of the expanded offices of the United Nations. And, in fact, John D. Rockefeller III was an early member of the League of Nations staff, as described in the following article by Albin E. Johnson in the September 1928 issue of the *Chronicle*:[2]

A slender youth, perhaps twenty-one or twenty-two, with serious mien and rather diffident air, sauntered through the halls of the League Secretariat. He was a new attaché of the organization and had been

1. Some years later Mr. Rockefeller, wanting to divest himself of property in Geneva, turned most of it over to the University of Geneva, except for that which had been given to the League. Included in the property that went to the university was the Villa Rigo, situated on the Avenue de la Paix, halfway between the International Labor Office and the new League buildings. This small but beautiful villa, located in a grove of chestnut trees until the city of Geneva erected some barrack-like school classrooms in the grove, was used as a headquarters for the International Federation of League of Nations Societies. I remember that at Federation meetings I was always intrigued—and sometimes beguiled—by the various angels and cherubs looking down from the ceiling.
2. Young Rockefeller was not the only scion of a wealthy American family to work at the League. W. Curtis Bok, heir to the fortunes of his grandfather, Cyrus H. K. Curtis, and of his father, Edward Bok, preceded him.

assigned to the job of "covering" a session of the Sub-Committee on Intellectual Cooperation. His task was to resume the proceedings for the newspapermen so that those plutocrats of the press need not sit through the long and uncomfortably hot meetings.

On the committee were such men as Einstein, propounder of the Theory of Relativity; M. Painlevé, France's leading mathematician as well as statesman; Mme. Curie, co-discoverer of radium; M. Tanakdate, Japan's foremost champion of "Romanization" of the Japanese written language; John Galsworthy, British author; Salvatore de Madariaga, Spanish writer; and others too numerous to mention.

When the meeting was over the diffident young man returned to a pigeonhole office on the fourth floor of the Secretariat and laboriously typed out his first piece of work. For which, if he collects his salary, he will receive around $1,000 per year. . . .

The lad was John D. Rockefeller III.

Almost from the beginning the number of American tourists and students visiting the League of Nations was quite large—in fact, at times more Americans seemed to be visiting the League than citizens of any other country. Some of these Americans could not understand why they could not secure tickets of admission to the League Assembly or go anywhere they wished in the Secretariat buildings. To assist the American visitors, a group was created called The American Committee in Geneva. It stemmed from the League of Nations Association and the Carnegie Endowment for International Peace. The committee recruited students and teachers from the United States who could spend some weeks at Geneva as guides. They supplemented the regular guides of the League of Nations without charge for their services, giving tours at the Palais des Nations and the ILO and pointing out things that would be of particular interest to Americans. Another activity of the American Committee was to assist in the arrangements at the summer school for college students, which was run by the International Federation of League of Nations Societies. On my own visits to

Geneva I always enjoyed seeing the enthusiasm with which touring Americans thronged through the League buildings behind their guides. American interest in the League was clearly on the rise.

3

The Geneva Protocol—Locarno—
The Pact of Paris

Although most of the contacts of Americans with the League of Nations in the period from 1921 to 1928 were in the technical field, twice Americans had a tremendous influence, directly or indirectly, on the political workings of the League.

The first occasion was in the matter of the Geneva Protocol, the purpose of which was to strengthen and supplement the League of Nations Covenant. It aimed to provide for the submission of all international disputes of every character to the Permanent Court of International Justice, or to arbitration, or to the Council of the League for final decision. It was to furnish a basis for the reduction and limitation of armaments—deemed indispensable in seeking world peace.

In the first drafts of the Geneva Protocol that were drawn by the Temporary Mixed Commission of the League, there was born the concept of making aggressive war an international crime. Then, however, loomed the complex problem of defining aggression. It was at this point, in the spring of 1923, that Colonel Requin, representative of the French government on the Commission, turned to the American James T. Shotwell, who had been attached to the United States delegation at the Paris Peace Conference and was currently professor of history at Columbia University. He agreed to have the question studied by a group of his eminent friends, among them David Hunter Miller, legal adviser to President Wilson at the Paris Peace Conference; General Tasker H. Bliss of the Supreme War Council, who was also at the Peace Conference; Frederick P. Keppel, president of the Carnegie Corporation; Professor Joseph Chamberlain of Columbia University; and Professor John Bates Clark, director of the Division of Economics and History of the Carnegie Endowment.

In the spring of 1924 Shotwell and Miller put the collective ideas of the group in the form of a draft treaty. It included the concept that aggression is resorting to force in violation of a given pledge to have disputes settled peacefully. Through Arthur Sweetser this "Draft Treaty of Disarmament and Security," which was accompanied by the qualification that it was an unofficial work by a private committee attached to no organization, reached the Secretary-General of the League of Nations, Sir Eric Drummond. The Secretary-General laid the plan before the League Assembly and it was voted unanimously to have it circulated as a League document. In the summer of 1924, Bliss, Miller, and Shotwell returned to Geneva to make sure that the "American Plan," as it was commonly called, was not being misunderstood.

Carrying the definition of aggression formulated by the American group, the Geneva Protocol was passed unanimously on October 2, 1924, by the forty-eight members of the League Assembly. Unfortunately, however, a change in government in Great Britain soon changed British support to opposition. In March 1925, Austen Chamberlain, the new British Foreign Secretary, announced formally to the thirty-third session of the Council his government's rejection of the Protocol.

According to Frank Walters, formerly Deputy Secretary-General of the League of Nations:

The real reasons [for the rejection] were four: the opposition of the Commonwealth Members, fear of trouble with the United States, a reluctance to underpin the territorial settlement of Eastern Europe, and the deep-seated dislike of the Foreign Office for compulsory arbitration. None of these reasons, however, appeared in the statement which Chamberlain read to the Council criticizing the actual terms of the Protocol. . . .[1]

For a while it looked as if all were lost in the effort to strengthen the League's system of security. But the Geneva Protocol did bear fruit. On February 9, 1925, shortly after a visit by Austen Chamberlain to Berlin, the German ambassador to Paris had proposed to French premier Édouard Herriot a Rhineland Security Pact which would be supplemented by arbitration treaties and deposited with the United States government as trustee. Long negotiations between France and Germany, and consultations with Great Britain and other nations, followed this proposal. Finally, the nations concerned met in Locarno, a small Swiss town on Lake Maggiore, on October 4, 1925, following the close of the Sixth Assembly of the League of Nations. On October 16 the final versions of a group of treaties were initialed.

The most important was the Rhineland Pact. Under its terms Germany and Belgium, and Germany and France, agreed to regard their existing frontiers and the demilitarized Rhineland as inviolable and that in no case would they attack, invade, or resort to war against one another. They would undertake to settle by peaceful means questions arising between them.

The signing at Locarno paved the way for German entrance into the League of Nations, on September 8, 1926, and the Locarno Treaties remained in effect until the morning of March 7, 1936, when Hitler, giving the Franco-Soviet Pact as an excuse —he claimed it was a violation of the letter and spirit of Locarno and that Germany therefore was no longer bound by Locarno

1. Frank P. Walters, *A History of the League of Nations*, Vol. I (New York: Oxford University Press, 1952), p. 284.

obligations—sent German troops to reoccupy the demilitarized Rhineland.

The second intervention of Americans that had a profound influence on the political work of the League of Nations was the Kellogg-Briand Pact or the Pact of Paris. Although technically this was not a League document, it affected the League deeply. In the thirties, when President Roosevelt and Secretary of State Cordell Hull wished to protest against aggression, they could not very well cite the League of Nations Covenant, since the United States was not a member of the League. But they could and did cite the Kellogg Pact. Through it, the United States committed itself to the peacekeeping objectives of the League of Nations, while maintaining its political aloofness from the organization.

On the tenth anniversary of America's entry into the World War, April 6, 1927, Aristide Briand, the French premier, addressed a message to the American people through the Associated Press. Its most significant passage was:

For those whose lives are devoted to securing this living reality of a policy of peace the United States and France already appear before the world as morally in full agreement. If there were need for those two great democracies to give high testimony to their desire for peace and to furnish to other peoples an example more solemn still, France would be willing to subscribe publicly with the United States to any mutual engagement tending to outlaw war, to use an American expression, as between these two countries. The renunciation of war as an instrument of national policy is a conception already familiar to the signatories of the Covenant of the League of Nations and of the Treaties of Locarno. Every engagement entered into in this spirit by the United States toward another nation such as France would contribute greatly in the eyes of the world to broaden and strengthen the foundations on which the international policy of peace is being erected. . . .[2]

2. James T. Shotwell, *War as an Instrument of National Policy* (New York: Harcourt, Brace and Co., 1929), pp. 41–42.

The reference in this message to the renunciation of war as an instrument of national policy was in harmony with the thinking of a large section of American peace advocates led by, among others, Professor Shotwell. It was Professor Shotwell who on March 22, in Paris, had suggested to M. Briand that a French initiative in the cause of peace would be particularly desirable because the French refusal to participate in the Geneva Naval Conference "had produced an unfavorable impression in America." The French premier asked Professor Shotwell if he "had any ideas as to the form the initiative should take. The answer was, in essence, that the French Government should appeal to the people of the United States to negotiate a treaty renouncing war as an instrument of national policy as between the two nations."[3]

In also using the phrase "to outlaw war" in his message, Briand made a gesture toward another growing section of American public opinion, which felt that the way to eliminate war was to outlaw it. The author of the phrase was Solomon O. Levinson, a Chicago lawyer who wrote extensively on the subject in the early twenties. One of the virtues of his presentation was its simplicity. He refused to be drawn into a discussion of the distinction between aggressive and defensive warfare: nations should outlaw the institution of war; for a nation to engage in self-defense is not war.

In the beginning there could not help but be some feeling of competition between the Shotwell and Levinson schools. When Mr. Levinson went to Paris in the spring of 1927 and met with

3. David Bryn-Jones, *Frank B. Kellogg* (New York: G. P. Putnam's Sons, 1937), p. 224. Professor Shotwell never publicly revealed his part in the origin of the Pact of Paris, although in his book *War as an Instrument of National Policy,* he gave a detailed history of the negotiations leading finally to the ratification of the Pact. His role was revealed by Secretary of State Frank B. Kellogg's biographer and others. It should not have taken a literary detective to discover it, however, because Briand's message included the words "war as an instrument of national policy."

Briand, some felt that the visit would deepen the opposition of the French to the idea of a pact renouncing war as an instrument of national policy: Europeans would be alarmed by the fact that isolationists who were anti-League and anti-World Court supported the idea of the outlawry of war. On the other hand, Mr. Levinson was afraid that Professor Shotwell's intervention would make the whole subject too complex. In an interview with Secretary of State Kellogg, he is quoted as saying that he resented the intrusion of Professor Shotwell into the discussion.

Here were two great Americans with different backgrounds, who came from different parts of the country, taking different roads to the same objective. As director of the Midwest office of the League of Nations Association, I worked with Professor Shotwell continually, and thanks to frequent communications from the national office giving details of his program, I was able to make it known to the press and to the people of the Midwest. At the same time I was a close friend of Mr. Levinson and lunched with him frequently at the Chicago Standard Club. Again and again, he would insist upon the simplicity of the idea of outlawing war and express his fear that certain of my friends would make the treaty too complex. Eventually, however, I think I helped him see and understand the point of view of Shotwell and others who supported the League of Nations, and the relationship that the League might have to the Pact of Paris. Indeed, the January 1929 issue of the League of Nations Association *Chronicle* carried Mr. Levinson's first written statement after the ratification of the treaty. The headline read: "Violation of Covenant or Locarno Treaty Would Be Breach of Peace Pact, Declares Levinson." In my editorial, "Peace Forces United," in that issue I wrote:

The *Chronicle* is proud to be able to publish the first written statement of Mr. S. O. Levinson since the signing of the Multilateral Treaty in which he played such a great part. By his vigor and imagination he had projected the words "Outlawry of War" into the most distant parts of the world. It goes without saying that the *Chronicle* and the Midwest Office are pleased with the ratification of the Multilateral Pact, for they have supported the treaty from the first. Neither is it necessary to repeat the reasons why the pact is considered of such infinite importance. They have been enumerated in these columns as well as elsewhere. The unity among the peace forces which the debate over the treaty indicated and promoted is an observation which might be made at this time. In the last few months the advocates of world peace, who have been too often split into academic and theoretical groups, have become united on two points: the need for the moral renunciation of war and the need of machinery to enable nations to solve their problems by peaceful means. A year ago this unity was perhaps more evident in Europe than in the United States.

The negotiations between the United States and France and later with other countries to eliminate war were conducted admirably by Secretary Kellogg over a period of almost a year. It was Mr. Kellogg who was largely responsible for the decision to make the treaty multilateral: he felt that the Senate would not accept a bilateral treaty between France and the United States. It was also feared that other nations would resent such a treaty.

Fifteen states signed the Pact of Paris at a dramatic ceremony in Paris on August 27, 1928. It was a very important step in the development of the laws against war. The League of Nations Covenant had one gap: after the member nations had exhausted the means for peaceful settlement of disputes, it would be no violation of the Covenant for them to go to war. The Kellogg Pact closed this gap. Paradoxically, however, as the United States had suggested the League but would not join it, so the United States had proposed the Kellogg Pact but would not support the machinery—the League of Nations—to give it effect. This marks the tragedy that helped produce the Second World War.

In the *League of Nations Chronicle* of August 1928, my editorial summed up the tragic irony of the American position:

Embarrassment is felt in Paris over the technique of signing the Multilateral Treaty. The presence of our Secretary of State rather necessitates the presence of Foreign Ministers, [Gustav] Stresemann and Chamberlain. But the German foreign minister finds it embarrassing to visit Paris while the French are in the Rhineland. At Geneva he and Briand may walk arm in arm about the Assembly Hall or sip champagne in the cafes of Thoiry, but not in Paris. The French would prefer, so would the Germans and all of the rest of the multilateral signatories, that the signing take place in Geneva, but Mr. Kellogg cannot go there.

As a matter of fact, the very next day Briand, Stresemann and Chamberlain as well as other foreign ministers will be en route to Geneva for the meeting of the Council, commencing the thirtieth. And one week after the signing in Paris the delegates of fifty-five nations will gather in Geneva for the Ninth Assembly. Even more significant, the Multilateral Treaty may be one of the Assembly's chief topics of discussion; it is virtually on the agenda as a result of Great Britain's note; it is quite possible that the Assembly may by resolution incorporate the outlawry pact in the League's fundamental program—all of this without the presence of the American Secretary of State.

Mr. Kellogg is not to be criticized; he sympathized with the League at the beginning; he has been more than fair and cordial in his treatment of the League in his multilateral negotiations. Pacing the deck of the *Leviathan* the third of September, he cannot but reflect on the peculiarity of our American situation which would permit him to go to Paris—but not to Geneva.

The Briand-Stresemann period was the most ideal in the history of the League of Nations. It began in 1925 with the Locarno Treaties and lasted for six harmonious years.

On September 10, 1926, the first German delegation was welcomed into the League Assembly. The German foreign minister was almost overcome by emotion as he began his address. The foreign minister of France, the only orator capable of expressing the drama of the occasion, replied. The unique

friendship of Gustav Stresemann and Aristide Briand tran-
scended the problems of their two countries and lasted until
Stresemann's death in 1929. They shared the Nobel peace prize
in 1926. For years, the world hung on their every word, believing that to eliminate the enmity between France and Germany
was the beginning of permanent peace.

Interesting stories circulated about the friendship of these
two men. Once, for example, they were locked in difficult
negotiations in a private room in a lakefront hotel in Geneva.
Newspapermen and some of the general public crowded the
lobby waiting tensely for them to appear. Finally, arm in arm,
they walked down the stairs to the lobby and announced that
they were agreed upon the next step to be taken. Everyone
relaxed. The two men confided later, however, that the only
thing they had agreed upon was to go to bed.

So close were the two statesmen that even such a sensitive
matter as German reparations could be the subject of a joke. A
small but famous restaurant in the little town of Thoiry attracted them. They would meet in a private room and eat the
best food that the management could provide. The restaurant
took on an added luster because Briand and Stresemann went
there. At the close of one of the meetings at Thoiry, each man
reached in his pocket to pay the check. But Briand said to
Stresemann, "Better let me pay it; you've got to pay the reparations."[4]

I was in Geneva a number of times during the Briand-
Stresemann period, and I still remember the glow generated by
the two leaders as they spoke in the League of Nations Assembly. Briand was handsome and a great orator. I heard him speak
in the Assembly a number of times. I have never heard a
greater voice. Sometimes his tones rumbled deep in his chest;
at others they rose in a smooth crescendo to a great height.

4. I am indebted to Clarence Berdahl, professor of political science at the
University of Illinois, for this anecdote.

Stresemann on the other hand was undistinguished in appearance, with a voice, as one observer said, "reminiscent of the experimental days of the radio." He enjoyed spending evenings in the old Café Bavaria, the political café for statesmen and the press, although in the last few years of his life failing health forced him to forego his beer and frankfurters.

In 1930, Aristide Briand made a moving speech at the annual dinner given by the foreign correspondents for the delegates to the Assembly.[5] Stresemann had died the year before. Briand called upon the world to witness that he had kept faith with his late friend by fulfilling his promise to withdraw French troops from the Ruhr five years before the treaty called for it.

More has been written about Briand than about his German colleague because Briand served in the League for a longer period. His wisdom was intuitive. One of Briand's compatriots remarked that Raymond Poincaré, president of France during the First World War and four times premier, knew everything and understood nothing, whereas Briand knew nothing and understood everything.

As French minister for foreign affairs, on May 17, 1930, Briand even addressed a memorandum to twenty-six European governments on the organization of a régime for a European federal union. The League of Nations Assembly at its meeting in September took the position that any European union must be within the framework of the League, and approved the appointment of a Commission of Enquiry to look into the matter. Unfortunately, the Commission's recommendations were weak, and Europe had to suffer the agony of the Second World War before the nations would move toward unity, as expressed in the Common Market and NATO. Briand was very much disappointed at the Commission's recommendations. But throughout a long life in French and world politics, he never

5. The menu cards made each year for this occasion by the Hungarian artists Derso and Kelen have become collectors' items.

lost his idealism, once remarking, "It is a great compliment they pay me when they call me an idealist. Can one be an idealist who has been twelve times premier of France?"

The Stresemann-Briand period came to an abrupt end not with the death of Stresemann, but in 1931 when the Japanese invaded Manchuria. Aristide Briand would spend the last months of his service to the League presiding at the Council as it tried to deal with this violation of the Covenant.

CHAPTER

4

❦

Rumbles of War—Invasion of Manchuria

The Japanese invasion of Manchuria in 1931 was the first of a series of aggressions that weakened the League of Nations organization and demonstrated that every crisis to come before the League was of worldwide importance. It began the train of events which reached its climax ten years later in the Japanese attack on Pearl Harbor.

China, of course, made an appeal to the League of Nations under the Covenant. The Council of the League first met to deal with China's complaint against Japan in Geneva on September 22. Despite a resolution passed on September 30 calling upon both sides to prevent any extension of the conflict, the situation became worse. When the Council met again on October 16, the United States government agreed that Prentiss Gilbert, the American consul in Geneva, should sit with the Council in its deliberations. There was great acclaim in the League and throughout the world on learning that the United States would throw its weight behind a peaceful settlement through the League of Nations. Unfortunately, the significance of Gilbert's taking his seat with the Council was weakened by the limitations on his authority:

Secretary of State [Henry L.] Stimson was disconcerted by the strength of Japanese opposition: the isolationist press attacked him, and the very

39

warmth with which his decision was greeted in Geneva increased his embarrassment. The State Department reverted, therefore, to its usual prudence. Gilbert's instructions were to the effect that his government could not join in formulating any action envisaged under the Covenant, but was willing to give its moral support and to take counsel, if required. . . .[1]

After a series of private meetings, the Council in public session on October 24 considered a resolution submitted by Aristide Briand. Japan, however, would neither consent to a time limit for withdrawal nor admit that the start of negotiations should wait for the time when military occupation had ended, and refused to accept the resolution. The Council set a deadline of November 16 for the withdrawal of Japanese forces. If such action had not been accomplished by that date, the Council would meet again.

In an address given over a radio forum of the Wisconsin League of Women Voters on November 10, 1931, I said:

Now consider what may be the effect of the Manchurian situation upon China. The representative of this very old people but albeit a new nation in modern life—a nation representing one-fourth of the population of the world—said to the League in effect: "We have ordered our people not to resist; we will not fight back; we place our cause in the League of Nations and Kellogg Pact." Suppose China is now told that the signatories of the Covenant and Pact cannot give her justice and peace; that she can only find security by the force of arms in the old-fashioned way. Then you have the militarism of one-fourth of the population of the world. Suppose China is made to feel that her security will be guaranteed by the world community; a great victory will have been gained.

When the Council met on November 16, it met in Paris. The statesmen of a few of the great powers had deliberately transferred the Council meeting there because the atmosphere in

1. Frank P. Walters, *A History of the League of Nations,* Vol. II (New York: Oxford University Press, 1952), p. 476.

that city, the capital of one of them, would not be as liberal as that at Geneva. Briand presided over what were to be his last League of Nations meetings. He died three months later, in March 1932.

The Council meetings in Paris were not attended by Prentiss Gilbert. Secretary of State Stimson had retreated, choosing now to keep in touch with the proceedings by diplomatic methods. General Charles G. Dawes, the United States ambassador to London, was sent to Paris to maintain contact in any way he wished. Dawes stayed at the Ritz Hotel. There he conferred with individual members of the Council who called upon him, while official contact between Dawes and the Council was maintained by Arthur Sweetser, then on the Secretariat. And although Stimson evidently told Dawes that sanctions imposed by the Council against Japan would have the support of the American people and that the government, while not officially endorsing sanctions, would not interfere, "it is not apparent that Dawes made any use of this message."[2]

In the face of further Japanese army preparations, the Council on December 10 adopted a resolution, by unanimous vote, providing for a League of Nations Commission of Enquiry in the Far East. Its task was to study and report on all circumstances of an international character which threatened peace and good relations between Japan and China.

The Commission was not completed until early January 1932. Its members were the Earl of Lytton, as chairman; General Henri Édouard Claudel; Count Luigi Aldrovandi-Marescotti; Dr. Heinrich Schnee; and, from the United States, Major General Frank McCoy.

Since there was no commercial air travel the Lytton Commission traveled by boat to the United States, by special train across the United States, and by boat, waiting for it in San Francisco,

2. *Ibid.*, p. 479n.

to Asia. By the time they had traveled this long route and had made some investigations, the members of the Commission were confronted with a *fait accompli.* The Japanese had taken Manchuria, which they declared to be the state of Manchukuo in February 1932. From April 20 to June 4, 1932, the Commission took testimony in Manchuria. It returned to Tokyo and then went on to Peiping to draft its report. The Commission found that Japan's action of September 1931 was not justified by reasons of self-defense and recommended that the powers should not recognize Manchukuo and that Japan should evacuate all of Manchuria except the railway zone.[3]

The report of the Lytton Commission, which was signed in Peiping on September 4, was adopted by the League of Nations Assembly on February 24, 1933. Shortly after, on March 27, Japan gave notice of her intention to withdraw from the League.

The failure of the Lytton Commission to affect the result in Manchuria and Japan's withdrawal from the League had a profound effect upon the League of Nations Conference for the Reduction and Limitation of Armaments, which had been convened in Geneva in 1932. In my radio speech of November 10, 1931, I had pointed out that

Many people now are asking what will be the effect of Manchuria upon the [coming] disarmament conference.

The Manchurian incident is not yet over, and its finish will have a decided effect, for good or bad, upon the conference. If the Manchurian problem is not settled peacefully, if the League and Kellogg-Briand Pact suffer a rebuff, there will be a reaction in favor of large

3. On January 7, 1932, the government of the United States, in a note addressed both to Japan and China, had declared that the United States would not recognize any agreement between the two nations which might impair American treaty rights in China, nor any situation brought about by means contrary to the Kellogg Pact. Enunciated by Stimson, this became known as the "doctrine of nonrecognition."

defenses. Some unthinking nations will be led by the militarists, always looking for an excuse, who will say, "It has been proved that the world's peace machinery can't keep peace. The conclusion is that each nation must be prepared to take care of itself." On the other hand, if the League and Kellogg Pact win the issue in Manchuria, the people will conclude that world public opinion, mobilized by the machinery of the world community, is able to maintain peace, and the conclusion will be that since nations no longer need to depend entirely upon themselves, they can afford to disarm in proportion to the security they feel in the world community.

Japan, however, was not as important to the Disarmament Conference as Germany was. It was Germany's activities, even more than Japan's, which brought about the failure of the conference, and were most shattering to the League itself. As Japan's withdrawal from the League of Nations was associated with the League's adoption of the Lytton Report, so the withdrawal of Germany from the League was associated with, although not entirely caused by, the League's conferences on disarmament.

The discussion of disarmament is a thread that runs throughout the history of the League, beginning with the First Assembly, which opened on January 20, 1920, and which was responsible for the setting up of the Temporary Mixed Commission for the Reduction of Armaments. Following the signing of the Locarno Treaties of 1925 and the entrance of Germany into the League of Nations in 1926, a stronger disarmament body was created—the Preparatory Commission for the Disarmament Conference. Hugh Gibson, the United States ambassador to Belgium, was head of the American delegation to the Preparatory Commission, which paved the way for the Conference for the Reduction and Limitation of Armaments itself. (Norman H. Davis, with the title of ambassador-at-large, represented the American government at the conference.)

At the Geneva meetings a fundamental difference was evident between France and certain other continental states on the one side, and the United States on the other, with the United Kingdom somewhere in the middle. The United States continued to approach disarmament on the basis of mathematical formulas following the pattern of the Washington Naval Conference of 1921.[4] The French approached disarmament as part of the overall problem of security, believing that collective security arrangements must accompany whatever formula was agreed upon or the formula would be meaningless. In 1932–33 there were two disarmament programs introduced at the conference. According to Professor Shotwell:

The program of France was set forth in its memorandum of November 1932. This stated in the clearest possible terms that France was ready to lessen its armaments in proportion as nations organized themselves for peace. Never was the collective system of security better described than in this document, which put in the foreground the obligation which a nation owes to the community of nations to ensure peace. It was not merely peace for itself but peace among other nations as well which created that condition of security necessary for any major steps in the reduction of armaments. The paramount issue in the eyes of France was the upbuilding of that "organization of peace" which, as M. Briand pointed out on the occasion of the signing of the Pact of Paris, was called for by that Pact, although not definitely provided for in its terms. The primary obligation is a universal one, that all signatories of the Pact of Paris engage themselves never to be a party to any breach of it, even by financial or commercial support of the aggressor. Nothing was said about military measures for international policing. The "Stimson Doctrine," that conquest does not constitute title, was accepted by all. Thus upon the background of a universal concept of security the French memorandum proceeded to grade the responsibilities of nations for the maintenance of peace. It then proposed a

4. Held outside the auspices of the League of Nations, the Washington Naval Conference was called by the American Secretary of State to meet in Washington, D.C., on November 12, 1921. It was this conference that reached the famous formula of 3:5:5 for the ratio of Japan's navy to those of the United States and Great Britain.

scaling down to armaments which would be measured by the increased security brought about by this realistic plan.[5]

This policy was accepted by the British government and was incorporated in the plan it introduced in March. The British draft became the basis of negotiations at the Disarmament Conference in the ensuing months.

The position of the Americans changed gradually during the conference. The United States came to recognize that limitation of arms by ratios depended less on finding the correct ratios than on "finding how far nations will participate in that kind of procedure which is designed to prevent war from breaking out at all."[6] Unfortunately, the United States itself was not ready to go very far. On May 22, 1933, Mr. Davis summed up the position of our government:

I wish to make clear that we are ready not only to do our part toward the substantive reduction of armaments but, if this is effected by general international agreement, we are also prepared to contribute in other ways to the organization of peace. In particular, we are willing to consult the other states in case of a threat to peace, with a view to averting conflict. Further than that, in the event that the states, in conference, determine that a state has been guilty of a breach of the peace in violation of its international obligations and take measures against the violator, then, if we concur in the judgment rendered as to the responsible and guilty party, we will refrain from any action tending to defeat such collective effort which these states may thus make to restore peace.[7]

Despite the United States recognition of the relationship between security and disarmament, however, the Disarmament Conference could not be saved after the virtual defection of Germany. The German government was under strong pressure

5. James T. Shotwell, *The Great Decision* (New York: The Macmillan Company, 1944), pp. 147–148.

6. *Ibid.*, p. 149.

7. As quoted in *ibid.*, p. 148.

from the Nazis and others not to participate in any arrangement that would imply Germany's acceptance of the disarmed and therefore second-class status imposed on her after the First World War. When Mr. Davis made his speech, Germany had already withdrawn once from the Disarmament Conference on September 14, 1932, but an agreement among the great powers, which Norman Davis was active in producing, had brought the German delegates back for a few months. In January 1933, however, the German Republic had its final collapse and Hitler became chancellor of the Third Reich. On October 14, 1933, Germany withdrew finally from the conference and on October 21 gave notice of its withdrawal from the League.

The conference resumed on October 16 and continued for some months, while Arthur Henderson of the United Kingdom, president of the conference, visited many capitals to see what could be done to save it. Finally, on June 11, 1934, it was generally agreed that the conference should recess.[8]

Despite the failure of the Disarmament Conference, a surprising amount of progress was made in the technical field while the statesmen were bogged down by political considerations. Some years later, after the Second World War was ended and after the revelation that the Soviet Union had the ability to produce atomic bombs, Major General George V. Strong, who had been chief military adviser to the United States delegation in the League's Disarmament Conference, told Professor Shotwell that the technical progress at Geneva had been so far-reaching that if a preparatory committee were called, it would take no more than three months to bring technical matters up to date so that a disarmament agreement would be possible.

8. I say "recess" because the League of Nations never abandoned a conference.

5

Campaign to "State the Terms"—Defeat of the World Court

The Disarmament Conference of 1932 took place under the cloud of the worldwide depression which had followed the collapse in October 1929 of the American orgy of speculation of the 1920s. Lasting longer than any previous depression in modern times, the Great Depression could not help but color the deliberations of nations in the tragic days of the thirties.

In the beginning, it was not realized how far the American collapse would go, how long it would last, or how it would affect the entire world. I remember hearing James J. Forstall, the Chicago financier who had made commitments to safeguard the property surrounding the site of the new League buildings, talking on the telephone from Geneva with his partners in New York. They were urging him to liquidate everything he had in the stock market. He, in turn, was holding out and preaching faith in the United States.

The Hoover administration could not believe that what had happened had really happened. After all, books had been written to prove that the new productive capacity of the United States and other nations ruled out the seasonal depressions that had been known in previous years. Frantic efforts were made to stem the tide and revive prosperity. The slogan became

"Prosperity is just around the corner." But no fundamental remedies were undertaken until Franklin D. Roosevelt, elected President in 1932, assumed office in March 1933.[1]

Meanwhile, there was pressure for a world economic conference from workers' delegates to the International Labor Organization's annual conference in April 1932, and from powers meeting at about the same time in Lausanne for a reparations conference—Germany, France, Great Britain, Italy, Japan, and Belgium. Preparatory meetings began in the autumn of 1932. Unfortunately, between then and the scheduled start of the conference in June 1933, a number of events whose effect on the conference could not help but be adverse occurred. Germany left the Disarmament Conference, and although she returned in December 1932, she was to leave again in the fall of 1933. The German Republic collapsed and Hitler and the Nazis seized power. Japan gave notice in March 1933 of her withdrawal from the League. And, not least, in April the United States went off the gold standard suddenly, without consulting other nations.

Nevertheless, the cordial exchange of views early in 1933 between the French premier, Édouard Herriot, and President Roosevelt on the one hand, and Prime Minister Ramsey MacDonald and the President on the other, as well as Mr. Roosevelt's famous appeal on May 16 to the heads of state to see to it that the Disarmament and World Economic Conferences should not fail, led to the belief that the United States would cooperate to the fullest in the Economic Conference, and that it had a chance to succeed.

1. President Hoover did commission a group of experts to make a study of the economic collapse, and thousands of words were written. But although the connection seems obvious today, there was scarcely a reference to the relationship between the destruction and dislocations of the First World War and the temporary prosperity of the twenties and subsequent depression. The American people, having chosen the road of isolationism, were living in such an unreal world that they failed to understand the effect of war debts and reparations on the world's economy.

The conference was scheduled to open shortly after the remarkable first 100 days of President Roosevelt's term, in which the most far-reaching steps were taken to restore public confidence, to give constructive relief, and to avoid what otherwise might have been a complete collapse of the American system. The President had a way of making people feel that he was concerned with them and consequently they wanted to follow him. I remember in the 1950s, when Mrs. Roosevelt was chairman of the board of directors of the American Association for the United Nations and I was its national director, we made a tour of chapters in Minnesota and the Dakotas. In one town, the mayor described to Mrs. Roosevelt her husband's special train traveling through the region in the depths of the depression. This man had been asked by the presidential party to come to the train and talk with the President. He said the President had asked him very human and practical questions, such as, Are your people getting enough to eat? and, How is their health? The mayor said that from that day he had supported President Roosevelt in everything. It was this personal attention that gave people hope and saved the country from social upheaval.

Unfortunately, just before the Economic Conference opened, on June 12, conditions in the United States grew worse. Mr. Roosevelt began to feel that recovery at home had not gone far enough to justify the constructive steps he had hoped would be taken in London, and his concern for domestic recovery gave him little time to think clearly about some of the problems of the conference. Secretary of State Cordell Hull, who headed the United States delegation, was a thorough internationalist, particularly in the economic field.[2] But even before he arrived

2. Before the President had selected his cabinet, Professor Shotwell had called upon then Senator Cordell Hull to ask him if he would support Norman Davis for Secretary of State. The senator had said he would be glad to, for Davis was also his choice. Mr. Shotwell was therefore quite chagrined when Hull himself was made Secretary of State. But Hull and Shotwell quickly became close friends, and Shotwell a valued adviser.

in London, a message from the President seemed to cut the ground from under him.

Assistant Secretary of State Raymond Moley, a professor of public law on leave of absence from Columbia University, persuaded President Roosevelt to permit him to go to London to try his hand at an agreement. Secretary Hull considered this an offense, although as things turned out, the milder currency stabilization plan that Moley, who was known in the State Department as a conservative, believed would be acceptable to the members of the conference, as well as to President Roosevelt, was repudiated in harsh terms by the President. The divisions within the United States delegation to the conference made it evident that this country had not yet decided on what approach to take to international economic affairs and considered that its job was to set its own house in order first. The self-interest radiated by the government of the United States at the conference in turn caused other nations to react with more nationalistic policies. There seemed to be nothing to do but adjourn the conference until the fall. Tariffs continued high and economic warfare unabated.

Despite the disappointing result of the Economic Conference, on December 28, 1933, President Roosevelt, in an address to the annual dinner of the Woodrow Wilson Foundation, spoke in constructive terms about the League of Nations, giving new hope to those of us who had been working so long for United States membership in the organization. His address was doubly welcome because some nine months earlier the John Day Company had published a book written by the President entitled *Looking Forward,* in which he stated:

In common with millions of my fellow countrymen, I worked and spoke, in 1920, in behalf of American participation in a League of Nations, conceived in the highest spirit of world friendship for the great object of preventing a return of world war. For that course I have no apology to make.

If, today, I believed that the same or even similar factors entered into the argument, I would still favor America's entry into the League; and I would go so far as to seek to win over the overwhelming opposition which exists in this country today. But the League of Nations today is not the League of Nations conceived by Woodrow Wilson. . . .

American participation in the League would not serve the highest purpose of the prevention of war and a settlement of international difficulties in accordance with fundamental American ideals. . . .[3]

The officials of the League of Nations Association had seen advance proofs of the book and realized that this statement was devastating to the program of the Association and cooperating organizations. They had made appropriate protests, but their efforts to have the manuscript revised were not successful. Fortunately, and surprisingly, the book had attracted little comment.

In his Woodrow Wilson Foundation dinner address the President said:

Through all the centuries and down to the world of conflict of 1914 to 1918, wars were made by governments. Woodrow Wilson challenged that necessity. That challenge made the people who create and who change governments think. They wondered with Woodrow Wilson whether the people themselves could not some day prevent governments from making war.

It is but an extension of the challenge of Woodrow Wilson for us to propose in this newer generation that from now on war by governments shall be changed to peace by peoples.

And he made a practical endorsement of the League of Nations:

The League has provided a common meeting place; it has provided machinery which serves for international discussion; and in very many practical instances it has helped labor and health and commerce and education, and, last but not least, the actual settlement of many disputes great and small among nations great and small.

3. Franklin D. Roosevelt, *Looking Forward* (New York: The John Day Company, 1933), pp. 254–255.

Today the United States is cooperating more openly in the fuller utilization of the League of Nations machinery than ever before.[4]

This was the first of a series of principles and proposals on the organization of peace that President Roosevelt was to announce in subsequent years, most of them following Pearl Harbor. Because of my position in the League of Nations Association and, later, in the Commission to Study the Organization of Peace and the American Association for the United Nations, I was in increasingly close touch with the President from Pearl Harbor until his death in April 1945. I was able to watch his ideas unfold and develop until he had a well-worked-out concept of what should take the place of the League of Nations, and had come to believe that it must be established before the war ended.

It was shortly before President Roosevelt made his speech in honor of Woodrow Wilson that I was appointed national director of the League of Nations Association. In June 1933 Philip C. Nash, who had been director since 1929, had resigned, and, after some searching, Hilton Railey, an old friend of Raymond Fosdick's who had the reputation of being a good fund raiser, had been appointed in his place. There was some embarrassment on the part of the national officers because after years of service in the Association I had been passed over, but I myself saw good reason for Railey's selection. He and I became acquainted immediately, and I offered to help him in every possible way.

It was thought important that Railey go to Geneva in the fall of 1933 to be introduced there to the many people interested in the Association, including representatives of other organizations and delegates with whom we had contact. I went to Geneva to prepare the way for his visit, and then on to Berlin,

4. *The Public Papers and Addresses of Franklin D. Roosevelt, Volume Two, The Year of Crisis, 1933,* compiled and collated by Samuel I. Rosenman (New York: Random House, 1938), pp. 547, 549.

where, according to plan, Railey was to catch up with me and we would continue on together.

In Berlin I had a very good visit with Ambassador William E. Dodd, who had been a member of the board of directors of the Chicago branch of the LNA, and who had asked me to call on him at his new post. The ambassador was anxious that I express to the Germans I met the distaste of many Americans for the growing excesses of the Germans. I remember he sent me to a comparatively liberal member of the German Foreign Office; a year later such a visit or protest would have been impossible.

From Berlin, Railey and I went on to Vienna, where John Gunther, whom I had known for some time, was the Chicago *Daily News* correspondent. Mrs. Gunther took me to dinner at the home of a distinguished Viennese family by the name of Sheue. They were Socialists, very liberal, and lived in one of the amazing buildings Vienna had erected for the working people. It was only a year later that Chancellor Dollfuss was shot by the Austrian Nazis in an attempted coup and left to bleed to death. Although the Nazis failed in their efforts to seize power at that time, they continued to grow in strength and in a few years liberal Vienna was no more.

From Vienna, Railey and I returned to Geneva, and upon adjournment of the League of Nations Assembly, I went with him to Paris to see him off for New York, confident that he was anxious to move ahead as the vigorous new national director of the Association. However, Germany's final defection from the Disarmament Conference in mid-October, and the notice of her intention to withdraw from the League of Nations, proved devastating to Railey's morale, as indeed they were to the morale of many Americans, who felt it was downhill to disaster from then on. It was only a matter of time until Railey resigned his post. He did so on November 17, recommending me as his successor. I remember waiting uncomfortably in a New York restaurant that was also a speakeasy, not far from the Coffee

House Club where the executive committee of the Association was considering whether or not I should be appointed. Finally, I was appointed acting director for four months, after which I became director.[5]

I was to make one other visit to Nazi Berlin, in 1934. Ambassador Dodd, no longer new to the post, gave me a pretty grim picture of what was by then happening in Germany. I had some personal experiences as well, one of which stays vividly with me. I was acquainted with a British newspaperman who had been expelled from Berlin. On finding out that I was going there, he had asked me if I would contact a friend of his, a Jewess, with whom he did not dare communicate himself.

She was a most attractive young woman, a secretary in the German dye trust office, whose plant was in Frankfurt. I wanted to talk to her but not in any way embarrass her. She seemed to believe that boldness was the best tactic, so she suggested that for dinner on the night we were to meet we go to a rather notorious Nazi café. The Brown Shirts were drinking beer at their tables and saluting each other, and no one expected that a Jewess would take an American guest—one who had made speeches against the Nazis—to this restaurant. She told me that, so far, she and her immediate family had not been troubled, although a cousin had been taken away by the Nazis. When he returned he had been in frail health and his hair had turned white; he told them never to ask what had occurred.

The next day we had a long excursion to the Tiergarten. We took a boat ride and ate at an outdoor café. Suddenly some Hitler youth appeared, shouting enthusiastically. Goebbels was

5. I knew most members of the New York board quite well. One of them afterwards told me that one of the women on the board—a very charming lady —had raised the question of whether I, as a Midwesterner, had the social background for the post of national director. She wondered if I would be accepted on Park Avenue. Spencer van B. Nichols, a member of the board and later treasurer, replied that inasmuch as Mr. Eichelberger was accepted in Paris, London, and Geneva, Park Avenue must adjust itself.

at the head of a Nazi parade taking Nazi salutes. We were surrounded. I felt something had to be done, for my companion was not going to salute. I brought my arm up stiffly across her back so that her instinctive reaction might be taken for a Nazi salute. If neither of us had appeared to make the gesture—she being a Jewess, and I an American who must have been known in Berlin as anti-Nazi—I shudder even now at what might have happened.

She was a young woman of courage who had hope that all this might pass, but who at any moment could expect the worst. I never heard from her again, and thought it better not to try to communicate with her as conditions grew rapidly worse for Jews in the months that followed my visit. I have always feared that at some time in the years after I met her she went to the gas chambers with the rest.

In 1934, the Association began its program with a campaign urging that the government state the terms under which it would be willing to enter the League of Nations. Our petition, on which it was hoped to get 1 million signatures, read:

We, Citizens of the United States,

Anxious to avoid war and organize peace in which prosperity can thrive,

Believing that the collective system of the world community which includes the Kellogg-Briand Pact (Pact of Paris) to which the United States is a party, and the League of Nations, can best prevent war,

Mindful of the fact that the United States is participating in many activities of the League of Nations,

Aware that without the privilege of membership in the League the United States is placed at a disadvantage, and the moral integrity of the world community is weakened,

Urge that the United States reinforce the League's contribution to peace by stating the terms under which full membership would be possible; and by appointing in the meantime an official diplomatic

representative to the League of Nations to participate in its deliberations.

Raymond Fosdick, president of the Association, in his letter
presenting the petition to "Friends of the League of Nations,"
wrote:

As President Roosevelt so clearly pointed out in a recent speech [De-
cember 28, 1933], "the old policies, alliances, combinations and bal-
ances of power have proved themselves inadequate for the preservation of world peace." We believe that the alternative to such a
procedure is the League machinery. . . .

We raise the issue now because while during the last decade and a
half the United States has declined to join the League of Nations as it
was organized in 1919, we have never stated what kind of a League
we *would* join or the precise conditions under which we would consent to sit down in common counsel with the other nations of the
world. It cannot be true that we would refuse to sit down under any
conditions whatever. Such a decision would be too completely unintel-
ligent, too blindly suicidal. The United States has participated in plenty
of international conferences in the last fifty years—on all sorts of subjects. What are the conditions under which we would participate in the
continuous international conferences that take place in Geneva?

Quite obviously, the suggestion that the United States state the
terms under which it would enter the League meant that the
United States would be proposing modifications of the traditional obligations of League of Nations members—in short,
changes in the Covenant, particularly in the obligation of members to take collective sanctions against an aggressor. As Joseph
Paul-Boncour, successor to Briand, had pointed out in a recent
speech, the nations of the world were in an abyss shaped, like
Dante's *Inferno,* in concentric circles; those on the outer rim
were less threatened by and had suffered less from war than
those closer to the center, and therefore it was not realistic to
expect them to assume the same obligations for preventing it.
The United States was on the outer rim, and the organization

of peace should adjust itself to this fact if it were to succeed.

Although the LNA recognized that exempting the United States from the obligation to participate in collective sanctions would weaken the League in one respect, we believed United States membership on an equal basis would strengthen the organization immeasurably, and would therefore be worth the price. And, after all, a great number of member nations had historically treated sanctions as an optional matter, despite the wording of the Covenant. Thus, we concluded, the United States might join the League by pledging only to the lesser obligations of consultation and non-interference with League measures against aggression.

This position was further developed in the resolution which Senator James P. Pope of Idaho introduced in the United States Senate on May 7, 1935. Pope credits Professor Shotwell with the major part in drafting his resolution—indeed, Shotwell had been largely responsible for the idea of "stating the terms." The resolution stated that

Whereas the League of Nations has in the course of its history established the principle that its members assume no obligations to aid in the enforcement of peace without the consent of their respective governments, acting in accordance with their own constitutional methods and with the regard of their traditional policies and geographical situation; and

Whereas it is therefore apparent that membership in the League of Nations upon these understood and agreed conditions would be consonant with and in furtherance of the vital interests of the United States . . .

the President should be authorized to notify the League that the United States accepted its membership in the organization on the following terms and understandings:

(1) That the obligations of the Pact of Paris not to resort to war as an instrument of national policy is recognized as the fundamental and guiding principle of the Covenant; and

(2) That the provisions of the Covenant of the League of Nations relating to cooperation in the prevention of war shall not be interpreted as obligating the United States to adopt measures which might involve the use of armed force; and that the decision as to what action shall be taken by the United States in case the peace of nations is threatened or violated shall rest with the Government of the United States acting according to the Constitution.

The petition campaign enrolled the cooperation of many national organizations. A letter that I wrote to officers and secretaries of the Association on February 5, 1934, reads:

. . . We have practically the unanimous support of the country. The Cause and Cure of War group endorsed it [the petition] as a program of work; such different organizations as the Catholic Association for International Peace, the National Council for the Prevention of War and the National Council of Jewish Women are circulating it. The World Alliance for International Friendship through the Churches is working shoulder to shoulder with us and has agreed to mobilize 65,000 clergy. . . .

It was not long, however, before those opposed to United States membership in the League were heard from. The petition's recommendation that the President appoint "an official diplomatic representative to the League of Nations" while the process of stating the terms was under way in particular attracted attention. On March 10, 1934, an article and a petition appeared in Hearst's *New York Evening Journal,* with the headline: "Plea Launched to Block U.S. League Entry." The article went on to say:

The *Evening Journal* and other Hearst newspapers throughout the country today gave the American public its first chance to voice organized disapproval of entanglement in the League of Nations and World Court. Through a huge petition, printed in these papers and circulated by patriotic organizations, those who are opposed to this nation becoming involved in European affairs may register their protest. Speedy action is necessary. International propagandists, fed with millions of dollars, have long been working to draw the United States into an entangling alliance with Europe. . . .

Despite the vociferous anti-League faction, the Association continued to enlist national leaders and responsible national organizations. But it did not have the facilities that were open to William Randolph Hearst to push his "Petition Against Participation in the League of Nations and World Court." On May 9, Hearst's Chicago *Herald and Examiner* indicated that more than 310,000 "loyal men and women have already registered a protest to Congress. . . ." Additional signatures were to be secured.

The Association's signature campaign continued throughout 1934. A statement by Raymond Fosdick entitled "Why Raise the Issue Now?" was circulated in leaflet form. It answered the question posed by its title in the following way:

We raise the issue now—

because the world is face to face with another 1914 . . .

because war hysteria grows as the influence of the League of Nations wanes . . .

because we do not know of any way of avoiding the impending disaster except as we build on the foundations that have already been laid in Geneva . . .

because the growing nationalism of the last five years has gotten the world nowhere . . .

because while during the last decade and a half the United States had declined to join the League of Nations as it was organized in 1919, we have never stated what kind of League we *would* join or the precise conditions under which we would consent to sit down in common counsel with the other nations of the world . . .

International conditions grew worse as the petition campaign was being presented to the country. In July Dollfuss was killed in Vienna. On the death of President von Hindenburg in August, Hitler consolidated the offices of president and chancellor and became Führer. In October, King Alexander of Yugoslavia and French Foreign Minister Barthou were assassinated in Marseilles. The one bright spot in the grim international picture was the Soviet Union's entrance into the League of Nations on September 18.[6]

In the face of international events and the hostility of the anti-League press, the petition campaign failed to achieve its objectives. Nevertheless, through the campaign millions of people became more aware of the League's significance and of the likelihood of war as the alternative to it.

Another of my early concerns as national director of the LNA involved United States participation in the World Court.

In 1926, the United States Senate had consented to the entrance of the United States into the Permanent Court of International Justice with five reservations. Of the five, the first four did not present serious problems for the League of Nations. The United States would pay its fair share of the expenses of the Court; the United States would have an equal share in the selection of the judges; the United States would assume no legal relationship to the League of Nations nor any obligation under the Treaty of Versailles; the United States might at any time withdraw its adherence to the protocols and the protocols would not be amended without the consent of the United States.

It was the fifth reservation which presented the problem. This stated that the Court should not render any advisory opinion except publicly after due notice to all states adhering to the Court and to all interested states, nor should it without the consent of the United States entertain any request for an advis-

6. I wrote at the time in a letter to the Association's branches that if Russia were not to be admitted to the League, she would be the victim of an attack by Germany and Japan.

ory opinion touching any dispute or question in which the United States had claimed an interest. The League of Nations was concerned that being able to block an advisory opinion would give the United States a preferred position over any other members of the Court, and asked the United States to explain the reservation. Unfortunately, the United States government found it inadvisable to make explanations.

There the matter rested until 1929. At that time Elihu Root, at the suggestion of the United States government, took advantage of his attendance at the League of Nations Conference for the Revision of the Statute of the Court to draft the so-called Root Protocol, designed to furnish a procedure to give effect to the fifth reservation. The Protocol provided that in case the League wished to ask the Court for an advisory opinion, it would notify the government of the United States. Should the United States government object to the granting of the advisory opinion, it would consult with the Council of the League. Should the League not feel free to withdraw its request for the advisory opinion, the United States could exercise its right of withdrawal from the Court without any imputation of unfriendliness. A prominent American jurist remarked that there might be only one case in a thousand in which an advisory opinion would concern the interest of the United States, and only one case in a thousand of those cases in which the League's request could not be rewritten or withdrawn to meet American objectives.

A few of us, anxious to avoid another Senate debate on the subject, felt that the Secretary of State could simply declare that acceptance of the Root formula constituted an acceptance by the League of the five American reservations and therefore that the President had only to confirm the 1926 Senate decision for this country to become a member of the Court. Unfortunately, however, the question of U.S. membership in the Court and the protocols were resubmitted to the Senate, where the administration believed they would easily pass with the required two-thirds majority vote.

The administration had not taken into account the "radio priest" Father Charles E. Coughlin, and William Randolph Hearst. In a hysterical speech one Sunday—January 27, 1935— Father Coughlin was able to mobilize his listeners to send 100,000 telegrams to the Senate opposing the move to join the Court. I reprint here an editorial I wrote in the *Chronicle* of January 30, 1935, because it not only expresses the indignation which friends of the Court felt but describes the kinds of maneuvers that kept the United States out of the Court and defeated the LNA petition campaign.

In the cold sober morning after the vote on the World Court, the Senators who were stampeded into switching their votes by the flood of telegrams secured over the week-end by Father Coughlin and William Randolph Hearst can well turn their minds to the wisdom of their change. Those Senators, such as Hiram Johnson, who from the beginning worked against the Court may well ask themselves whether they did not pay too great a price for the defeat of the Court in allying themselves with Father Coughlin and William Randolph Hearst.

It is not too much to say that the means used to defeat the Court witnessed the birth of the American Fascist movement. Certain terrible forces of demagoguery were let loose which may well make the American people tremble for their democracy.

On Friday, January 25, there were clearly enough votes for the entrance of the United States into the World Court by the required two-thirds majority. It was clear that the opposition was preventing a vote, hoping for some important development over the week-end. Sunday, Father Coughlin stepped to the radio and delivered a speech that, for vituperation, prostitution of religion, misrepresentation and demagoguery, is unexcelled by any utterance of the French Revolution or of American history. He paid $8,000 for this opportunity. Added to his broadcast, William Randolph Hearst used every trick of which he is notoriously capable in support of Father Coughlin's campaign.

The result was a flood of 100,000 telegrams received in Washington over the week-end. It was clear on Monday that the opponents of the Court had taken the aggressive; Father Coughlin's campaign had put the Court advocates on the defensive. In the face of such misrepresentation, backed by unlimited resources to buy radio time, the friends of the Court, dependent upon the reasonableness, intelligence and an appreciation of fact, were in a bad way.

What happened? Senators were stampeded. For illustration, the two Senators from Massachusetts were considered pledged to vote for the Court. There was plenty of evidence that the thinking people of Massachusetts wished them to so vote. Bar associations, all of the great church bodies, women's groups had spoken favorably and, if the League of Nations was a factor at all, the voters in one-fourth of Massachusetts had urged American entrance into the League of Nations itself in the Massachusetts election. In a moment all this expression of the intelligent people of Massachusetts was forgotten in the panic which seized the two Massachusetts Senators because of a few thousand telegrams inspired by Father Coughlin, and because half the members of the legislature, it is reported, at the suggestion of a Hearst reporter signed a telegram urging the two Senators to vote against the Court. They forgot their pledges and abandoned the thinking people of their state to be stampeded by one unfortunately wearing the cloth of the church that would gladly repudiate him and a newspaper editor who, since the time of the Spanish-American War, has been the scourge of American life.

Father Coughlin, William Randolph Hearst and Huey Long—there are the leaders of the American Fascist movement. Their progress at the moment is certainly farther than the headway Hitler had made at the time of the "beer putsch" in Munich. These men are united by three basic appeals. They breathe hatred of all things foreign in exactly the same language. Second, they are united in taking advantage of the impatience of the people for quicker economic recovery. True, Hearst has criticized the President for being too radical and the other two men criticize the President for not being radical enough. But this gulf can be easily breached if William Randolph Hearst is given a position of power to satisfy his so far insatiable inferiority complex. Finally, these men are united in their common unscrupulousness. No charge was too base to make, no language too vile for them to use in their efforts to defeat the Court.

The foes of the Court, in order to defeat American entrance, have turned loose upon this country a demagogue who has demonstrated that, by securing 100,000 telegrams in a hysterical radio appeal, he can stampede the Senate into disregarding the sober judgment of the majority of American people.

The Senators who voted against the Court at the suggestion of William Randolph Hearst have admitted that he has the balance of power in their respective states. Having tasted power on this important issue, they may expect that on other issues this year if he cracks the whip they must jump, contrary.even to the wishes of the President, to save their necks from Hearst's political guillotine.

Senator Long has already organized his "share-the-wealth movement." One United States Senator, a very conservative gentleman, told the editor that at the present moment Huey Long could overthrow the political balance of power. What he is now doing in Louisiana in the destruction of the freedom of speech and the orderly process of government could be duplicated on a national scale if these American Fascists got control. News from Louisiana about armed resistance, the seizure of government buildings, the organizations of secret groups and the accounts of suppression of political enemies by Senator Long's troops read very similarly to the dispatches from Vienna and Berlin.

Following in the trail of these men is the American court jester, Will Rogers. Somewhere there is a fable about the court jester who lost his head because he took himself too seriously and wished to be the king. Democracies have a sense of humor and the people in their enjoyment of freedom of speech laugh at Will Rogers' amusing quips. However, Will Rogers might well pause to consider the fact that in Germany it is a concentration camp offense to poke fun at the powers that be. The Fascist movement to which he is unconsciously allying himself will not tolerate his humor once American democracy is destroyed.

The defeat of the World Court is not simply defeat of one of the agencies of the organized world community to give effect and meaning to the Kellogg Pact. Defeat of the World Court is an admission that one newspaper chain plus a demagogue who can let loose upon the United States Senate 100,000 telegrams are sufficient to block the will of the people by stampeding the national legislature. From now on the issue is not only peace or war and world cooperation against isolationism; the issue fundamentally is democracy vs. fascism.

The defeat of the World Court showed that, despite increased United States cooperation with the League of Nations, the American people could still be mobilized against any imagined political commitment to the organization. Europeans were discouraged. They had been led to believe that the United States would accept the Root formula, but the Senate debate had brought out unusually bitter opposition: a Midwest senator in the heart of the debate had shouted, "To hell with Europe!" Yet a day or so after the vote was taken, the same senator saw no inconsistency in joining a group of senators who had called a meeting to consider how they might promote a greater sale of American agricultural products abroad!

6

Munich and the Approach of the Second World War

By 1938 the moral and legal foundation of international society had been declining for some time, although up to September of that year there was hope that respect for the League Covenant and the Kellogg Pact might revive. Unfortunately most of the small states, whose loyalty had not swerved, were dependent upon the wishes of a few great powers—the United Kingdom, France, and the Soviet Union. The moral test of two of these three powers came when the British and French ambassadors to Czechoslovakia knocked on the door of the president of the Czechoslovak republic, Eduard Beneš, at two o'clock in the morning of September 21 to demand that he accept a virtual surrender to Hitler. The small states had been deserted. By the end of the year it was clear that the League of Nations system could not be saved without being rebuilt, or that something else must be created to take its place if there should be the tragedy of world war.

Nevertheless, even in 1938 there was much that the League of Nations was doing in the economic, health, and social fields. Many countries, including the United States, continued to place great emphasis on economic and social cooperation through the League in the hope that non-political cooperation might reverse the tide of aggression. In particular, the United States, which was recovering from the depression, supported broad economic policies that might lead to worldwide recovery, and enlisted the support of the National Peace Conference, of which the LNA was a member, in its efforts.

The National Peace Conference was an umbrella organization composed of about forty organizations devoted to world cooperation and peace. Some were devoted exclusively to these causes; the rest—civic, business, and labor groups—had these among other objectives. The organization included groups, such as the LNA, which supported a policy of collective security against aggression. Most of these were in favor of revising the Neutrality Law so that it would make a distinction between an aggressor and the victim of aggression. They did not believe that the United States could stay out of world involvement. Other members of the National Peace Conference, including some pacifist organizations, wanted this country to take no sides. They were opposed to any revision of the Neutrality Law, and the darker the international situation became, the more anxious they were to follow a policy of withdrawal and neutrality.[1]

In spite of their differences, however, all of the peace organizations were concerned with world economic cooperation, due

1. As an illustration of how deeply the members of these groups felt, I refer to an incident that occurred in Berlin in 1934. On one occasion after seeing Ambassador Dodd, I met a member of the National Peace Conference—the head of one of the large American peace organizations—and his wife at a café on Unter den Linden. He asked me to take tea with them. I had spent the evening before with some people who had much to fear, because they were Jews, and I was deeply worried. My colleague from the peace movement, however, was concerned with one thing and that was disarmament. He said, "If France does not accept the German proposals for disarmament, let France look out." I was bemoaning what Hitler was doing to the German people and to Europe, and my friend was predicting the destruction of France if she did not agree to the German disarmament proposals! And although I would not say that he enjoyed the prospect of a Europe dominated by Nazi Germany, he did not abhor it as much as I thought he should.

largely to the influence of Secretary of State Cordell Hull. They were generally in agreement on the need for supporting the reciprocal trade program and for doing everything possible to promote international economic cooperation through the League of Nations. If some of them followed this program to escape confronting the political facts, all of them believed that if nations which felt that they were in an inferior economic position had a better opportunity in the world, some of the causes of war would be eliminated. Consequently, the peace groups adopted a program of world economic cooperation at an economic conference they held in Washington in early 1938. Professor James T. Shotwell, Eugene Staley, professor of economics at the University of Southern California, and many others took an active role. It was an effort in which the League of Nations Association played an important part—the last program which all sections of the American peace movement could support.

In addition to its work with the National Peace Conference, in late fall 1937 the LNA helped to organize the Committee for Concerted Peace Efforts, composed of those organizations that shared the LNA's belief in collective security. The committee's members were concerned to find means to halt the spread of Japanese aggression in China, and the majority were deeply troubled by the intervention of Germany and Italy in the Spanish Civil War. They did not believe the United States could avoid becoming involved in a world catastrophe, and felt that if this country became involved before the catastrophe developed it might yet be averted.

In May of 1938 the committee encouraged the United States to participate in the only collective resistance on the part of the powers to the German threat to Czechoslovakia. Hitler's troops were menacing the Czech frontier. The Czechs had mobilized, demonstrating not only the efficiency of their army but the degree of unity in their country. Their mobilization was accompanied by a show of firmness on the part of France, the Soviet Union, and Great Britain, and the committee believed that an appeal under the terms of the Kellogg-Briand Pact by the American Secretary of State would add to the collective moral weight against the use of force by Germany. On May 26 a telegram was sent on behalf of the committee to President Roosevelt and Secretary Hull, stating:

. . . We feel that the Government of the United States could, with all propriety, remind the German government of its mutual obligations with the United States as one of the signatories of the Kellogg Pact. We are not clear as to whether the admonition to Germany should be public or through quiet diplomatic channels, but we urge that the United States impress upon Germany its desire that the dispute with Czechoslovakia be settled peaceably.

On May 28, Secretary Hull issued a statement in which he said:

With reference to the critical situation involving countries in Central Europe. . . . Nearly 10 years ago the Government of the United States signed at Paris a treaty providing for the renunciation of war as an instrument of national policy. There are now parties to that treaty no less than 63 countries. In that treaty the contracting parties agree that "the settlement or solution of all disputes or conflicts of whatever nature or of whatever origin they may be, which may arise among them, shall never be sought except by pacific means." That pledge is no less binding now. . . .[2]

The German advance stopped. A rough form of collective security had indeed functioned effectively. What happened during that week of May 21, 1938, shows how Czechoslovakia might have been saved had the powers demonstrated the same devotion to the concept of collective security in September.

Between 1934, when the "state the terms" petition had been

2. *Documents on American Foreign Relations: January 1938–June 1939,* edited by S. Shepard Jones and Denys P. Myers (Boston: World Peace Foundation, 1939), p. 286.

circulated, and 1938, the officers of the League of Nations Association had not ceased to feel that United States participation on an equal basis with the members of the League of Nations was of paramount importance. A meeting of the International Federation of League of Nations Societies was scheduled to meet in Copenhagen in the summer of 1938. Before leaving on June 15 to attend the meeting, I sought a conference with President Roosevelt and saw him on June 9.

As was so typical of the President, he opened the interview by asking me what was the news. I got right to the point and said that I was going to Europe to "see how much suffering there is," and I wanted to talk to him first. The President said that some observers who had returned from Europe had reported that there was much unrest against fascism in Germany and Italy. Others reported the opposite.

I told him I was going to the meeting of the International Federation for two reasons: to urge the Federation to back a program of expansion of the League of Nations economic work and to discuss the wisdom of the revision of the Covenant. Referring to the latter, the President said, "That's the thing. That's good, I believe it's about time for something to be done along that line." I told him I felt that the majority of the member associations would agree to a system of providing automatic membership for all nations that had undertaken the two obligations of the Kellogg Pact—renunciation of war as an instrument of national policy and settlement of disputes by peaceful means only—which were the most fundamental obligations of human society.

After some speculative conversation on other changes that might improve the workings of the League (see Chapter 15), I returned to this idea for automatic membership so that I would not miss a definite answer. I said that the whole concept of "membership" must be discarded. The weakness of the system had been that the League of Nations had been a club admitting applicants by a two-thirds vote. Instead, *all* nations who accepted the obligations of the Kellogg Pact should be entitled to equal use of the League. Some 200 percent interpretationists might disagree, but I believed that when the League was given the moral and legal standing of the community of nations, conditions would be much better. I asked the President if he agreed and he said that he did.

I explained that it might not be necessary to consult Congress because the delegates we sent to the League of Nations would support the two purposes of the Kellogg Pact, the obligations of which we had already undertaken. I added that if I asked a statesman from some small state what he thought of the idea of revising the Covenant, he would probably say, "Don't destroy what we have left." However, if he knew that the United States would be in the League as a result of the revisions, he would gladly accept them.

The President said he was glad I was going to Europe. I told him I would like to do two things—observe and report to him, and appoint a committee on Covenant revision, if he did not object. He said no, just so the public didn't think the initiative came from the White House.

I reminded the President of a previous interview in which he had said he did not want to make a speech about international organization, "but that when the time came . . ." I said I believed the time had now come for a world conference, which would be the occasion for such a speech, and that it should be called in August, the twenty-fifth anniversary of the outbreak of the World War. He said he agreed. I added that all of the nations would probably come except three (Germany, Italy, and Japan) and that the conference could go ahead without them. We were then interrupted, and the interview was brought to a close, the President asking me to see him on my return.

In a memorandum to the President on June 12, I again mentioned the idea for a world conference:

The world has reached the point where possibly disaster can be averted only through a dramatic appeal on your part for a world conference. It might be of the greatest psychological advantage to use the month of August, which is the anniversary month of the outbreak of the World War, for the calling of a conference to promote economic equality and political stability so that the world may enter a new era of human history.

En route to Denmark, I spent a few days in Paris talking with old friends about the growing crisis. Among others, I had an interview with the former premier of France, Léon Blum, who lived in a quiet apartment on the Île de la Cité. In a letter to President Roosevelt on August 31, I reported on this meeting as follows:

My appointment with Blum was on a Sunday morning in his apartment, on one of those rare occasions when a man speaks very frankly. He said he felt the time had come for a disarmament conference. In reply, I asked him if he did not mean a conference for both economic and military disarmament, as they had become parts of the same problem. He agreed. Then in reply to my query as to how such a forward movement could be started, he said, "There are only two men in the world who could call a conference successfully at this moment—the Pope and President Roosevelt. It is obvious that the former will not do so, and consequently, your President is the only person who can issue such an appeal."

In reply to my remark that I hoped sometime to have the pleasure of repeating his remark to you, Mr. Blum said he would be delighted to have you know how he felt. Consequently, I have felt a responsibility to tell you of this interesting conversation, although I am certain you are receiving the same observations from many sources.

I talked to quite a number of statesmen and many of the so-called common people on my trip. All of them felt that while they might muddle through this particular crisis, or that particular crisis, the constructive leadership for the final pull to political and economic peace must come from the United States.

I returned from Europe more convinced than ever that the United

States alone had the moral and financial reserve capable of giving leadership in this crisis. I returned home more impressed than ever with the fact that your leadership is world-wide, and that the spiritual implications of "The New Deal" are more than matters of domestic influence and have in them the possibilities of world reconstruction.

On June 9 I had found Mr. Roosevelt sympathetic to the idea of a world conference, but he never publicly called for one. As I think back over Léon Blum's message to him, I wish that the President had taken that one last chance before the nations surrendered at Munich. A world conference with the moral forces of mankind behind it might have lifted the nations above the immediate crisis and set them on a new path, even if a few of the great powers stayed away. We will never know.

The International Federation of League of Nations Societies brought together in Copenhagen over 150 delegates from League of Nations groups in 26 countries. Many of the delegations, including that from the United States, were more liberal than their governments. Others, such as the French delegation, while nominally independent, were virtual government representatives. Discussions were lively.

The United States delegation introduced a resolution urging the Federation to appoint a committee to discuss revision of the Covenant. After much friendly discussion, in which a considerable part was played by Senator Henri Rolin of Belgium and René Cassin of France, it was decided to ask a number of societies to express their views on Covenant revision before December 1938. A committee of the Federation would then discuss the proposals and formulate a report for the next plenary session of the Federation in the summer of 1939, which was to be held in New York City. Tragically, the rapid deterioration of the international situation prevented the Federation from meeting in 1939 and the Committee of the Federation for Covenant Review never met.

The other resolution which our Association introduced at the Copenhagen meeting called for support of the economic work of the League. It was likewise accepted, with some changes to which we were delighted to agree.

After the meeting in Copenhagen I went to Prague. I was a little hesitant about crossing Germany, considering the speeches I had made about Hitler, but I traveled in the company of the secretary of the Czechoslovak League of Nations Association, who was not at all concerned. I was in Czechoslovakia for the better part of a week. In Prague I was fortunate to be able to talk to the foreign minister, a number of other officials and, as a climax, with Eduard Beneš. He was confident that Czechoslovakia could weather the storm, primarily because of the support of Great Britain, France, and the Soviet Union. He did not believe the allies would abandon Czechoslovakia, and for a very special reason: the Czechs accounted for thirty military divisions; if the allies deserted Czechoslovakia, these thirty divisions would vanish and the allies must necessarily compensate for them. On July 18, I broadcast from Prague to the United States:

I am preparing this address on a restaurant terrace high above Prague, on the hill of Saint Peter. It is a night such as all citizens of Prague love. The sky is clear, many stars and almost a full moon. Prague has been named the golden city of a hundred towers. And it seems as if all these towers are alive tonight in the moon and flood lights. . . .

This is Prague, capital of the country that has held so much interest for the world the past few months. The city has grown very rapidly within the past two decades. At the close of the war the population was less than half a million. Today it is a city of almost a million. This growth is most impressive. On the hills surrounding old Prague are many fine residences and apartment houses built within the past few years. The contrast between the city of today and the city which I visited shortly after the war is very great indeed. Greater Prague is a modern city, with good transportation and fine shops yet does not lose the beauty and picturesqueness of a city whose traditions enjoy the rich inheritance of many centuries.

I think I can anticipate some questions which my American listeners would like to have answered today. Is Czechoslovakia calm? Yes, one of the calmest places one can imagine. The people are not placid—they know the political and economic problems which they face, and the worldwide responsibilities which events have placed upon their shoulders. But they are calm because they are determined to meet those responsibilities with righteousness and firmness. And such firmness often produces tranquility. The people carry on their daily occupations; enjoy life; and seemingly read every one of the many editions of their newspapers.

German pressure inside Czechoslovakia was being exerted through Conrad Henlein, head of the Sudeten area of the country. The Sudeten Germans were a minority on Czechoslovakia's western frontier with Germany who had never been a part of Germany, always remaining outside the German frontier. The Czech government had agreed to make certain concessions to this German minority, but what Henlein wanted was a Nazi Party, which he would direct within the Czech state. In a speech on April 24, 1938, he had said: "Notwithstanding the practical bond of the state, we cannot —being part and parcel of the German nation—withdraw from a political philosophy, an outlook on life and society which is today joyfully confessed by Germans all over the world."[3] I crossed the Sudetenland by train, by plane, and by bus, and I was convinced that not all the Germans in the Sudetenland supported Henlein. If the minority had not been urged on by Hitler, the Czechoslovakian government could have worked out an arrangement with them.

3. The last phrase of this statement is an indication of the nationalistic hysteria that governed Hitler and some of the German Reich. Certainly, all Germans all over the world did not confess this particular German way of life.

In Copenhagen I had received a letter from Sean Lester, Deputy Secretary-General of the League of Nations, asking me to be a "temporary collaborator" for three weeks of the Assembly, starting September 8. I also received a letter from Adrian Pelt, head of the Information Section, telling me that the pay for a temporary collaborator was 880 Swiss francs toward expenses.[4] At least this amount would pay for my hotel for a few weeks, and on the strength of it I decided to return to Geneva for the League Assembly. I reported to the Secretary-General's office ready to fulfill my assignment, but that is as far as I got. The crisis facing the Assembly became so acute that I concentrated on it instead of the quiet observations I should have made as a temporary collaborator.

The nineteenth session of the League of Nations Assembly opened on September 12, 1938. It was an unreal Assembly. Day by day, it pursued its routine agenda. The only word said about the Czech situation was Maxim Litvinov's address on September 21. In his speech, the delegate of the Union of Soviet Socialist Republics analyzed the situation, adding, "We intend to fulfill our obligations under the pact and, together with France, to afford assistance to Czechoslovakia by the ways open to us."[5] On the closing day of the Assembly, the delegates did such ritualistic things as adopt the budget and caution the organization against excessive expenditures. In contrast, *outside* the Assembly Hall very little was spoken of except the increasing threat of Germany to Czechoslovakia and the efforts of the British and

4. Occasionally people of some academic standing who supported the League were invited to Geneva for a few months, generally during the Assembly. The duties of these "temporary collaborators," as they were called, consisted mostly of studying documents so that they could teach about the League more satisfactorily when they returned. I was not a professor, of course, but I was involved in teaching about the League, which I suppose qualified me for the post.

5. League of Nations, *Official Journal,* Records of the Nineteenth Ordinary Session of the Assembly, Plenary Meetings, Special Supplement, No. 183 (Geneva, 1938), p. 78.

French governments to force Czechoslovakia to a hideous surrender.

Shortly after arriving in Geneva, I had had a telephone call from Edward R. Murrow, then director in London of the European office of the Columbia Broadcasting System. Murrow said that he had transferred William L. Shirer from Geneva to Berlin so Shirer could better broadcast on the crisis. He wondered if I would go on the air at critical moments to explain the attitude of the League Assembly to developments. I made my first broadcast the night of September 11:

Tomorrow, as was pointed out, the delegates of fifty nations will meet in the annual parliament of Nations. At least several great contributions to world peace will be made. Despite the absence of some nations the habit of cooperation and the principles of international morality will be maintained as the delegates discuss problems that touch every phase of human activity from economic cooperation to intellectual cooperation. Even though there is not the will to make great decisions, for the settlement of the great world's ills, the League of Nations Assembly will furnish a forum in which the problems of Czechoslovakia, China and Spain, as well as economic maladjustment will be discussed. And it is also possible that before the month is over with certain very constructive suggestions for real world reconstruction will be undertaken.

Tonight the League's new buildings shine white in the deepening twilight. There are many statesmen, many Secretariat officials, and many people throughout the world who refuse to believe that these buildings are a white sepulchre in which are buried the dead hopes of peace of our generation. They have faith in man's capacity to control his economic and scientific forces with the power of the human spirit. For this task the League of Nations is the symbol. To those people everywhere who have visions of a better day, I take the liberty of saying we must not permit immediate events to discourage us. We must not permit any catastrophe to destroy our faith. No adversity should stop us for a moment from fulfilling the task of our generation which is the outlawry of war and the establishment of the institutions of peaceful international society.

I was scheduled to make a broadcast on September 23 or 24, but unfortunately I could not find the Swiss censor, who had a date with his girlfriend, so at the last moment I had to phone Ed Murrow that I couldn't deliver the speech. Although the League had its own broadcasting facilities, the Swiss were afraid that something might be said to compromise their neutrality.

My next broadcast, therefore, was the morning of September 26, and followed immediately one that Chancellor Hitler had given. Since CBS kept the facilities open, my address had a very wide audience. In my speech of September 11, on the eve of the Assembly, I had made only general observations as to the possible uses of the Assembly. In my September 26 address, I spoke of the hope and then of the disillusionment:

There was undoubtedly in many circles admiration for Chamberlain's first visit to Berchtesgaden. Since prestige is not an issue with democratic statesmen as it is with dictators, Chamberlain could afford to fly to Hitler for the first talk. There was a general sigh of relief that his visit meant negotiations and, as President Roosevelt said in his telegram this morning, as long as negotiations continue there cannot be war.

A day or so after Chamberlain's first visit the feeling of satisfaction gave way to stupefaction, then indignation at the position in which Czechoslovakia was placed. It will be remembered that President Beneš was awakened at two o'clock in the early hours of the morning [of September 21] by the French and British Ambassadors who demanded that he accept the terms immediately which Mr. Chamberlain was to take back to Germany. The Czechoslovakian government, in a radio broadcast, has characterized the brutality and the haste of this démarche as unparalleled in history.

These circumstances, plus the fact that in the second interview Hitler rejected the terms which Mr. Chamberlain had reason to believe would be accepted and made further impossible demands which have been transmitted to Prague in the nature of a German ultimatum, have maneuvered Prague into the position of a defeated power being presented with ultimatums from friends and enemy alike. There is universal resentment characterized by a stiffening of opinion here, in London and in Paris, that a law-abiding democratic state such as Czechoslovakia should be placed in this position.

Margaret Olson, my assistant in the New York office of the League of Nations Association, was also in Geneva, where I had arranged for her to be a member of the American Committee. In preparing the broadcasts for CBS, we used the typewriter in the office of the American Committee, which was on the second floor of the International Club, writing the broadcast in the middle of the evening after we had picked up the latest news. Since there was no time for dinner, we arranged with the chef of the International Club to let us have coffee and sandwiches. Following completion of the speech we found the Swiss censor, a very amiable person who was simply doing his duty in looking over the manuscript. Then we proceeded to the Swiss broadcasting office to broadcast the speech, which was heard sometime in the evening in New York.

Almost daily there were cable communications between those of us who were in Geneva and my office in New York. We sent messages to be distributed to all Association branches and all cooperating organizations. For example:

September 19. Geneva, Switzerland. Czechs firm against further concessions having already gone limit. Increasingly control Sudeten as Henlein fled. Sudetens renewing pledges loyalty. Nevertheless danger powers urge dismemberment stop Hitler. Urge following. First Board LNA send me strong message urging peaceful settlement respecting Czechoslovakian frontiers for use here. Second International Peace Campaign requests members Concerted Efforts plus few others notably Scott send joint cable IPC Geneva for publicity Europe. Third Czech-American Committee mobilize expressions opinion emergency mass meetings protesting dismemberment immediately. Press erroneously reports recrudescent United States isolation with quotation presumably Neutralists. Have you secured cooperativist statements and released foreign press agencies. Transmit portions this message all concerned with full text branches board.

Another dated September 23 read:

Accelerate meetings resolutions statements over weekend. Have prayers all churches for Czechoslovakia. Original British French satisfaction partially giving way to humiliation at appalling betrayal Czechoslovakia. Possibly too late prevent Chamberlain plan but still time prevent something worse. Danger that Hitler will demand more or will send troops without waiting Delimitation Commission. Huge demonstration London yesterday. Two thousand British meetings Sunday. Three French Ministers resigned. Your meetings should pay tribute heroism Czechs and demand settlement with justice dignity. Point out bankruptcy alliance system and that collective system security and peaceful settlement through League only alternative. Important you send me for use full account total activities sentiment resolutions.

On September 25, a mass meeting sponsored by the Save Czechoslovakia Committee was held in Madison Square Garden in New York City. There was an overflow crowd of 23,000. In Chicago on the same day 65,000 attended a meeting. There were twenty-eight other meetings across the United States. I sent the following message to the New York meeting:

If the threats to Czechoslovakia succeed it will appear that after twenty years of armistice German militarism has won the World War. These threats will be followed by other similar attacks. A long dark night will be settling over Europe and casting its twilight over the Western Hemisphere. The refusal of the United States to join the League of Nations twenty years ago and the abandonment of its principles by other great powers is finally bearing fruit.

Whether light or darkness prevails will depend upon those who mobilize their faith in the standards of international morality. You are contributing to this effort tonight. Let no American feel that his country is not interested in this great issue. We were partly responsible for the creation of Czechoslovakia that has taken the inspiration for its democracy from us. The United States cannot escape the results of world assault upon international law and order and democracy. Indeed, it may be that only the United States can issue the call that would lift the ills of the world above the Sudeten issue and resolve its problems again on a basis of broad principles and ideals.

Czechoslovakia has become the symbol of the world issue between dismemberment, secret diplomacy, broken promises and strengthened dictatorship against international law and order, democracy, the peaceful settlement of disputes, the League of Nations and the Kellogg-Briand Pact. The events of the moment are the strongest argument for the revival of the system of collective security and world cooperation through the League of Nations. Only a determined effort of the peaceloving nations can stop aggression.

On September 26, the President of the United States in a message to Beneš and Hitler pointed out the tragedy that confronted the world and urged that the nations not break off negotiations. This message, of course, was acclaimed by Daladier, Chamberlain, and Beneš, and repudiated by Hitler. As I read the President's message, I was impressed by the weakness of his position, due to no fault of his own. The United States accepted none of the obligations under the League of Nations Covenant. It was not represented at Geneva and therefore was in no position to make its way felt. The President was handicapped by a Neutrality Law which, if it were invoked in case Czechoslovakia were attacked, would penalize Czechoslovakia rather than Germany or Italy. Most of the principles to which the President appealed were principles that had originated in the United States—the League's Covenant and the Kellogg-Briand Pact—but we were not in a position to defend them.

Chamberlain and Daladier surrendered to Hitler at Munich at two o'clock Friday morning, September 30, 1938, when they signed the agreement with him and Mussolini that became known as the Munich Pact. This Pact so mutilated the State of Czechoslovakia that it was hard to see how it could exist as a valid entity, and indeed Poland and Hungary were to claim their slices of the country a few days later.

The League of Nations Assembly adjourned the morning of September 30. In his closing speech President Eamon de Valera of Ireland gave thanks that a crisis had been averted. After calling attention to the useful and beneficial activities of the League of Nations in many fields, he concluded by saying, "There is hardly a domain of human life or action in which the League does not take an interest and cannot play an active part."[6]

The president of the Council, Garcia-Calderón of Peru, however, was not so temperate. He concluded with a tribute to Neville Chamberlain:

I pay a tribute of admiration to Mr. Neville Chamberlain, the great English statesman, "the grand old man." As you are aware, this expression of affection and respect has not been used in England since the time of Gladstone. This knight of peace, this hero of peace, who scorns hatred and envy, has attained the highest peak of human greatness, a glory greater than that of all conquerors. His name today is blessed in every home in the land.[7]

I could hardly contain myself as I listened to the hypocritical tributes and the explanations of why the sacrifice of Czechoslovakia was the road to peace. I believed it was the beginning of the Second World War.

That night I was the guest of Carl Hambro, president of the Norwegian Parliament. The affair had nothing to do with the Munich settlement. Hambro had invited Frank Buchman, who was leader of the Oxford Movement, later known as Moral Rearmament, and several of his younger associates. The *pièce de résistance*, so to speak, was Eamon de Valera. It was a strange

6. *Ibid.*, p. 100.
7. League of Nations, *Official Journal*, 103rd Session of the Council, 2nd Meeting, Sept. 30, 1938 (Geneva), p. 877.

dinner party, somewhat of an antidote to what I had lived through during the day. The next day I took the train for Paris.

As a Midwesterner I was called to active duty in the American army in Chicago in 1917. We were shipped by troop train to Jacksonville, Florida, and after some months at Camp Joseph E. Johnston in Jacksonville, we entrained for Newport News to embark for France. Thus I am one of those Americans who saw Paris before I saw New York. In contrast to the experience of some soldiers, Paris was very kind to me. For example, I remember wandering around to the Louvre only to find it was closed on Sunday. A young woman led me by the hand to a window where I could see the statue of the Winged Victory, and tried to point out other things through the windows.

After I became director of the League of Nations Association, I visited France frequently en route to Geneva to attend meetings of the League Assembly. I was always very comfortable in Paris, and had many like-minded friends there. At Geneva I saw that many of the ideas presented to the League of Nations were of French origin and many of the ablest statesmen who appeared there were French. Of course, the greatest was Aristide Briand, really the spiritual leader of the League of Nations. Another distinguished Frenchman was Albert Thomas, director of the ILO. An important member of the League of Nations Secretariat told me one time that in the early days, when a plan was to be drafted for the League to consider, there were usually two plans, the plan of the Secretariat and the plan of the French.

Suddenly, that day in early October 1938, all that France had meant to me seemed to vanish. France had betrayed the League of Nations. She had been false to her alliance with Czechoslovakia. Paris seemed like ashes. I walked certain streets that I had walked for many years, but the streets, the buildings, the restaurants—none of these things meant anything.

I sought out a number of friends. There was one I think of particularly, Pierre Comert, who for years had been director of the Information Section of the League of Nations. Comert was heartbroken at what had happened in Munich. When I asked him why France had agreed to the Munich settlement, he explained that French public opinion was quite confused. He pointed out that there were a number of important Frenchmen, men of economic and political influence, who would rather have Germany win than the Soviet Union and Czechoslovakia. They were more afraid of the Soviet Union and communism than they were of Germany and Nazism. This was not all but it was one of the main reasons.

I left Paris for London and then sailed back to the United States. My romance with France had ended.

7

War—Salvaging the Technical Work of the League

The statesmen left Geneva at the close of the League of Nations Assembly in 1938 disillusioned and fearful as to the future; a few derived a hypocritical satisfaction from what had occurred. The decade of the thirties, which had opened auspiciously following the signing of the Kellogg Pact, had been a period of gradual deterioration from the principles of the League of Nations. Germany, Italy, Japan, and a number of other states had withdrawn or given notice of withdrawal from the League. Ethiopia and Austria had disappeared because of the aggression of the dictators and the refusal of the statesmen of other countries to stand by the principle of collective security. The Munich betrayal was the most humiliating of all for the League of Nations. Its Assembly was in session, yet it was ignored in negotiations over the future of Czechoslovakia. As the previous chapter spells out, after days of mounting crisis, statesmen of the United Kingdom and France journeyed to Munich—not to Geneva— to meet with Hitler. In the Council chamber at Geneva on the day that Czechoslovakia agreed to the Munich "settlement," some representatives of the great powers explained that it was the road to peace and praised Czechoslovakia for her courage in making "a great sacrifice for peace."

Now, as the statesmen faced 1939, the question was what would be the next price of the dictators for the illusion of peace? What other countries must sacrifice their frontiers? What other changes in the order of Europe must be made to satisfy Mussolini and Hitler?

The League of Nations Association of the United States, I am proud to say, adopted a courageous and prophetic program. The Association was not certain, but it was fearful that there would be a final dénouement which would come in the last part of 1939, when total war would break out. If this happened, there would be no alternative but to create another international system to maintain peace after the war was over. The United States would have to assume much of the responsibility. As the Association policy statement of March 27, 1939, stated:

The tide of world events seems to be running against it; at the same time the majority public opinion in the United States is for the first time in sympathy with the fundamental principles for which the Association stands. More and more we are presenting the problems in terms of American leadership. For some reason difficult to analyze, the rest of the world seems very tired. Indeed, many of the ideals which make up the principles of the League of Nations had their inception in the United States. The League of Nations, the International Labor Organization, the Kellogg Pact, the Principle of the Good Neighbor, the doctrine of non-recognition of a situation brought about in violation of the Kellogg Pact, etc., etc., these ideals will be carried into practice to the extent that the United States is willing to give leadership for them.

The League of Nations Association stands on its present policies and will expand its program and its activities to achieve those objectives at this dark moment.

That fateful League of Nations Assembly of 1938 had taken one constructive step which went almost unnoticed in the overwhelming tragedy of Czechoslovakia. A few Americans attending the Assembly, including Senator Claude Pepper of Florida and myself, were very much interested in the maintenance of the non-political activities of the League of Nations in the face of political chaos. Support of such activities had been one of the major concerns of the League of Nations Association since its founding. Indeed, much of the participation of the United States, informally and formally, in the work of the League of Nations was in its economic and social activities.

We believed it would be important for the Assembly to call the attention of non-member states to those activities and ask for increased cooperation. After several informal meetings with two old friends of mine, Arthur Sweetser and Benjamin Gerig, of the League Secretariat, a draft resolution to this effect was prepared. On September 30, 1938, the Assembly adopted a resolution reaffirming the importance of the non-political activities of the League and noting the League's policy of inviting the collaboration of non-member states in such work, which had steadily increased. The resolution also stated that "any comment or suggestion for the wider development of such technical and non-political collaboration which non-Member states would care to make would be welcomed by Members of the League. . . ." The resolution was duly transmitted by the Secretary-General to non-member states.

Support of this resolution and the possibilities it opened up was one of the points made in my report to the board of directors of the League of Nations Association at its meeting October 24, 1938. Professor Shotwell, then president of the LNA, and I were in agreement that it would be important to talk with Secretary of State Hull as soon as possible to urge a strong and constructive reply from the United States.

I sought an appointment with Secretary Hull in Washington. However, preparations for his departure to the Lima Conference of American States prevented his seeing me. But he suggested that I call on him at the boat November 25. In the letter which I presented to him, I called his attention to the League resolution of September 30, pointed out that "this may afford an excellent opportunity for you to make some constructive suggestions to the League for the development of its non-political activities," and asked if Professor Shotwell and I might prepare a memorandum on the subject. Mr. Hull replied that he did not know exactly when he would return and therefore suggested that we get in touch with Mr. Abbott Low Moffat or Mr. Theodore C. Achilles of the Department of State.

Professor Shotwell and I then set to work preparing a memorandum giving the background of the Assembly resolution and offering suggestions for the furtherance of the League's economic and social work. Our memorandum was submitted to Mr. Achilles on January 12, 1939. We urged a sympathetic response to the League resolution.

On February 2, Secretary Hull sent an encouraging reply to the League Secretary-General, Joseph A. Avenol. Mr. Hull noted that the League had been "responsible for the development of mutual exchange and discussion of ideas and methods to a greater extent and in more fields of humanitarian and scientific endeavor than any other organization in history," and that the United States government was "keenly aware of the value" of this interchange and "desires to see it extended." The reply ended by pledging continued collaboration on the part of the United States with these activities, and stated that the government would consider "in a sympathetic spirit means of making its collaboration more effective."[1]

Mr. Hull's reply was warmly welcomed in League circles. Mr. Sweetser, at an LNA board meeting on March 6, 1939, spoke of the "great satisfaction with which the American reply was received in Geneva."

Responding to the Assembly resolution of September 30,

1. *Documents on American Foreign Relations: January 1938–June 1939*, edited by S. Shepard Jones and Denys P. Myers (Boston: World Peace Foundation, 1939), p. 463.

1938, the League Council on May 27, 1939, appointed a special committee, under the chairmanship of the Right Honorable Stanley Bruce of Australia, to consider and report to the Assembly on the further development of the work of the League in the economic and social fields. It was generally agreed that Mr. Hull's letter was a considerable inspiration for this action.

For some time a number of statesmen had wanted to segregate the economic and social activities of the League of Nations so that they might proceed more vigorously. And some of the policy statements of the League of Nations Association looked forward to such decentralization. .

The Bruce Committee met in the summer of 1939. Its report to the Assembly recommended far-reaching changes in the League's structure. It proposed that a Central Committee for Economic and Social Questions be set up, to which would be entrusted the direction and supervision of the League's activities in these fields. The Central Committee would be composed of thirty-two members. Eight would be selected in a personal capacity because of their competence in the related fields. The remaining members would be representatives of governments, selected without distinction between member and non-member states. The Central Committee would consider the budget for the League's technical work; it would appoint the members of the principal technical committees, who at that time were appointed by the League Council. One of the first tasks of the committee would be to study the conditions under which non-member states might participate in the economic and social activities. It would coordinate its work with the International Labor Organization.

Here was a proposal in effect calling for a league within the League. The economic, social, and technical activities of the organization would be segregated; non-member as well as member states could belong. The Council and the Assembly would be delegating their powers of control over the economic and social work to the new Central Committee. Indeed, the proposed technical organization would have practically as much autonomy as that enjoyed by the International Labor Organization. The fateful unanimity rule would no longer block the road for needed advances in technical matters, because the committee's decisions would be taken by a majority rule.

The Bruce Committee report was adopted by the Twentieth Assembly of the League on December 13, 1939, and an organizing committee of ten was set up to implement it.

The long-threatened war broke out in the first few days of September 1939 when the Germans attacked Poland, and France and Great Britain went to Poland's support. For the first time in twenty years, September passed without the meeting of the League of Nations Assembly.

Cautious plans were made for a limited Assembly in December to consider the immediate non-political work. But a meeting was not absolutely essential, and the risks were considerable. Many states felt that it was inopportune and the idea was abandoned. A plan then developed for calling the fourth committee of the previous Assembly into session, simply to vote the budget and to attend to other necessary administrative matters. This procedure would avoid the question of credentials: all states present at the Assembly session in 1938 would naturally be qualified to reappear.

However, as the delegates began arriving in Geneva, they were met with Finland's appeal to the League of December 2 against the Russian invasion. Finland had concluded that despite the fate of Czechoslovakia, she could lose nothing and might gain some advantage by appealing to the League. The Secretary-General immediately called for the Council to meet on December 9 and the Assembly, to which Finland had also appealed, on December 11. An observer in Geneva at the time wrote: "On the greater war, the lull continued. All eyes, even in the belligerent countries, were turned on the Russo-Finnish conflict."

The Assembly condemned Russian aggression and called upon League members to give Finland all material help they could. It further resolved that Russia, by refusing to be present at the Assembly, had placed herself outside the Covenant and called on the Council to draw "an appropriate conclusion." Later that day, December 14, the Council exercised for the first and only time its authority under Article 16 to exclude from membership any member who had violated the Covenant. Thus Russia became the only power to be expelled from the League. It is ironic that the Soviet Union, the only great power to support the Covenant against Germany's action in Czechoslovakia in 1938, was now the only country to be expelled from the League for violating it.

In assessing the work of the Twentieth Assembly, Arthur Sweetser wrote to Dr. Frank G. Boudreau of the LNA on December 19 that he regarded the adoption of the Bruce Report as "the most fundamental change in the Organization of the League since its start," and that the organizing committee would be meeting shortly. He went on to say: "We have just lived through a most extraordinary week when from a situation of extreme quiet we suddenly burst onto the center of the world's stage with condemnation and expulsion of Russia. This was a very grave decision which was taken with full consciousness of its possible consequences, but in the circumstances no other outcome was considered possible. . . ."

Mr. Sweetser also spoke of the cuts in the League budget and said that further compressions would be necessary; in fact, letters of dismissal had gone out to 140 members of the Secretariat that day.

The Assembly adjourned on December 14, although it did not close its Twentieth Session. A small notice appeared in the League of Nations *Journal* of December 13, 1939, telling those who planned to travel through France on their way home how to secure the necessary travel papers and directions before they left Geneva.

Six years were to pass before the Twentieth Assembly could resume. The Bruce Committee, or rather the organizing committee created by the Twentieth Assembly, did meet at The Hague in February 1940 to plan its work, but only for a few days and then it, too, suspended its labors.

The Assembly resolution of September 1938, the Hull reply, and the Bruce Committee had been concerned with the expansion of the League's non-political activities. However, by 1940 it was no longer a question of expanding those activities but of safeguarding what already existed.

After the outbreak of the war, a small, courageous group of Americans, members of the American Inter-organization Council, had stayed on in Geneva. They were deeply disturbed at the situation facing the League. Its revenues had shrunk because of the decrease in membership; the staff was being reduced and its activities curtailed as the war spread. At any moment an effort might be made to surround Geneva or even to bomb the League buildings—to try to destroy the idea by destroying the physical plant which helped to sustain it.

The members of the American Inter-organization Council wondered if something could be done in the United States. Might it be possible to secure a congressional appropriation of $100–150,000 to help the technical work of the League, in which the United States had always cooperated? Mrs. Laura Puffer Morgan of the Inter-organization Council wrote to her friend, Dr. Mary E. Woolley, president emeritus of Mount Holyoke College.

In early 1940 Dr. Woolley consulted with friends in the League of Nations Association, including myself, and then called on President Roosevelt to present him with the idea of a congressional appropriation. It did not seem to be too unreasonable a request inasmuch as Canada and some other members of the League of Nations then at war were keeping up their contributions to the League. However, it was felt in Washington that such a congressional appropriation would be impossible at that time.

After further consultations, with the war spreading and the situation becoming more serious, a plan was developed to create a special committee of perhaps fifty persons to make a public appeal for support of the League's non-political activities. Dr. Woolley agreed to serve as chairman, with such persons as Dr. Frank Boudreau, William Allen White, and others associated with her. The plan had the approval of Washington and President Roosevelt agreed to send a letter to Dr. Woolley supporting her initiative. I was asked to send the President suggestions, and with revision, the President's letter, dated April 4, was duly received. It was understood that we would release it when announcement was made of the creation of the committee.

Clearance was also sought from Geneva. Dr. Boudreau, then president of the League of Nations Association, cabled Mr. Avenol on March 27 that in view of the growing anxiety in this country for the fate of the League's technical work and the "present hopelessness of obtaining government appropriations," leaders here proposed to raise $100,000 "with endorsement from highest quarters."

Mr. Avenol replied on April 3. He minimized the dangers to the League, advised further consideration, and explained that the Central Committee of the League would have to decide about accepting private funds. He also mentioned that the Rockefeller Foundation was contemplating offering a grant of $100,000, following an earlier precedent. I showed Mr. Avenol's letter to friends in Washington; a revision of our plans seemed necessary.

Dr. Woolley, Dr. Boudreau, and I consulted again. It seemed advisable to create the committee on a broader, educational basis. Dr. Woolley's letter of invitation to join the committee had to be revised, and approval for the modified plan again sought in Washington.

After obtaining Washington's approval of the modified plan, I wrote several members of the board of directors describing the functions of the committee, and suggested that we organize it as already planned, using the President's letter. The committee would inform the people as to these non-political activities that continue during the war, the necessity of keeping them active so that they would be ready for reconstruction and the foundation of the organization of peace at the close of the war. The committee would hold itself in readiness for any emergency. Suppose, for illustration, that Italy were to enter the war and that the League would be forced to leave Geneva at the request of Switzerland in order to preserve her neutrality. It is not fantastic to say that this country might have to give asylum to the non-political work of the League for the duration of the war. The committee would not, however, raise money at the moment, but would hold itself in readiness. I secured agreement for the organization of the committee on the broader base.

The invitations to join the committee started going out at the end of April and in early May. After stressing the importance of maintaining the non-political activities of the League during the critical times, Dr. Woolley said in her letter that the "committee would keep the public informed about the situation as it affects these activities, and would be ready to assist in any emergency, even to the extent of appealing to the country for financial contributions to the technical budget as the need arises."

About fifty persons agreed to join the committee. Announcement of its formation, however, was held up until June 1 because of the difficulty of getting attention in the press: The Lowlands had been invaded on May 10 and the war was spreading over Europe.

Dr. Woolley, in announcing the committee, described some of the League's technical work and then said,

This work must go on even in time of war if the extremity of human suffering is to be averted. It will be indispensable when peace comes to a war torn world. . . . Now the tide of war threatens to ruin those most hopeful attempts to harness science to the service of man. Without them the future peace conference will be gravely handicapped. If they are destroyed, the task of rebuilding a peaceful world may fall short of success.

Dr. Woolley further stated that inasmuch as the United States had cooperated wholeheartedly in these activities, it was natural that Americans "should view with concern their possible destruction." She concluded her statement with the President's letter:

My dear Dr. Woolley:

I have received the preliminary announcement that you are forming a committee to support the non-political and humanitarian activities of the League of Nations, which have been crippled by the outbreak of the European war. Please allow me to say that I hope your committee will get full and adequate support.

Without in any way becoming involved in the political affairs of Europe, it has been the continuous policy of this government for many years to cooperate in the world-wide technical and humanitarian activities of the League. Certain of them indeed are not only worthy, but definitely essential.

The League's health organization, for example, must in no way relax its efforts in preventing the spread of epidemics: wartime conditions definitely increase the danger. The world-wide efforts for better nutrition standards have already shown that the way towards solution of health problems may also be the way towards definite improvement of economic conditions.

The international Narcotics Control system has been of the greatest value in combating the drug traffic. The child welfare work has won the sympathies of every friend of children. The League's committees on intellectual cooperation have outlined non-political programs furthering the mutual appreciation of artistic and cultural values essential to common civilization.

Secretary Hull, in a letter to the Secretary-General of the League dated February 2, 1939, said:

> "The League . . . has been responsible for the development of mutual exchange and discussion of ideas and methods to a greater extent and in more fields of humanitarian and scientific endeavor than any other organization in history. The United States Government is keenly aware of the value of this type of general interchange and desires to see it extended."

Realizing, as we must, that these essential and non-political activities are handicapped under wartime conditions, I am glad that your committee has undertaken the task of providing support, to the end that their work may continue. However governments may divide, human problems are common the world over and we shall never realize peace until these common interests take precedence as the major work of civilization.

Very sincerely yours,
(Signed) Franklin D. Roosevelt

Following the invasion of the Lowlands, it was clear that the League of Nations technical services should be moved to the United States as soon as possible, while the ILO should move to Canada, which, as a member of the League, could more readily invite the organization to her shores.

A number of communications and cables concerning the possibilities of such a move were exchanged between Mr. Sweetser in Geneva and Dr. Boudreau in the United States, and Mr. Sweetser visited the United States to confer with various parties. Finally, on June 11 a cable was dispatched to Secretary-General Avenol on behalf of Princeton University, signed by

Harold W. Dodds, president; the Rockefeller Institute for Medical Research, signed by Carl TenBroeck, director of the Department of Animal and Plant Pathology; and the Institute for Advanced Study, signed by Frank Aydelotte, director:

During the past two decades we have watched with the greatest admiration the growth of the technical sections of the Secretariat of the League of Nations. They have provided leadership in the promotion of international collaboration between scholars, in the furthering of public health, in the control of opium, and in the international exploration of economic and financial problems. Recently we have become increasingly apprehensive that the war may do more than merely interrupt this work. With the involvement in hostilities of all countries surrounding Geneva, we are fearful that the trained personnel of these sections, so carefully built up, may be dispersed, and that the records so painstakingly accumulated may be destroyed.

Under these circumstances we should like to suggest to you very strongly that you consider the possibility of removing the technical sections of the Secretariat, including both the personnel and the records, to Princeton, New Jersey, for such period as may prove to be advisable. At Princeton are located, as you doubtless know, Princeton University, a branch of the Rockefeller Institute for Medical Research, and the Institute for Advanced Study. It gives us great pleasure to inform you that the governing authorities of these three educational and scientific institutions hereby unite in extending a most cordial invitation to the technical sections of the Secretariat to move from Geneva to this place. Should you find it possible to accept this invitation you may rest assured that the members of the three institutions indicated will do everything in their power to assist the technical sections in finding suitable offices and living quarters and to make it possible for these sections to continue their work in the most effective manner. They would, of course, be as independent in this work in Princeton as they are in Geneva.

We are extending this invitation because of the great importance which we attach to the scientific and scholarly work of the technical sections of the League. We understand the difficulty of building up such an effective personnel as these sections now contain, and are most eager that they should not be dispersed, and that the work of these sections may not be interrupted by the war.

A stuffy and bureaucratic reply was received from Mr. Avenol several days later. After expressing profound gratitude for the invitation from the three Princeton groups, he went on to say:

The statutory seat of the League being established at Geneva, I am certain that you will understand it is not within my power (a) even provisionally to alter this arrangement unless compelled by force majeure or (b) to transfer all or part of the secretariat unless the initiative were taken by one or more states. These would then have to envisage all responsibilities attendant upon such initiative, the final decision remaining subject to the approval of the states members.

This seemed to be the last straw. However, on June 16, Dr. Aydelotte put the dilemma to Lord Lothian, British ambassador to Washington, who wrote on June 24 that the British government had "sent a strongly worded message to Avenol saying that in its opinion the Princeton invitation should be accepted and asking that if the Secretary-General has already declined the invitation the British Government must ask that that refusal should be rescinded pending further discussion."

Meanwhile, Dr. Woolley and others were becoming increasingly alarmed at the situation. Private representations were made to the President urging the United States government to issue an official invitation to the League to accept the Princeton offer. Friends in Geneva also urged a more favorable response from the League.

The Princeton offer was repeated on July 12, this time with more success. Secretary-General Avenol replied in part:

After careful consideration of the problems involved in consultation with the heads of departments concerned I am glad to respond to your generous invitation by authorizing Mr. Loveday, Director of the Economic and Financial Department, and those of his collaborators whom he considers essential for the prosecution of their work to proceed to the United States on mission. Eight officials accompanied by wives and children to a total of twenty-two persons will start for United States as soon as formalities can be completed including United States appropriate visas. I should be greatly obliged to you if you could inform the State Department that applications for such visas are being made forthwith through the proper channels.

The idea of sending the Secretariat officials to the United States "on mission" apparently relieved the Secretary-General's anxiety about moving the technical services without "proper" authority.

Avenol resigned not long afterwards. On leaving his post August 31, he issued the following statement:

... The crippling effect of the war on our activities, far from discouraging our American friends, led them to consider how the light of international cooperation might be kept burning.

A committee organized by Dr. Mary E. Woolley for this purpose met with wide support, and her efforts, as well as those of Dr. Frank G. Boudreau and Mr. Clark M. Eichelberger, deserve the recognition of all who have our cause at heart.

As this war went on further evidence of American determination to help was forthcoming, and in this connection I would gratefully mention the offer to place the facilities for work at Princeton University at our disposal, received from President Dodds of Princeton University, from Dr. TenBroeck, director of the Rockefeller Institute for Medical Research, and from Dr. Aydelotte, director of the Institute for Advanced Study. To all these men I am deeply grateful.

So, while most of the League's services languished in Geneva during the war, able to do little more than preserve their records and enough staff to begin again whenever it might be possible, the Economic and Financial Section at Princeton continued with its work. Besides its regular publications it issued a series of valuable studies on postwar reconstruction and was active in the formation of new international agencies as the war neared its end. "The last dying exertions of the League thus merged almost imperceptibly into the prehistory of the United Nations."[2]

2. Frank P. Walters, *A History of the League of Nations,* Vol. II (New York: Oxford University Press, 1952), p. 810.

8

Revision of the Neutrality Act— Commission to Study the Organization of Peace

By September 1, 1939, several member states of the League of Nations had disappeared, among them Austria and Czechoslovakia. However, until then there had not been a formal declaration of the war that finally engulfed the British, the French, and much of the civilized world. During most of 1939, the world seemed to be waiting for the dénouement.

As the international situation unfolded in that fateful year, there were at least three opportunities for constructive activity on the part of those organizations working for the restoration and the maintenance of world peace. One was the opportunity to preserve what was possible of the League of Nations. The story of this effort, much of which involved Secretary of State Cordell Hull, was told in Chapter 7.

The second was to plan the future League of Nations system or to determine what was to take the League's place.

Finally, the Association and many of the organizations working with it were deeply concerned about what they could do to aid the cause of the allies if open warfare should break out. Of primary importance would be the revision or repeal of the Neutrality Act. It seemed to me that there was a chance for success. After I had returned from Geneva at the close of the disastrous "Munich" Assembly of 1938, I had traveled some 8,500 miles, delivering addresses to chapters of the Association and other groups in the leading cities of the country. In a memorandum to the members of the LNA following my trip, I had written:

In the first place, the American people are the most informed of any people on international affairs. This is a rather sudden development. . . .

In the second place, I did not find the isolationist reaction which one might have anticipated following the Munich settlement. The smug self-sufficiency of the more contented periods of postwar history has pretty much disappeared. The people are worried; they feel insecure and their sympathies have been deeply stirred by events in other parts of the world.

In the third place, there is a growing feeling that the United States has become an adult nation and must take a share of responsibility commensurate with its stand on international morality. . . .

The swing of the country from isolationism to a position of world leadership was well under way.

As I analyzed the situation in an editorial in the September 1939 issue of *New World*,[1] one approach to revision of the existing Neutrality Laws of 1935 and 1937 would provide for "a difference in the application of our neutrality legislation so that it would favor the nation attacked and be applied against the nation at war in violation of treaties with the United States, presumably the Nine-Power Treaty and the Kellogg Pact. . . . [It] would put a moral foundation under our neutrality law. . . ."

The administration urged adoption of a second approach, through repeal of the arms embargo provisions of the current acts, with certain safeguards, such as requiring that title of

1. The name of the LNA publication had just been changed from the *Chronicle* to *New World*. The format was also changed—from newspaper to magazine.

goods be transferred to the purchaser before leaving United States shores, that American ships be kept out of war zones, and that no loans be given to the belligerents. This approach, I wrote in *New World*, "while not attaining the moral objective, at least meant a return to fundamental principles of international law and advance assurance that we would not be the ally of Hitler if he made war this fall." The Association and those working with it favored the first approach. However, they threw their weight behind the administration proposals when the time came. On July 11, 1939, the Senate Foreign Relations Committee had voted 12–11 to defer further action on the neutrality legislation until the next session of Congress. Afterwards, President Roosevelt had called a conference of congressional leaders, at which he stated that failure to take action would weaken any influence the United States might have in trying to preserve peace. It was at this conference that Senator William E. Borah made the statement that he had "better private information" than the Department of State regarding the imminence of war. Others shared his belief that there would be time to consider neutrality legislation when Congress returned in January in regular session, and on this note, Congress had adjourned.

Events, however, confounded the politicians. When war broke out in September, the President scheduled a fireside chat for September 3. Several officers of the Association wired him on September 2 urging that in addition to stressing the need to keep this country out of war, he "emphasize the vital national interest of the United States in the maintenance of law and order in the world," and that the United States desire to keep out of war did not mean "that we are indifferent to the outcome of the conflict."

In his broadcast the President urged the people to be calm, to discriminate between news and rumor, and made a plea for national unity. He stated that it was an "unalterable fact" that "when peace has been broken anywhere, the peace of all countries everywhere is in danger." In concluding, he said:

This nation will remain a neutral nation, but I cannot ask that every American remain neutral in thought as well. Even a neutral has a right to take account of facts. Even a neutral cannot be asked to close his mind or his conscience. . . . I hope the United States will keep out of this war. I believe that it will. And I give you assurance and reassurance that every effort of your Government will be directed toward that end. As long as it remains within my power to prevent, there will be no blackout of peace in the United States.

Several presidential proclamations followed, on September 5, setting forth rules and regulations with respect to ships, U.S. citizens, loans, and so on, and, as required by the Neutrality Law of 1937, an embargo on the export of arms and munitions to belligerent powers.

I had an appointment with the President on Thursday, September 7. Among the topics we discussed was revision of the neutrality legislation, now most urgent. I told the President that we might as well face the fact that the American peace movement was hopelessly divided between the isolationist, pacifist, peace-at-any-price appeasement group on the one side and the group that I was associated with on the other—a group that stood for revision of the Neutrality Law and believed that the best way to keep America out of war was to give the British and the French any possible arms, ammunition, and so on, because if they lost, the struggle for civilization would be a lone battle for the United States.

The President said that one of the greatest services the Association could perform would be to disillusion the American people as to the certainty of allied victory; that the odds at present were fifty-fifty, not ten to one, as many Americans believed; that no one could be certain that the British and the French would win, and that the American people must face this fact. If the democracies won, there would be one kind of peace, and if the democracies lost there would be another kind of peace. Picture a world, he said, in which Hitler and Stalin, and possibly the Japanese, not only dominated Europe and Asia but could swiftly take the Philippines and our outposts in the Pacific, which we could not easily defend, and imperil our interests in South America, leaving nothing but the continental United States. He felt that the American people must know that there were two sides in this war, evenly matched. Either side might win, and the people faced one kind of world if one side won, and another kind of the other side won.

I suggested that we faced two problems in regard to the Neutrality Law: the kind of revision to propose, and the kind of arguments to make. Should we work for revision or outright repeal? My belief was that the sentiment of the country was: "Let's repeal the whole damn thing and go back to international law." The President replied that he did not care how it was done—the important thing was to get rid of the arms embargo feature, and if this were done he had enough authority to enforce cash-and-carry on any other products to protect American interests. I told him that we were going on the presupposition that a special session of Congress would be called to revise the Neutrality Law, and I asked his advice as to what kind of arguments we should make. We could make the technical argument that by repealing the Neutrality Law we would be returning to international law; or we could take the courageous line and advocate repealing the arms embargo as the surest way to keep America out of war because it would give supplies to the British and the French and help them do the job we would have to do if they didn't win. He said that obviously we could make stronger arguments than the administration could officially—we could use the second argument while he could not.

We then spoke about the fireside chat on Sunday. I told the President that I had sympathized with his position and had sensed the embarrassment and conflict under which he had labored. Obviously, the law required that he proclaim neutrality, but how much more he would have liked to have told the American people about the international situation! He remarked that it was a terrible situation to be in, that he had written a speech including all the things that seemed important, and then had had to take them out. I commented, "Your statement that you were not asking people to be neutral in thought is what saved the speech." He agreed.

Here one may make a comparison between President Woodrow Wilson's position on neutrality in the First World War, and President Roosevelt's in the Second. President Wilson, urging neutrality, had asked the American people to be neutral in thought and action, whereas President Roosevelt, as he proclaimed neutrality, had saved the situation by saying that he was not asking people to be neutral in thought.

On September 13, Congress was summoned to meet in special session on September 21 to consider revision of the Neutrality Act. President Roosevelt's message to Congress when it reconvened urged that action be taken with respect to the embargo provisions of the Neutrality Act, which he felt were a "danger to our neutrality and our peace." He asked for "repeal of the embargo provisions and a return to international law."

It seemed to us that we should now give all possible support to the administration so that its efforts this time would not fail. It was vital to overcome the considerable opposition of well-organized, well-financed, and highly vocal minority groups, and especially the followers of Father Coughlin. The organization of a special ad hoc committee for this purpose seemed to be the answer. I consulted with friends in the Department of State and in the Senate about the best possible person to be chairman of such a committee. Most names were brushed aside quickly except for that of William Allen White. Mr. White was a Republican; he lived in a small town in the Midwest; as editor and publisher of the Emporia *Gazette,* he was a well-known writer. But above all those things, there was about him an unusual integrity which revealed itself as time went on.

The American Union for Concerted Peace Efforts,[2] which now brought together all of the organizations that were supporting the program of giving aid to the allies, agreed that a nation-wide ad hoc committee was needed. It was to be called the Non-Partisan Committee for Peace Through Revision of the Neutrality Law. I was authorized to approach Mr. White to ask him to serve as chairman of the committee.

I telephoned Mr. White that day and there followed a letter to him signed by Henry A. Atkinson, Hugh Moore, and myself, as officers of the American Union, outlining the proposal and offering to go see him in Emporia to discuss the matter further. This was the first of an exchange of communications. On September 28, Mr. White wired that he was "slipping a little" and wanted the names of at least ten persons who would definitely go along. We quickly wired him the names of persons we could reach immediately, including Frank P. Graham, Charles G. Fenwick, Carrie Chapman Catt, James T. Shotwell, Mary E. Woolley, Frederic R. Coudert, Roscoe Drummond, Dorothy Thompson, Dorothy Canfield Fisher, and Frank Aydelotte. Anne O'Hare McCormick and Raymond and Betty Gram Swing also urged his acceptance. The situation looked promising, and as I wrote Adolf A. Berle, Assistant Secretary of State, on September 28, "I am leaving tonight for Emporia, Kansas. We have only had tentative acceptance, but I believe the trip is justified."

I saw Mr. White on September 29 and we agreed on the sort of telegram to go out to a "first" list of persons inviting them to serve on the committee. He asked that Professor Shotwell ap-

2. Formerly the Committee for Concerted Peace Efforts.

prove all the names. He also wanted to be assured about the financial backing: "We must have no money from international bankers or from munition makers which includes big and little steel." He asked that a separate bank account be set up for the committee, and said that we could consult him daily. He would be in New York on October 13.

The invitation to join the committee went out almost immediately. In it Mr. White said, "The present Senate Bill to revise the neutrality law goes as far as human ingenuity can to lessen the danger of American involvement. Moreover, by repealing the arms embargo our country is no longer aiding Hitler to the disadvantage of the democracies who are resisting the spread of dictatorship."

Announcement of the formation of the committee was made on October 2. There followed an intense month of trying to reach all segments of the American public through every possible means. Even before the announcement of the formation of the committee was made, we had secured the support of former Governor Alfred E. Smith who, on October 1, gave an address over CBS resolutely backing the administration's Neutrality bill.

Within a few days of the committee's formation, 269 men and women prominent throughout the country in civic, religious, educational, and business affairs had been recruited. "As the only national organization of its kind, created for the special purpose of educating and mobilizing public opinion throughout the country and developing ways and means for its effective expression, the Committee quickly became the spearhead of the public movement for revision and repeal, and rallied to its support the efforts of vast numbers of individuals and existing groups."[3] Among the means urged to get the committee's message to the public were daily spot news releases; a special state-

3. A Report of Activities of the Committee dated October 30, 1939.

ment from Mr. White and photograph to go to those small-town areas where sentiment for revision was less strong; telegrams to newspaper and magazine editors to stimulate editorial comment; press conferences by Mr. White in New York and Washington; sponsorship of live radio broadcasts and transcriptions of speeches to stations without network affiliation, including one especially prepared to counterbalance the effect of Father Coughlin's broadcasts; public opinion polls among university and college presidents, faculty and college students, the American Legion, and various communities, the results of which were given wide publicity; printing and distribution of leaflets; cooperation with other organizations; meetings with speakers, the first of which was a luncheon hosted by Frederic R. Coudert, Sr., at which Mr. White spoke to distinguished business leaders, educators, statesmen, and publicists; direct mail, telephone, and telegraph contact; and information supplied to Congress.

It was quite within the policy of the LNA to cooperate with the American Union for Concerted Peace Efforts and through it with the White Committee. A letter to the Association's branches, dated October 4, 1939, explains:

The traditional stand of the Association in the interests of international order has been reflected in its program in recent years which has stood for discrimination in whatever neutrality law is on our books as between an aggressor and the victim of aggression. . . . The present Administration bill does not embody the principle of discrimination against an aggressor which we had most desired. On the other hand, it puts an end in terms of practical effect to the unwanted discrimination in favor of aggression which our present law contains.

Mr. White came to New York in the middle of October. He gave personal attention to the activities and direction of the committee, writing many of his friends both in Congress and out to enlist their support for repeal of the arms embargo. With the aid of our Washington office, close attention was paid to the mood of Congress, and Mr. White and I went to Washington for the last crucial days of the debate.

On October 27, the Senate finally passed the administration's bill repealing the arms embargo and providing for arms sales to belligerents on a "cash-and-carry" basis by a vote of 63–30. The House passed the bill on November 2, by a vote of 243–181. Subsequently the Senate adopted the conference committee bill by 55–24 and the House by 243–172. The bill was signed by the President on November 4.

In a telegram typical of his style, Mr. White wired me from Emporia on November 3: "When vote seemed safe I pulled out. Congratulations upon final issue. Give my warm regards to all your force. It was a happy adventure. You were most efficient and I was just your friend and an old stuffed shirt."

Senator Claude Pepper and others wrote expressing their appreciation for the work of the committee. Adolf Berle, with whom I had consulted during the planning stages of the committee, wrote on November 6:

The Neutrality Act fight is now over; and I think all of us owe you a very great debt of gratitude for your very effective work.

The situation was anything but easy; but the result has been virtually a vote of confidence in the foreign policy of the Administration. I think the Administration was entitled to it; but public opinion in this matter needed leadership other than the kind it was getting from Father Coughlin; and that I think your Committee very largely provided. You have every right to be proud of the result.

In a handwritten addition to a letter of November 11, Mr. White, always aware of his Republicanism, wrote: "I had a swell note of gratitude from FDR. I feel like America's No. 1 Hypocrite!"[4]

4. A warm friendship and deep mutual admiration, despite their political differences—differences that could be felt very deeply in the Midwest—existed between the President and Mr. White. I remember President Roosevelt asking me during one of our conversations if I had heard from Bill White lately. He

Mr. White wrote to the members of his committee on November 14, thanking them for their support in the campaign and dissolving the committee, its immediate task and purpose having been accomplished. A number of persons replied, expressing their appreciation for the committee's work and for Mr. White's leadership. Mr. Coudert, however, to name one member, felt its demise should be only temporary. He suggested that

it might be just as well not to disband the Committee for the moment. After having talked with some of the other members, I am convinced that very grave questions will arise in the future which may require more Congressional legislation to protect the peace, honor and dignity of the United States. Under such circumstances, a committee such as that which was formed under your wise auspices might be of utmost utility and therefore I trust that there may be no formal dissolution of the Committee until we are back to something like a real peace.

Within a few months, events were to demonstrate Coudert's wisdom.

The League of Nations Association began its work of helping plan for revisions in the League or, if need be, for a new organization, by bringing together a group of individuals and representatives of organizations to set up what became known as the Commission to Study the Organization of Peace. Originally, it was thought that this group might produce its first, and possibly its final, report in six to twelve months. We could hardly have known that the Commission would continue and grow in influence not only through the planning of the peace and the San Francisco Conference, but on to this day.

There were a number of developments before the Commis-

said, "I was in Emporia speaking some time ago and Bill was on the platform, grinning from ear to ear. I said to the audience, 'You know, Bill White is with me three and a half years out of every four.'"

sion took its final shape in the fall of 1939. After the adjournment of the League of Nations Assembly in 1938, I had had a
few days of talks with friends in Paris and London. On my
return to the United States, I had long conferences with Professor Shotwell and other officers of the Association. I also conferred with people outside the LNA throughout the country
and in Washington, including Sterling Fisher of the Columbia
Broadcasting System, who was to play an important part in
implementing our immediate plans. Speculating about the future of the League machinery, we reasoned that the world
might go to the brink of war and then pull back. Should that
happen, there would be a movement to revise the League Covenant; more than that, a movement to reorganize the League
itself. American public opinion might be frightened out of its
isolationism and be willing this time to fulfill the obligations of
full membership. If not, the effort to reorganize the League
would be abortive. On the other hand, if formal world war
broke out, it seemed likely that something new would have to
be created to take the place of the League of Nations system.

I put my thoughts in a memorandum to Mr. Fisher on October 27, 1938. I started out by saying, "One of the most important contributions that could be made to the solution of international problems would be a discussion over the air of the subject
'What kind of international society does the world need?' " The
memorandum outlined four possible programs and speakers.

The proposal grew. At the LNA board meeting on January 24,
1939, I spoke of the "proposed radio program and conference
which it is hoped to put on with the cooperation of the Columbia Broadcasting System"—a series of radio broadcasts followed by a two-day conference. By April 12, the plan called for
the establishment of an "Unofficial Enquiry." "Enquiry" had
been the name for a commission of outstanding citizens
brought together by Woodrow Wilson in 1917–18, to plan the
peace terms and the League of Nations. Professor Shotwell had

been a member of that original "Enquiry."

Although war was not to break out until the following September, it seemed inevitable in April 1939. Indeed the first paragraph of the memorandum dated April 12, 1939, proposing the "Unofficial Enquiry" makes reference to "the organization of international society to follow the present state of war." I quote further from this memorandum:

The fundamental need of the world is a dynamic process of international community life capable of providing for advancement of peoples within the bounds of justice and peace. The efforts of the League of Nations to provide for the peaceful settlement of disputes, collective security, international justice and peaceful change, are manifestations of a great effort that must be made to provide the dynamic organization of a changing world.

Such a task necessitates the expansion of the League of Nations far beyond that which now exists. Indeed the League should be less thought of as a building or a Covenant, than in the freer sense as the vital processes of community life.

The United States must take the lead in this effort. Most of the concepts for world cooperation have had their origin at least partially in the United States. Among these are the League of Nations, the International Labor Organization, the Pact of Paris, etc., etc. The United States, supplying one-third of the raw materials of the world and accounting for 40% of its industrial output, can be one of the most powerful factors in planning the future of international society.

The League of Nations Association proposes to appoint a commission to perform the task herein outlined. The Association, which throughout its history has been devoted not to a rigid Covenant or a static piece of machinery, but to the dynamic processes of international life, is the logical organization to undertake and administer the "Unofficial Enquiry."

The memorandum concludes:

A very important task remains to be performed in transmitting the deliberations of the Enquiry to the public. They will be of value if

they may be widely accepted by the people on a non-partisan base
and form the basis of American foreign policy. The radio makes
possible an educational approach to millions of people. It has been
the plan for some time of the Columbia Broadcasting System, in cooperation with the League of Nations Association and other groups
asked to participate, to hold in New York a conference of leaders of
the country on the subject "What kind of international society does
the world need?"

Instead of holding a radio conference this spring, as originally
planned, it would seem better to delay the conference until the Enquiry was ready to present the results of its first six months of deliberations to the public. At the conference it is proposed that members of
the [conference] commissions speak to the nation and their addresses
be followed by a general discussion participated in by the delegates to
the conference. Ample radio time has been set aside by the Columbia
Broadcasting System so that millions of people may listen in to the
proceedings of the New York conference and thus learn the first conclusions of the Enquiry.

Under Dr. Shotwell's leadership, a few key people were enlisted during the summer of 1939 and we started outlining a
program of studies. Those invited to serve on the Commission
comprised many of the same people who later were to organize
the William Allen White Committee to support revision of the
Neutrality Law. As time went on, it seemed more and more
remarkable that pretty much the same group of leaders, in the
same office, with the same staff, and supported primarily by the
same national organizations, should undertake planning for the
future and for giving maximum support to the allies as the war
grew more intense.

In a memorandum of August 10, I was able to state that the
Enquiry would "start work in early October and take six months
to produce its conclusions." The plan at that stage was that
other organizations would co-sponsor the Enquiry, which
would be composed of well-known authorities. A radio broad-

cast would launch the program. At the conclusion of the Enquiry's deliberations, a conference would be held to present the findings to the general public.

Then, in the first week of September, Germany invaded Poland. France and the United Kingdom responded, and war was formally declared. Now the allies missed the thirty Czech divisions that they had thrown away when Czechoslovakia was sacrificed. Since Poland had helped dismember Czechoslovakia, it was hardly as ideal a cause to which to rally as had been Czechoslovakia, but the great powers could no longer ignore Hitler's aggression.

In my September 7 interview with President Roosevelt, in addition to discussing the war situation and the problem of the revision of the Neutrality Law, we talked about the future. I gave the President a very brief outline of the plan of the Enquiry and told him the Columbia Broadcasting System was willing to give unlimited facilities to the effort. He thought the scheme "grand," although of course this was to be an unofficial Commission, unlike the earlier Enquiry.

The Commission was about ready for its first meeting in the early fall, but the outbreak of war naturally changed our thinking and our timing: the William Allen White Committee's work took precedence. Only when the embargo provisions of the Neutrality Law had been repealed and the repeal signed into law on November 4 were we free to devote our attention to the Enquiry. The first meeting of the Committee for the Study of the Organization of Peace was held on Sunday, November 5, at the old Murray Hill Hotel in New York. This was to be our regular meeting place during the early years of the Commission's existence. Inasmuch as our meetings were normally held on Sunday, we frequently had to compete for an hour or so in our deliberations with the services and hymns of the "Great I Am's" who met in an adjoining room.

Twenty-seven persons attended the first meeting of the

"Committee for the Study of the Organization of Peace."[5] A method of work was agreed upon, as well as an outline of studies and the organization of the Commission itself. Its officers and committee chairmen were: Professor Shotwell, chairman; William Allan Neilson, president emeritus of Smith College, executive committee; Clyde Eagleton, professor at New York University, studies committee; Evans Clark of the Twentieth Century Fund, publications committee; and Lyman Bryson, radio committee. I was elected director. Among the other Commission members at that time were such well-known citizens as Frank Aydelotte, Frank G. Boudreau, Esther Caukin Brunauer, John Foster Dulles, Charles G. Fenwick, Frank P. Graham, Thomas W. Lamont, Charles F. Taft, and Quincy Wright. Clarence A. Berdahl and Richard R. Wood were among the original members of the Commission; they have been active throughout the years and are currently members of its executive committee. It was assumed that the LNA would act as the secretariat for the project.

For various reasons, including the formal outbreak of war, the national conference which had been planned was not held. However, two weekly radio series began at the end of January 1940. As previously planned, one was an "adult" program over which Professor Shotwell presided; the other a "student bull session." The overall title for the series was "Which Way to Lasting Peace?" The programs met with success and reached a large audience. After they had been on the air for only two weeks, it was learned from CBS that seventy-one of their stations carried the Shotwell program and seventy-five the student session. Only 26 of their 115 stations did not carry either one.

The letters inviting persons to join the Commission had in-

5. The title was changed a month later to the present name, "Commission to Study the Organization of Peace." At times we have thought of changing the name to something shorter and more "dynamic," but this name so well defined the purpose of the Commission that no catch phrase ever seemed as appropriate.

cluded the statement that we would not be rushed in our deliberations, "although it is hoped conclusions might be ready in about six months." On May 19, 1940, Dr. Neilson reported to the Commission that the executive committee, of which he was chairman, "was proceeding on the assumption that the Commission would continue." There was no opposition to this statement.

What was to become the "Preliminary" or First Report of the Commission was discussed at this meeting. The document was revised by the drafting committee during the summer months and presented to the Commission again on September 29. It was agreed at that time that after further revision the draft would be circulated among members for their general approval and signature. Members could withhold their signature if they disagreed with the findings. This pattern, established for the First Report, would become the practice for the Commission throughout its history.

The final draft of the First Report went out for signature on October 26, setting a deadline of November 6 for replies. Thus a year after the Commission's inaugural meeting, its First Report was ready to be published.

Many drafts were submitted for discussion by the executive committee, which was really the drafting committee. One member submitted a twenty-five-page document for consideration as the preliminary report. It seemed to some, however, that the First Report should be very brief, in a sense a proclamation of faith and intention. The report begins with the following sentences:

As the shadows of the second world war deepen, the Commission submits the following statement of principles which it considers fundamental to the organization of peace. It does so because it has sufficient faith in man to deny that war is inevitable, and to believe that if he can be brought to see and understand the nature of the world in which he lives, he will be capable of organizing international order and justice, and thereby making possible the continuous development of the social well-being of all peoples. . . .

No one could have foretold back in 1939 that the Commission would continue discussing the adjustment of the world to the problems that would develop after the United Nations was established. And who could have foretold, during the war or immediately afterward, the advent of atomic energy, the revolt against colonialism, the conquering of outer space, the effort to develop a régime for the sea, and the other problems with which the Commission has concerned itself in the postwar years?

9

The Committee to Defend America
by Aiding the Allies

No one could quite tell, in the fall of 1939, what Hitler and Mussolini would do next. Hitler had invaded Poland on September 1. Great Britain and France had declared war two days later. But the armies did not move rapidly; a blitz did not occur. People talked about the "phoney war," and there were those, like Senator William E. Borah, who seemed to find comfort, and possibly an escape from reality, in the phrase. Some observers thought that after a time there would be long discussions leading to a peace settlement, which at that point would necessarily be to the advantage of Germany and Italy, and to the humiliation of France and Britain. Others, including William Allen White, members of his former committee, and myself, believed that the world faced a long military road. The aggressors had not been definitely challenged.

After the campaign for the revision of the Neutrality Law, I had kept in touch with William Allen White, certain that it would only be a matter of time until we would need his leadership again. There were continual consultations among members of his old committee both in New York and throughout the country, particularly in Washington.

Mr. White came East at the end of April 1940 to speak at a

dinner on May 1, given by *The Nation* in honor of Mrs. Roosevelt. On April 29 Frederic Coudert arranged a small, private luncheon for him at the Downtown Association, inviting many of the same people who had been present at a luncheon he had given during the days of the Committee to Revise the Neutrality Law. The guests included Frank L. Polk, Thomas W. Lamont, Wendell Willkie, Nicholas Murray Butler, James T. Shotwell, Henry Breckenridge, Thomas K. Finletter, and Henry L. Stimson.[1] The talk ranged over several subjects, including the coming political conventions and the need to ensure strong foreign policy planks in the party platforms. But the subject most on our minds was inevitably the war and what could be done to secure aid for Britain and the allies. One immediate step, it seemed to us, would be to prepare for the revival of the William Allen White Committee to mobilize public opinion in favor of such aid.

Other Americans shared our concern for the allies, ill-equipped to meet a threatening Germany. For example, George Field, program director of Radio Station WEVD, had told me of plans he, Frank Kingdon, Christopher Emmet, and others had for a national committee to mobilize public opinion. I met with Mr. Field and his group several times at the Town Hall Club in early May and we discussed the possibility of a new William Allen White Committee to aid the allies. Kingdon and Field agreed to go along with our plans because ours were further advanced and also because William Allen White would be a natural chairman for such a program. They offered all possible assistance and said they would look after the New York City end of the committee. Indeed, Frank Kingdon became

1. Wendell Willkie's attendance at this luncheon was important, bringing him as it did into a group planning strategy on aid to the allies. Willkie was, at that time, a controversial utility magnate from Commonwealth and Southern, but he was becoming more and more a public figure noted for liberal views. He and I were to become good friends.

chairman of the New York City branch of the committee and George Field its director.

Suddenly the "phoney war" was over. On May 10, 1940, the Germans marched into the Low Countries—Belgium, The Netherlands, and Luxembourg. (Norway and Denmark had been occupied in April.) It was time to act.

At the meeting of the executive committee of the League of Nations Association on May 14, the Association took a threefold position: first, to support the allies in all methods short of war, because their defeat would make impossible the realization of the principles for which we stood; second, to continue directing the attention of the American people toward the future organization of peace; third, to assist in safeguarding the non-political activities of the League. And, the executive committee voted that the facilities and staff should be made available to the White Committee for its forthcoming campaign.

As news of the fighting grew worse, telegrams and messages flew back and forth between New York and Emporia. Mr. White wired various drafts of the statement he would make calling upon the American people for aid to the allies, and I sent suggestions for revision after asking the advice of people in New York and Washington.

The first telegrams asking people to join the committee went out the night of May 17. On May 18 I had a telegram from Mr. White saying, "Wire quickly copy of telegram to [Alf] Landon. Knox has signed." Landon, unfortunately, did not become a member of the committee, but in addition to Frank Knox, publisher of the Chicago *Daily News,* some of the first signers were Governor Herbert Lehman of New York, Nicholas Murray Butler, Gene Tunney, Bishop Henry W. Hobson of Cincinnati, Reinhold Niebuhr, Robert E. Sherwood, and Mary E. Woolley.

On May 20 the formation of the Committee to Defend America by Aiding the Allies[2] was announced to the press; many papers carried the complete text of Mr. White's statement:

As one democracy after another crumbles under the mechanized columns of the dictators, it becomes evident that the future of western civilization is being decided upon the battlefield of Europe. Here is a life and death struggle for every principle we cherish in America, for freedom of speech, of religion, of the ballot and of every freedom that upholds the dignity of the human spirit. Here all the rights that the common man has fought for during a thousand years are menaced. Terrible as it may seem, the people of our country cannot avoid the consequences of Hitler's victory and of those who are or may be allied with him. A totalitarian victory would wipe out hope for a just and lasting peace.

The time has come when the United States should throw its economic and moral weight on the side of the nations of western Europe, great and small, that are struggling in battle for a civilized way of life; that constitute our first line of defense. It would be a folly to hold this nation chained to a neutrality policy determined in the light of last year's facts. The new situation requires a new attitude.

From this day on, America must spend every ounce of energy to keep the war away from the Western Hemisphere by preparing to defend herself and by aiding with our supplies and wealth the nations now fighting to stem the tide of aggression. This is no time for leaders to consider party or factional advantage. All men and all creeds and clans may well call upon our President to confer with leaders of all parties looking to a foreign policy providing for an increase in arma-

2. By the time the committee was formed in May, Britain stood virtually alone: Norway and Denmark had fallen; The Lowlands were soon overrun. Vichy France was to sign an armistice on June 22, 1940. However, the phrase "by Aiding the Allies" was retained officially in the committee's name until the last few months of its existence, when it became simply the "Committee to Defend America." The philosophy behind this choice was stated in a speech Mr. White made on June 8, 1940. He said that the committee was carrying the banner "not merely for Great Britain and the British Empire, but also for Scandinavia, for Czechoslovakia, for Poland, for Holland, for France, for Abyssinia. All these captive peoples are our allies. For these oppressed nations now enslaved by the dictators, we are making our fight. Wherever one man suffers injustice, the rights of all men are endangered. . . ."

ments to defend ourselves and for every economic effort to help the Allies. In foreign affairs we must present an unbroken, non-partisan front to the world. It is for us to show the people of England, of France, of Holland, of Belgium and of Scandinavia that the richest country on earth is not too blind or too timid to help those who are fighting tyranny abroad. If they fail, we shall not have time to prepare to face their conquerors alone.

Will you join with me and several hundred others in the formation of a committee which would carry these points of view to the American people?

The response was instantaneous. *The New York Times* of May 26 described it in a special dispatch from Emporia:

The always cluttered desk of William Allen White at the office of the Emporia *Gazette* is cluttered a few inches higher these days by the telegrams and letters of the correspondence of the Committee for Defense of America Through Aid to the Allies. The affairs of this Committee constitute Mr. White's chief occupation these days.

Ten days ago in the New York office of the Committee, of which he is chairman, he wired to a hundred prominent men and women asking them to join. Responses began immediately to pour in to Emporia and New York and today he has 150 important persons allied with him in this endeavor. Included are the presidents of Yale, Harvard, Columbia and Dartmouth.

Mr. White concluded the interview with the *Times* correspondent by saying: "We are entirely candid in our aims. We have nothing up our sleeves, nothing to conceal. We are trying to crystallize the overwhelming sentiment that exists in America favoring the cause of the Allies and to make that sentiment real and vital in Congressional and administrative action."

A great deal of emotion surrounded the founding of the second William Allen White Committee. The lobby of the building at 8 West 40th Street where the committee was located was crowded with visitors. Some were curiosity seekers; some were volunteers who wanted to help; some wanted jobs. Police patrolled the lobby, for not all the reaction was favorable. The committee received threatening letters, some of them addressed to prominent members of the committee and its officers.

Important national figures were quick to agree to go on the radio for the committee. James B. Conant, president of Harvard University, in a nation-wide program over CBS on May 29, pointed out the dangers of a Nazi victory and the necessity of releasing army and navy airplanes and other implements of war, without impairing national security, to France and England. Mrs. Dwight Morrow, then acting president of Smith College, spoke on June 4 over NBC. Her subject was "Does America Deserve a Miracle?" In her talk, Mrs. Morrow said, "the French and British are fighting tonight for all the things we honor in life. Why not support them as a first line defense? If Hitler's world as he has outlined it sounds tolerable to you, my pleas will be unavailing. If not, write or wire tonight to the President, to your senators and your congressmen and urge that every possible aid be given at once to the Allies. The need is immediate—it is a matter of days."

By this time, the evacuation of Dunkirk had been completed. No one knew what Hitler intended to do, launch an invasion against England or turn south to Paris. Most of the American public was aroused and frightened, and ready to respond to Mrs. Morrow's plea. The Western Union Telegraph Company told us the next day that they had been swamped throughout the country and in Washington by the thousands of messages that had poured in as a result of her talk. They asked that the committee let them know ahead of time whenever a radio speaker would be requesting telegrams to Washington so that they could be prepared with an adequate staff.

Other prominent persons volunteered to help the committee in other ways. For example, Henry Steele Commager, then at Columbia University, sent a letter on his own initiative to 250 persons asking them to join with him in a committee of historians, with aid to the allies as their focal point.

Perhaps the biggest impetus given the Committee to Defend America by a volunteer was from Robert E. Sherwood. I remember his coming into the office one day early in June with the draft of an advertisement he had prepared. He wanted our approval to run it as an official advertisement of the Committee to Defend America by Aiding the Allies. This, of course, was readily given. Mr. Sherwood not only gave the ad to the CDA, but arranged for it to run June 10 in ten or more newspapers in strategic places throughout the country and raised the money among his friends to finance it. This was the famous "Stop Hitler Now" advertisement, which received considerable comment in the press. *The New York Times* story of June 12 about the presidential press conference of the previous day reported:

A copy of the full-page newspaper "Stop Hitler Now" advertisement was on the President's desk as reporters filed into his office for the usual Tuesday afternoon conference and he had been told that a request for comment would be made. Eyeing the bold headlines, Mr. Roosevelt said he did not want to be placed in a position of endorsing every phrase of the advertisement.

Then he noted that the advertisement had been prepared by Robert Sherwood, leading playwright, and remarked that it was a very good thing that Bill White was able to get such messages across for the education of the American people. William Allen White, editor of the Emporia, Kan., *Gazette*, is national chairman of the Defense Committee for Aiding the Allies.

The "Stop Hitler Now" ad gave a big boost to the committee financially, attracting many new supporters and inspiring new chapters. Branches of the League of Nations Association transformed themselves into CDA branches, which became the backbone of the nation-wide organization. Other national organizations threw their weight behind the CDA and some of their branches affiliated with the CDA.

The genius of the Committee to Defend America was to get information and suggestions for action out to the country and in turn to channel expressions of opinion to Washington. The chapters were crucial to this operation, and the nucleus of the field organization was the staff of the LNA. In some other localities a particular person was asked to assume responsibility for organizing a chapter, but for the most part, the chapters just sprang up. By the end of June, there were over 300. There were over 500 members of the committee; contributions from over 3,000 people had been received at headquarters, totaling over $85,000. This, of course, was in addition to funds the chapters raised locally for their own purposes.

To support our cause and to convince the public that we did not want to weaken this country's defense capabilities, we asked distinguished military authorities for their opinions. For example, the Boston chapter arranged a rally at Faneuil Hall for June 28. Admiral Harry E. Yarnell was the chief speaker. To balance the navy point of view, the Washington, D.C., group wanted General Pershing to send a message to the meeting. Roger Greene, who directed our activities in the Washington office at that time, contacted the general and secured the following message from him:

The time has come for all Americans to lay aside partisanship and work together to build up the defenses of their country and the defenses of our democracy against the greatest peril with which America has ever been faced. We need material equipment of every kind for our Army and Navy at the earliest possible moment. Our only chance of security lies in the wholehearted and energetic cooperation of all who can contribute in any way to the arming of democracy. Without such team play and readiness to make sacrifices we cannot hope to get what we need when we need it, and cannot use it effectively when we get it.

So long as Britain stands the danger may be kept at a distance.

Therefore, while organizing and equipping ourselves it is sound sense to do all that we can to keep Britain supplied with the food, arms, and munitions of which she must have a continuous supply if that outer bulwark of democracy is not to crumble. If we do that the last sacrifice may not be demanded of us. . . .

I earnestly hope that you may be successful in awakening our people to the real situation, for I am sure they will then play their part worthily as they have always done throughout our history. There is no time to lose.

General Pershing's statement, of course, had wider use than just at the Boston meeting. It was sent out to all committee members and chapters. Mr. White wrote, on July 5, that he was using it in all his committee correspondence and suggested that it be used as a stuffer in all mailings. He went on to say, "Next time you write to Mr. Greene tell him that I think that is a classic—one of the best things we have got out."

General Pershing's statement came at a moment when Britain needed munitions of all kinds, when her forces stood on the beaches practically unarmed. The committee strove desperately to secure immediate aid. John L. Balderston, who for a few weeks conducted a news service for the committee for a selected list of newspaper editors, sent the following telegram from Washington on August 27, giving a summary of the arms to Britain sent during June, July, and August:

One night in July message came to Washington from Winston Churchill for President Roosevelt. It announced in effect, the writer hasn't seen it and doesn't pretend to quote it, arrival British ports of huge mass of weapons, cannon, machine guns, rifles and stuff to shoot out of them too.

After describing successful convoy precautions Churchill told President trains were waiting with steam up in all ports, into which ships were being warped and he said weapons would be in hands of British soldiers awaiting them within twenty-four hours.

During this period of extreme crisis when Churchill's already famous cry of defiance to Hitler, his fight on the beaches speech, was ringing through the world, fifteen ships containing roughly hundred thousand tons American weapons and explosives reached Great Britain. Invasion was thought matter of days or hours by those who knew tragic lack means of defense caused by loss almost whole modern equipment British army in Flanders and France.

Eighty thousand Hotchkiss and Lewis machine guns were sent from this country and now guard shores of England.

Some seven hundred fifty seventy-five millimetre field guns with mountain of shells were sent and are now in service.

Half a million Lee Enfield rifles were in those consignments. Churchill said last week that two million soldiers armed with rifles now stand ready in Britain. One man in four of Britain's defenders now carries rifle sent from United States since battle of France became the catastrophe of France.

There has been no invasion but there might have been and there may be and a high British authority has expressed himself to an American to effect that these shipments "repaired at any rate patched up a situation desperate in the exteme."

In addition to weapons mentioned huge quantities which must be unspecified in amount of shells small arm ammunition other materials were shipped across.

These shipments were far from gifts by United States to Great Britain. They were rounded up by British purchasing agents and bought from holders in this country in strict compliance provisions Neutrality Law for good prices paid in American dollars, the purchaser taking the risk of loss in transit and then seeing to it there was no loss in transit. Method of transfer of government property to individual firms is well known and the transfer of airplanes at this time by these or similar methods received full publicity, but few outside inner circles were aware of the successful attempt in progress to help rearm British land armies before the Germans could strike.

Among those who were aware were members of the ubiquitous German intelligence service and this fact causes smiles among those who know what has been going on at the cries arising from Capitol Hill and elsewhere that turning over fifty old destroyers will somehow constitute an act of war against Hitler by a nation until now at profound peace with that potentate. Methods of transferring destroyers will necessarily be legally technically and tactically different from those employed in helping rearm British army but result will be precisely the same, the implementing of the pledge made by the President at Charlottesville. We have sold the British more than most people realize as this dispatch shows, sold not given a distinction we should keep in mind.

In the last paragraph of his statement, John Balderston refers to the pledge to the allies made by the President at the University of Virginia in Charlottesville on June 10, 1940:

In our American unity, we will pursue two obvious and simultaneous courses; we will extend to the opponents of force the material resources of this nation; and, at the same time, we will harness and speed up the use of those resources in order that we ourselves in the Americas may have equipment and training equal to the task of any emergency and every defense.

All roads leading to the accomplishment of these objectives must be kept clear of obstructions. We will not slow down or detour. Signs and signals call for speed—full speed ahead.[3]

On June 4, 1940, with the evacuation of Dunkirk virtually completed and the situation of the French armies deteriorating, Prime Minister Winston Churchill had addressed the British people and issued his famous rallying cry: ". . . we shall defend our island, whatever the cost may be, we shall fight on the beaches, we shall fight on the landing-grounds, we shall fight in the fields and in the streets, we shall fight in the hills. . . ."[4]

President Roosevelt responded to the prime minister's pleas

3. *The Public Papers and Addresses of Franklin D. Roosevelt: 1940 Volume, War—and Aid to Democracies,* compiled and collated by Samuel I. Rosenman (New York: The Macmillan Company 1941), p. 264.

4. Winston S. Churchill, *Their Finest Hour* (Boston: Houghton Mifflin Company, 1949), p. 118.

to some extent in his Charlottesville speech. He did not, however, proclaim a state of belligerency as Churchill would have liked him to do. Mr. White was full of praise for the President's speech and wired me the next day: "It was a powerful and moving speech delivered by the President yesterday afternoon. It was so moving that it moved America out of neutrality up to the deadline of belligerency. It moved the United States into a twilight zone. We are now unbelligerent unneutrals. We are where we belong."

As a result of fighting in the North Sea and the Mediterranean the British fleet of destroyers had dwindled from about 176 at the beginning of the war to fewer than half that number by June 1940. Ships were being lost or damaged every day, and the remainder of her fleet was clearly inadequate to keep open Britain's sea approaches and protect her supply convoys, to block the sea exits from continental Europe and the Mediterranean, to provide for the defense of Gibraltar, and to prevent the invasion of the British Isles.

In *Their Finest Hour* Winston Churchill writes,

On May 15 [1940], as already narrated, I had in my first telegram to President Roosevelt after becoming Prime Minister asked for "the loan of forty or fifty of your older destroyers to bridge the gap between what we have now and the large new construction we put in hand at the beginning of the war. . . ." I recurred to this in my cable of June 11, after Italy had already declared war upon us. . . . At the end of July, when we were alone and already engaged in the fateful air battle, with the prospect of imminent invasion behind it, I renewed my request. I was well aware of the President's good will and of his difficulties. For that reason I had endeavored to put before him, in the blunt terms of various messages, the perilous position which the United States would occupy if British resistance collapsed and Hitler became master of Europe, with all its dockyards and navies. . . .[5]

5. *Ibid.*, pp. 398–399.

The discussion of the need for destroyers went on for many weeks, while public opinion in the United States in favor of supplying them continued to mount.

On June 20 I wired the chapters as follows: "We recommend strong approval immediately to President Roosevelt for releasing to Britain twenty small torpedo boats and submarine chasers and an appeal for sale to Britain of some old destroyers urgently needed to protect supply lines. Congress should know public supports President in such measures to aid Allies. Most urgent."

After the conclusion of the two national political conventions in July, the committee could more fully turn its attention to the issues at hand. On July 23, Mr. White wired a selected list of chapters: "Confidential information highest authority convinces me British Government desperately short of destroyers. Successful defense of Great Britain may depend upon release through sale by the United States of fifty or sixty over age but recently reconditioned destroyers. President already has authority or could secure Congressional authorization if necessary. Urge you wire President immediately advocating this action."

On July 11 a dozen or so of us had met in New York to review the whole situation of aid to Britain. Known for a time as the Century Club group, because it frequently met there for dinner, or the Francis Miller group, because he took a leave of absence from the Council on Foreign Relations to take charge of the office the group opened, this was the nucleus of what was later formalized and expanded into the Fight for Freedom Committee. (I was not a member of the Fight for Freedom Committee, although I met with them from time to time.)

We met again on July 25 and according to the "Memorandum of Meeting" prepared by Mr. Miller, the British chances of success were "doubtful, but responsible British officials believe that they could successfully withstand invasion if they had 100 more destroyers." It was reported that American naval experts believed that British crews could take these destroyers to England without special training. During the discussion the suggestion was made that these destroyers "should be offered to Britain in exchange for immediate naval and air concessions in British possessions in the Western Hemisphere."

We went on to consider ways and means. There was general agreement that time was too short for congressional debate on the proposed program. Consequently, a few of us should see the President and urge him to take action, "on the reasonable assumption that Mr. Willkie would go along with him."

I had gathered from various sources that the President had been quietly consulting many people who had seen service in the Department of State about the possibility of sending the destroyers to Britain. He had also consulted the Republican minority leader of Congress, Senator Charles McNary. McNary was very anxious that all possible aid go to Britain, but since it was an election year he advised the President to try to find some way of doing it without confronting Congress with the question.

So on August 1, Herbert Agar, Ward Cheney, and I called on the President. We gained the impression that he was not certain as to his authority to transfer the destroyers without the consent of Congress.

Late that same afternoon I went to the office in the Interior Department of my close friend Benjamin V. Cohen. I always enjoyed visiting with Ben Cohen, but on this particular day I had a specific question for him. We discussed the problem of the destroyers and the President's uncertainty as to his authority for trading them without the consent of Congress. I asked Ben if such authority could not be found. He went to work consulting various books he had in his office. Finally, I returned to my hotel and went to bed while Ben worked all night, as usual. The next morning he called me at breakfast time and said, "I think I've got it."

I returned to New York for a meeting of the Eastern chairmen and officers of the White Committee. On arrival, I called Mr. White, who had just arrived in Estes Park, Colorado, for a few weeks vacation. On the basis of my call, he was able to send a telegram to the meeting from Colorado urging that the destroyers be put on the "must list," and saying, "I have information which persuades me that these ships may make the difference between success or failure. I am also sure that if President Roosevelt feels public opinion behind him, he will act. Time is urgent."

In the meantime, Mr. Cohen drafted a legal opinion stating that over-age destroyers could be released for sale to the British under existing statutory authority. He conferred with Dean Acheson (not then in the government), who suggested that he redraft the opinion as a letter to *The New York Times*, to be signed by Mr. Acheson and two or three other distinguished lawyers of national repute who were not in the government or in any way beholden to the Roosevelt administration. A week or so later the letter, signed by Dean Acheson; Charles C. Burlingham, a venerable leader of the New York Bar; Thomas D. Thatcher, a former solicitor-general in the Hoover administration; and George Rublee, a law partner of Dean Acheson and a former member of the Federal Trade Commission in the Wilson administration, was brought to our New York office. *The New York Times* had been advised of the letter and was waiting to carry it in the Sunday edition of the paper.

The statement, with the headline: "No Legal Bar Seen to Transfer of Destroyers," ran in *The New York Times* on Sunday, August 11, 1940, and was reprinted by many other newspapers throughout the country. On August 12, copies were sent out to local chairmen of the Committee to Defend America by Aiding the Allies, so that it could be made known to as many people as possible around the country. The final paragraph read, "When vital interests of the United States are at stake, when the sentiment of the country is clear, the government should not hesitate to exercise powers under existing law. To seek an unnecessary reaffirmation of these powers from the Congress now would be to run a serious danger of delay and by delay possibly to endanger the vital interests of the people of the country in keeping war from our own shores."

On August 13, *The New York Times* reported that Senator Claude Pepper had introduced a resolution to authorize the sale of the destroyers. He won the support of two colleagues, Senators Josh Lee, Democrat of Oklahoma, and William H. King, Democrat of Utah. Pepper predicted that the United States would release the destroyers "as soon as Congress and the public became accustomed to the idea." He felt that President Roosevelt would "take the initiative after some legal method, consistent with Federal and International Law, has been devised." In a lively debate in the Senate on August 15, Senator Lee cited the "recently published opinion of Charles G. Burlingham, Thomas D. Thatcher, George Rublee and Dean Acheson," and quoted several paragraphs of the statement.

Besides the acquiescence of Congress, Wendell Willkie's support, or at least his non-opposition, had to be sought. In early August, Mr. Willkie, having been nominated as Republican candidate for President, was in Colorado Springs for the candidate's traditional two weeks rest before opening the campaign. Since William Allen White was in Estes Park, it was natural that he should be the person to talk to Wendell Willkie. He got busy on the telephone to Colorado Springs and also, confidentially, to Washington. On August 9, he wrote me, "I had a telegram from Willkie just now indicating that something had popped but I didn't call him because he didn't call me. We'll see in the morning." He wired me again on August 12,

. . . here follows wire just sent to Hyde Park: "It's not as bad as it seems, I have talked with both of you on this subject during the last ten days.

I know there is not two bits difference between you on the issue pending. But I can't guarantee either of you to the other. Which is funny for I admire and respect you both. I realize you in your position don't want statements but Congressional votes, which by all the rules of the game you should have. But I've not quit. And, as I said, it's not as bad as it looks. With warm greetings I am cordially yours." Here's hoping.

Come early fall, the Whites were ready to return to Emporia. The local members of the William Allen White Committee gave a farewell party for them. In the course of the party, as told to me, the chairman said, "Our village has been greatly honored this summer. Scarcely a day has gone by that Mr. White has not had a talk with the President, the Secretary of State, with Wendell Willkie and so on and so on." The Whites almost fainted. Mr. White said to his wife, "Sally, what happened?" She said, "Well, you know, Will, that our servants are all loyal to us. I haven't any idea."

So she asked the chairman, "How did you folks know all about these things?" The chairman replied, "Bless you, Sally, you folks were on a party line. So when the phone rang we listened in on the conversations. They were very interesting, but people in Estes Park were too loyal to you to say a word."

I shocked the newspapermen by telling them this story. There had been many of them hanging around our committee's New York office that summer asking what the latest word was from Mr. White, Mr. Willkie, and the committee. They had only to go to Estes Park and get on a party line and they could have had all the information they wanted.

10

Base-Destroyer Deal—Lend-Lease— William Allen White Steps Down

On September 3, 1940, the long-awaited headline was blazed across the front pages of newspapers throughout the country: BRITISH GET DESTROYERS, WE GET BASES. The President had notified Congress of an agreement between the United States and Great Britain under which the United States would lease naval and air bases in British possessions in the North and South Atlantic and the Caribbean and in exchange transfer fifty over-age destroyers to Great Britain.

On September 4, the first three destroyers, freshly painted and repaired by crews throughout that day, sailed slowly out of Boston Harbor at sunset, bound for a Canadian port.

Immediately after we got the news, telegrams went out from our New York headquarters to all committee members and local chapters suggesting that messages be sent to the President in support of the action. In Washington on September 5 I had appointments with both the President and the Secretary of State. According to my notes, the President opened the conversation by saying, "First let me tell you that I had something over six hundred telegrams. I can't tell you exactly; we measure these things by inches and estimate them so many to the inch, and it figured up somewhat over six hundred, and of the lot a

136

great many, oh not half, but enough to make a considerable proportion of the lot, maybe a third, probably a little more, were from persons who signed themselves either as chairmen of your committees or as members of the committees, all over the country, and I want to tell you you have done a swell job and we are all deeply grateful to you."

I was extremely touched by the President's praise, but this was not why I had come to see him. I repeated the question I had asked him when I first came into his office: "What's next?" He said he thought it would be the little torpedo boats. Not much longer than his office, they were swift; they carried an 18-inch projectile, and we had somewhat more than the twenty the British were asking for. Of course, we could not sell them while they were in the process of manufacture, but now that they were practically finished, the navy had decided that the 21-inch shell was much more effective than the 18-inch, and was using it on all our boats and in all specifications for new boats. The President suggested that the torpedo boats could be turned back to the manufacturers as "unfit for our work and unsuited to our naval specifications," and then sold to the British, whom they would help greatly, without arousing much opposition to the deal.

I told him that we would try to make the country realize that we could spare the boats and that the British needed them. The President then wanted to know more about the committee. I told him that we had 600 branches or more, some of which had downtown staffs in various cities, and I explained how we raised the money and where it came from. He seemed to be greatly interested.

I also saw Cordell Hull that morning. He thanked me for all that we had done and told me how strongly he felt the backing of the committee all over the country. I answered his questions about the committee's organization, financing, methods of operation, and so on, explaining that it was purely a propaganda organization devoted to crystallizing public opinion and conveying it through letters, telegrams, and telephone calls to various administration officials and members of Congress. Secretary Hull said that we had been marvelously effective. He added rather apologetically that it had taken a long time to complete negotiations for the Caribbean bases. At first, he said, the British did not wish any kind of definite horse trade. They wanted the islands to come as gifts and the destroyers to be return gifts, as an afterthought, for the British kindness. Public opinion in Great Britain seemed to be squeamish about trading away bases but not about giving them away, while our public wanted a definite swap. American public opinion was the opinion of a trading nation that wanted to have no outstanding obligations after the trade was made. The British wanted to leave it open as evidence of friendly relations.

So, Mr. Hull went on, while it was agreed at the start that Great Britain should have the destroyers and we should have the bases, we were nearly a month arranging the deal. Finally, a compromise was reached by allowing Newfoundland and Canada to present us with two bases as a gift, and the rest were given with a *quid pro quo.*

Mr. Hull stated that he had insisted upon this closed account —that this was "a trade, a definite trade," and that the trade was ended with the transfer of the destroyers and the bases—not only because our own public opinion would not stand for an open account, but also because he wanted certain other things for the future needs of Great Britain which would be considered by our government as the British asked for them, and so he wanted it definitely understood that this destroyer base deal was "all under the four corners of one blanket."

I said I hoped he would be able to find other things besides cash which we needed that the British would be able to give us, like the Caribbean bases. He smiled and began talking about our needs in the Pacific, stating that so long as the British fleet was afloat we could keep our own fleet largely in the Pacific and could handle any situation that might arise there. He mentioned Singapore as the key to the Asiatic naval situation, and added that we also badly needed air bases in the area so that we could keep the lanes of trade between the Dutch West Indies and the United States open. Mr. Hull felt that such bases and Singapore would be just as valuable to us as the Caribbean bases. He also stated that the Japanese were conscious of the possibility of an understanding between the United States and Great Britain with regard to bases in the Pacific; he believed that Japanese awareness of this possibility, together with the fact that the British fleet in the Atlantic was still afloat, was one of the things making for continued peace in the Pacific.

Press comment for and against the destroyer base deal was immediate and continued for several days. Wendell Willkie, while not opposing the result, criticized the President for not submitting the matter to Congress. William Allen White, Willkie's ardent supporter politically, defended the President's methods and took issue with Mr. Willkie. Willkie's criticism, however, was mild, and he did not make the deal a campaign issue. So to that extent Mr. White's negotiations in Colorado in August bore fruit.

The destroyers themselves made news. By the time the arrangement had been announced, some of them were already in East Coast ports or scheduled to arrive there soon. *The New York Times* of September 5 had carried the story about the three destroyers that had left Boston for Canada. There was a further story on September 10 from a port in Canada describing the takeover by British sailors: "For the first time in years British tars will not sleep in hammocks. There were bunks for every one of them." The article went on to report that the ships' stores were complete—butter, meat, vegetables, coffee, sugar, etc.

British seamen had been sent to Canada in advance to await the destroyers. As Winston Churchill wrote later in describing the negotiations going on that August, Lord Lothian, then British ambassador to Washington, thought that "We should send some British destroyer crews to Halifax and Bermuda without any delay. It would create the worst impression in America if destroyers were made available and no British crews were ready to transport them across the Atlantic. Moreover, the fact that our crews were already waiting on the spot would help to impress the urgency of the case on Congress."[1]

On September 28 it was announced in the press that the first group of destroyers had arrived in Great Britain. Their arrival time had been kept secret, but word spread and crowds were there to welcome them. One press story pointed out that the crews were English, but everything else American, and the crews appreciated the steam heat and the soft drink machine on deck. They had already been at work on their way over, having picked up some downed airmen at sea.

William Allen White and I returned to New York on Saturday, September 7. While pleased with the expressions of appreciation of what the committee had done, we were saddened by the news from Britain, especially by accounts of the fires in London, and the possibility of an invasion from either France or Belgium, or even Norway, seemed very real.

The executive committee of the CDA met on Sunday, September 8. The following afternoon and evening the advisory policy committee convened for the first time. This committee had been formed in July, when Mr. White had sent letters to a distinguished group of Americans—from the academic and business worlds, from labor, the clergy, the arts, etc.—asking them to serve. Twenty-five persons had accepted. The group was to become more and more influential in matters of policy. At the meeting on September 9, Mr. White reported briefly on his recent interviews in Washington. I presented a draft state-

1. Winston S. Churchill, *Their Finest Hour* (Boston: Houghton Mifflin Company, 1949), p. 407.

ment of policy based on the discussions of the executive committee the day before. It was generally believed that the CDA should, for the moment, take one step at a time. Most important for now was to urge our government to send, in addition to twenty torpedo boats, flying fortresses to help the British defeat the German bombers that were bombing London every night.

The next day, September 10, Mr. White wired the heads of 662 leading chapters of the CDA as follows:

Not necessary to tell you German bombings of London very serious and this may be the most crucial hour in modern history. Our policy remains the same, that everything that can be legally spared, especially planes, from our armed forces or from American factories, should go immediately to Britain in this crucial hour. Our urgent suggestion is telegrams, letters, editorials directed to President Roosevelt urging government to send everything possible—especially planes—now. Your committees contributed much to destroyer victory and have reason to believe that similar support now can be of comparable importance.

In addition, Mr. White asked for the opinions of a few outstanding leaders, including General Douglas MacArthur, who cabled one of his vigorous replies from Manila on September 15:

You have asked my military opinion as to whether the time has come for America to give continued and further aid to England in the fight for civilization. The history of failure in war can almost be summed up in two words, too late. Too late in comprehending the deadly purpose of a potential enemy. Too late in realizing the mortal danger. Too late in preparedness. Too late in uniting all possible forces for resistance. Too late in standing with one's friends.

Victory in war results from no mysterious alchemy or wizardry, but entirely upon the concentration of superior force at the critical points of combat. To face an adversary in detail has been the prayer of every conqueror in history. It is the secret of the past successes of the axis powers. In this war it is their main hope for continued and ultimate victory.

The greatest strategical mistake in all history will be made if America fails to recognize the vital moment, if she permits again the writing of that fatal epitaph, "too late." Such coordinated help as may be regarded as proper by our leaders should be synchronized with the British effort so that the English speaking peoples of the world will not be broken in detail. The vulnerability of singleness will disappear before unity of effort—not too late, not tomorrow, but today.

On September 12 Mr. White addressed a comprehensive letter to the officers and chairmen of the chapters to put our step-by-step program in proper perspective:

I wanted to write this rather long and confidential letter to say a few things about what we have accomplished and our plans for the next few weeks.

The battle of Britain continues and is now reaching its full fury. We may expect within the next few days the destruction and loss of life to grow greater and greater and a strong possibility of an invasion from either the French and Belgian ports held by Germany or from Norway.

We believe that the fifty destroyers will be of the greatest physical and moral assistance to Great Britain in repelling the invasion. Their importance cannot be over-stated. As part of the arrangement, the United States secured air and naval bases which will be a tremendous factor in national defense. The public almost unanimously applauds the negotiations. I for one believe that the President acted absolutely correctly in negotiating the arrangement as an executive matter. There was no time for the long debate which Congressional consideration would have resulted in. I am proud of the part that this committee and its many chapters played in mobilizing public opinion in support of this great step.

But the battle of Great Britain goes on. Other materials will be needed. In fact we can for the sake of simplification think of materials for Britain in two divisions: one, material that will be needed this week or next to save Britain from destruction before the bad weather sets in. Two, material that Britain will need throughout the winter to be in a position in the spring not only strong enough to resist invasion but powerful enough to take the aggressive. Later on I shall write you about the latter material but today I want to say a word about what we believe could go quickly.

First, airplanes. We have approximately seventy-five flying fortresses in our army. These are incomparably more powerful with a longer range than anything that any other nation has. Also, we have many planes, not all first class, but out of which some could be spared for the defense of London. If an invasion is undertaken, little electric boats, called the "mosquito fleet," would be very helpful in turning back the transports. That would be second only in importance to the destroyers.

Therefore we strongly hope that our government dispatch immediately twenty-five flying fortresses and as many pursuit planes as possible, and twenty mosquito boats. Every day is important and a few weeks may be too late to save Britain and our first line of defense. . . .

This winter the British will need tanks for the desert campaign to protect Suez and Gibraltar; probably food on credit; and a large proportion of the products of American airplane factories. These latter materials we will discuss with you when the present emergency is over.

Many of you wired a few hours after the destroyer deal was completed asking what to do next. I wired Tuesday for letters, editorials, telegrams to the President urging that everything that can be spared from our American armed forces go now to help save London. We were very fortunate in the destroyer matter in being able to mention fifty destroyers and repeat the number constantly. It is not always easy to give as precise figures. Sometimes our instructions will have to be a bit more general. But please have faith in us, knowing that we are trying to do everything possible to secure correct information and that we will not urge anything that we do not believe is wise and possible. Although I know that you must be tired from the hard work over the destroyer campaign, I urge you to use every bit of energy and reserve you have in the next two weeks in support of our government sending every bit of material that can be spared to help Britain resist invasion from air and sea.

One word more, we are getting all sorts of letters and inquiries about our political position. Everything that is done as one moves toward an election naturally seems to have a political motive. A radio commentator referred to us the other night as a Willkie Committee and as if to balance that a wire came from one of our branches asking if the rumor was true that the Committee was about to come out for Roosevelt. May I say that the Committee contains many of the outstanding men of both political parties and I hope a few members of the Socialist party as well. The Committee's position will be absolutely non-partisan. As a non-partisan Committee we support the foreign policy of the President enthusiastically, not because the President is a Democrat but because he is our President, the Commander-in-Chief of our armed forces, and above everything else, because his foreign policy is one that we can enthusiastically support.

The campaign for the flying fortresses reached a climax in early November. On November 8, 1940, a letter from the committee to the chapter officers, and so forth, which I signed, said:

It has just been made public in Washington, and I presume there will be further details in the evening papers, that a rule of thumb policy has been established whereby Great Britain and Canada "would be supplied 50 per cent of American defense items now coming off factory lines, including large bombers and other things needed both here and abroad." Obviously, this policy involves flying fortresses and flying boats. Thus, before the end of the year Britain will have some of the new model flying fortresses, the necessity of which we have been pointing out for weeks.

As Winston Churchill indicated in his speech, and as the news of German submarine activity is carried in the press, British shipping is in a serious situation. It may be that our next specific objective will be in the line of ships as well as planes.

The administration has done very well in a policy of aid to Britain. I think all of us will agree, however, that the material which we are supplying Britain in the way of ships, planes, guns, tanks, etc., is but the beginning of the material that must be produced by American industry if Britain is to hold out and thus keep the war away from our shores.

Throughout that fall of 1940, while the committee was becoming bolder and more aggressive, William Allen White supported its statements and personally wrote many of the telegrams to the chapters suggesting points of emphasis and activity. For example a policy statement, agreed to at a meeting of the policy committee that Mr. White attended, and released for November 26, contains the following: "Also we say regretfully that no one can guarantee that the United States can avoid active military involvement. But one thing is certain; the only chance of avoiding war is by giving all material assistance to Great Britain and her allies immediately."

On December 23 at noon I was having a conference with several members of our policy committee at the home of Lewis Douglas, who belonged to both the executive committee and the policy committee. One of the members arrived late, bringing with him the noon edition of the *World Telegram.* The paper carried a sensational article to the effect that Mr. White had virtually repudiated the Committee to Defend America by Aiding the Allies.

Mr. White's statement, in answer to a query from the editor of the Scripps-Howard Press, Roy W. Howard, ran as follows:

Emporia, Kansas—In response to your query about the position on war of our Committee to Defend America by Aiding the Allies, let me submit the following:

The only reason in God's world I am in this organization is to keep this country out of war. I don't go an inch further or faster than Wendell Willkie or the American Legion, or the American Federation of Labor or the National Grange; nor an inch further or faster than you went this month in the *Philippines Magazine* on the Eastern question.

The story is floating around that I and our committee are in favor of sending convoys with British ships or our own ships, a silly thing, for convoys, unless you shoot, are confetti, and it's not time to shoot now or ever.

Another thing: Our loathed but highly esteemed adversaries keep insisting that we are in favor of repealing the Johnson Act, a stupid thing to do because it would not help Great Britain and there are half a dozen other good, legal ways to get aid to Great Britain. The President is following his own way. But the Johnson Act should not be repealed and we are not for it.

Still one more charge: It is not true even remotely that we favor repealing that portion of the Neutrality Law which forbids American ships to carry contraband of war into the war zone. That would be leading us to war and our organization and I personally are deeply opposed to it. If I were making a motto for the Committee to Defend America by Aiding the Allies it would be "The Yanks are not Coming." We could not equip them, transport them and feed them if they went. We have less than 200,000 ready and we need them worse at home on the assembly belt than we need them in Europe.

War would defeat the first and last end for which our committee is organized—to defend America by aiding Great Britain—and would bring on a 30-year conflict. The Yanks are not coming because if they went to war they would lose our cause. That is my firm, unshakable belief.

I have no doubt that some members of our organization who are not officially representing us are martial-minded. To condemn all of us for our more belligerent brethren is as foolish and unfair as it would be to call the Kinghts of Columbus appeasers because Joe Kennedy gave Roosevelt the Judas kiss. Not one official utterance of our organization has anything remotely suggestive that we feel the only alternative for American defense through aid to Britain is war.

Moreover, I have sat in all our executive councils, all our policy-making committees, and I have never heard war as an alternative objective seriously discussed by any official group of our organization at any time. America will go to war or stay out of war not because we make Hitler mad but only when, as and if Hitler thinks he can win the war. And so long as we arm behind the British fleet and England fights while we arm, Hitler never will think he can win the war, unless he starts war to slow down aid to Britain. Any organization that is for war is certainly playing Hitler's game.

I hope you know that I am not a liar and I hope you feel that I am not a sucker, and I trust you will believe what I am writing.

We were stunned by the fact that Mr. White would give such a statement to Roy Howard without consulting us or at least informing us in advance. I was particularly appalled because I had been the first to approach Mr. White to serve as chairman of the two committees and he had only recently expressed his deep appreciation of our cooperation and friendship, saying in a letter dated December 3, 1940, "You have been splendid. My own son could not have been so considerate of me, so thoughtful, so kind as you have been."

Several days after the *Telegram* article appeared, I received a letter from Mr. White dated December 23 which indicated that he did not realize the seriousness of his statement to Roy Howard. It began in a routine way—"The advertisement and the chapter letter signed by me turned up Saturday morning. I think it was a beautiful job"—and went on to say, "I hope you liked my piece I sent to Roy Howard. He may be leading me into a trap, but I shall fight my way out. The breaks last week were all ours."

Mr. White was thus very much surprised and hurt at the reaction of the members of his committee, the chapters, and the press throughout the country.[2] Although letters and telephone calls to Emporia tried to get a statement from him which somehow or other would unite the committee behind him again, and Frederick C. McKee of Pittsburgh, a member of the executive committee and its only bachelor, volunteered to make a trip to Emporia to see him just before Christmas, White was not in any mood to retract.

Finally it was agreed that, as he was determined to do so, Mr. White should submit his resignation. The members of the committee were almost unanimous in believing that Mr. White's great work for the committee must be preserved and his feelings spared. Therefore, upon his resignation, which was announced on January 1, 1941, he became honorary chairman of the Committee to Defend America and remained on the policy

2. The reaction in the Midwest and West was not as sharp as it was in the East. Mr. White said in one letter that he received as many telegrams of appreciation as of criticism from the Midwest.

committee, as well as the executive committee.

In retrospect I can see that the situation had been building up for some time. Mr. White was tired. His work for the committee occupied him almost full time in Emporia. He would not move to New York, although in one of his letters he stated that he could not fulfill his duties properly without doing so. The problem of partisanship, as the election approached, bothered him as well. While professing his deep appreciation of President Roosevelt's program of aid to the allies, Mr. White, as a Republican, did not want his committee to be involved in local political campaigns. However, inevitably in an election year, this had happened. In one case, for example, the Dutchess County Chapter of the CDA had severely criticized isolationist Republican Congressman Hamilton Fish. Mr. White had known Congressman Fish's father for many years, and sent a message of friendliness to the congressman which was read at a public meeting. Some regarded this as an endorsement of Mr. Fish's candidacy, although it was not meant to be one at all.

On November 27, 1940, Mr. White delivered an address before the National Association of Accredited Publicity Directors at a dinner at the Town Hall Club in New York—he was the recipient of their annual award for outstanding service in the publicity field. In his speech he explained some of the techniques the CDA had used in organizing public opinion in favor of sending destroyers and flying fortresses to Great Britain. He spoke of the committee putting General Pershing on the air. Then he added, "but the really smart trick we pulled was that, after Lindbergh made his speech [on radio on May 19, opposing U.S. "meddling" in European affairs], we put his mother-in-law [Mrs. Dwight W. Morrow] on the air—and was that a face card? It was."

On November 28 the newspapers reported the award dinner and the speech, and the trouble began. "Smart trick" had been a most unfortunate phrase. In the next few days *The New York*

Times, the St. Louis *Post-Dispatch,* and other papers ran articles about the phrase "smart trick" implying that the committee had put something over on the American people.

In a letter to *The New York Times* dated December 4, after
his return to Emporia, Mr. White wrote:

What I was trying to say, and my talk was entirely extemporaneous,
was that in bringing these citizens to our cause we had taken a trick,
not played a trick, and I used the word "face card" to indicate my
figurative intention.

. . . Three times in the speech I remember declaring that we had not
made a convert, that we were merely crystallizing existing public
opinion and implementing it to influence the government in our aims
to Defend America by Aiding the Allies. . . .

Over and over I tried to tell those publicity agents that I had done
nothing and our committee had done nothing that was not an essential
part of the picture of American democracy. Yet the editorial . . .
administered a rebuke to the work of the committee on the assumption that the speech was an exaltation of our work and in bad manners
and bad taste.

But the damage was done. Possibly the best one can now say is
that a great writer who is a poor public speaker should not
attempt to be amusing in an extemporaneous speech.

Mr. White was also constantly bothered by what he felt were
the criticisms of the Century Club group, whose members, distinguished citizens all, were individualists. Although many of
them were members of Mr. White's committee, they did not
feel the need of carrying the public with them as Mr. White felt
it should be carried. To them, Mr. White and his committee
seemed slow.

All these aggravations piled on the months of overwork and
fatigue reached their climax in Mr. White's letter to Roy Howard. Many times I am sure he wished he had not written it, but
he would not admit that it had been a mistake.

Had Mr. White's break with the CDA occurred shortly after

it was created, his disaffection might have wrecked the committee. It could not have been started without his name and leadership. But its work was now too far along and too well known and its supporters throughout the country were too well informed to abandon it at this time. Nevertheless it will always be remembered as the William Allen White Committee.

I remember Mr. White with friendship and admiration. I visited him in Emporia frequently, taking the Santa Fé Railroad out of Kansas City—the railroad seemed so much a part of Mr. White's Midwest. At his newspaper office he sat in a big chair behind an old-fashioned rolltop desk. Around him was a semicircle of newspapers and books that had been sent in for review. There were stacks of articles that he had written and discarded or set aside to pick up again in a few days. A smaller chair stood within that circle of papers. He would say, "Clark, step over that pile and come into the circle and we'll talk." So I would sit down in the chair next to him and we would have a long talk. As far as I could tell from his secretary, that disarray was always there, but it was a pretty systematic disarray. Mr. White knew exactly what was there and said that if his secretary filed anything he never would be able to find it.

Mr. White wrote many books and articles, but I think if one wishes to appreciate the simplicity of his prose, one should read *Mary White*, a tribute to his daughter published in the Emporia *Gazette* after she was killed in a riding accident.

As 1940 drew to a close, United States aid to the allies, now primarily Britain, moved into its second and most crucial phase. The public was more than ever aware of the magnitude of the threat to Britain from Hitler's armies and that more and more would be required of the United States. This country had been supplying the British with war material, but for cash. Even the fifty over-age destroyers, while not traded for cash, had been traded for "kind"—the leases on the British bases in the Caribbean.

But although the American public may not have realized it, those in offical circles were aware that Britain would soon be unable to pay for more material. After careful preparation Prime Minister Churchill had sent a letter to President Roosevelt on December 8, 1940, setting forth at length Britain's current needs and pointing out that her dollar credit would soon be exhausted and that "the moment approaches when we shall no longer be able to pay cash for shipping and other supplies."[3] As Mr. Churchill wrote later in *Their Finest Hour,* the British had already sold $335 million worth of American shares requisitioned from British owners, and had only $2,000 million, much of which was in investments that could not be easily marketed. Not only was the war demanding a terrific price from the British in burned and bombed-out cities, but added to this was the destruction of their economy and the loss of life. Payment for war material was forcing the liquidation of the savings of the British people and the wealth of the land.

President Roosevelt, aware of the impending crisis, discussed the problem in a press conference on December 17. He spoke again of the desperate need of the British for American help. He reminded the American people that the theory might still prove true that the best defense of Great Britain was the best defense of the United States.

As so frequently occurred in a press conference preceding a momentous decision, the President was not only preparing the way for the support of public opinion but was actually thinking certain things through. He said that several ways to make it possible for the British to continue ordering military equipment had been suggested. One was that we lend money to Great Britain to be spent over here, "either lend it through private

3. *Their Finest Hour,* p. 566.

banking circles, as was done in the earlier days of the previous war, or make it a loan from this Government to the British Government."[4] Another suggestion was that the United States pay for the munitions, ships, plants, guns, and so on, and make a gift of them to Great Britain. But he said he was "not at all sure that Great Britain would care to have a gift from the taxpayers of the United States."[5] Then he went on to say that there were other ways that were being explored, that he had been at it for three or four weeks. He suggested that the United States might

take over British orders, and, because they are essentially the same kind of munitions that we use ourselves, turn them into American orders. We have enough money to do it. And thereupon, as to such portion of them as the military events of the future determine to be right and proper for us to allow to go to the other side [of the Atlantic], either lease or sell the materials, subject to mortgage, to the people on the other side. . . . Now, what I am trying to do is to eliminate the dollar sign. That is something brand new in the thoughts of practically everybody in this room, I think—get rid of the silly, foolish old dollar sign.[6]

Then he used his famous analogy of lending a length of garden hose to your neighbor whose house is on fire. You do not ask your neighbor for immediate payment for the hose, but you lend it to him. If it should be damaged in the fire, the neighbor replaces the hose with a new one. If it is not damaged, it is returned intact.

Very clearly the President was pointing the way to Lend-Lease.

On December 18, the day following the President's press conference, a memorandum from William Allen White urged

4. *The Public Papers and Addresses of Franklin D. Roosevelt: 1940 Volume, War—and Aid to Democracies,* compiled and collated by Samuel I. Rosenman (New York: The Macmillan Company, 1941), p. 606.

5. *Ibid*

6. *Ibid.,* p. 607.

the members of the advisory policy committee to offer "our services to the President to be of any help in working out the plan and in helping mobilize sentiment for it through our chapters."

The President's press conference was followed by his fireside chat of December 30 stating that the United States "must be the great arsenal of democracy. For us this is an emergency as serious as war itself. We must apply ourselves to our task with the same resolution, the same sense of urgency, the same spirit of patriotism and sacrifice as we would show were we at war."[7]

On January 10 the historic Lend-Lease bill was introduced in Congress. On January 11 a statement from the Committee to Defend America by Aiding the Allies, signed by former Senator Ernest W. Gibson, the new national chairman of the committee; Lewis W. Douglas, chairman of the board; and myself, as national director, was issued to the press. It read:

The Committee to Defend America by Aiding the Allies stands squarely back of the President's plan for aid to Britain and to the other nations now fighting against aggression.

The time has come for Congress and the people to prove that they mean what they say when they agree that our security demands that the aggressors be defeated. We must show that our democracy is capable of defending itself energetically, that it will not allow itself to be paralyzed by inertia, suspicion and internal strife.

The Lend-Lease bill had two particularly important provisions. The first was that the United States would take over the orders of the British and any other allies and manufacture the requested supplies as part of America's needs. In a memorandum annotating his Annual Message to Congress on January 6, 1941, President Roosevelt said: "a mere loan of dollars would not be as quick and as productive of results as a loan of war materials, to be repaid in kind after the close of hostilities. By

7. *Ibid.*, p. 643.

manufacturing war supplies for all the democracies, we could fit our own needs into theirs, and provide more efficient and speedy production for all of us."[8]

The second provision of the Lend-Lease bill had ominous overtones of tragedy. It was clearly explained in the January 18 edition of the CDA Progress Report sent out by the Washington office:

The Bill provides authority to "repair" any defense article of Britain or one of her allies, a provision which would allow us to repair damaged units of the British Fleet. Such an arrangement might be of great value to the British Navy this year. It might prove of even greater value to American defense in the blackest contingencies we can envisage. If the British Admiralty can plan on using our repair facilities and even use them in some instances, the way will have been smoothed for the British Fleet to fall back on our bases in case the British Isles could not be maintained. In such cataclysmic circumstances, our Atlantic security would depend directly upon the fate of the British Fleet.

Edward R. Stettinius, Jr., director of the Lend-Lease administration for a time, in his book, *Lend-Lease: Weapon for Victory,* gives the following account of the Lend-Lease debates:

In the three months that followed, the American people debated Lend-Lease as no issue in our foreign policy had ever been debated before. As a nation we finally thought through the entire problem of our national security in a dangerous world. The debate reached from the halls of Congress to every fireside in America. The discussions grew violent and sometimes bitter, but that was all a part of our democratic way of talking matters out with ourselves.[9]

The William Allen White Committee played a major part. Our Washington office gave the chapters the latest information from the Capitol. Our hundreds of chapters, the officers, and

8. *Ibid.*, p. 674.
9. Edward R. Stettinius, Jr., *Lend-Lease: Weapon for Victory* (New York: The Macmillan Company, 1944), p. 4.

leading citizens who spoke for the committee were mobilized for the campaign as never before. Thousands of mass meetings were held; countless messages were sent to members of Congress.

The critical moment in the congressional debate came in February, when a few senators in opposition tried obstructionist tactics to see if they could gain sufficient momentum to man a successful filibuster. At a press conference held in Washington, D.C., on February 26, I reported one such incident:

Last Thursday an incident occurred that is almost unbelievable in view of the speed with which our hour glass is being emptied. The opposition, a very small minority, wasn't ready with its speeches, so the Senate recessed at 4:09 P.M. until Friday! Who knows what may be the consequences of these tactics upon our program of defense? All over America people are working after hours to insure success for the defense program. Why is it that the opposition, this small minority of die-hard isolationists, cannot work after hours in the Senate, too, in the interest of their country?

The Lend-Lease bill passed the House of Representatives on February 8 and the Senate on March 8. The Conference Committee agreed on its provisions on March 11, and the President signed it the same day.

Possibly because it involved a decision of Congress, possibly because it was the most advanced step that had been taken to aid Britain, it seemed to be our most signal victory. But it was not simply "aid to Britain." The Lend-Lease bill, more than any step our government had taken before, consolidated British and American defense.

11

Germany Invades Russia—The Atlantic
Charter—I Visit London

By spring 1941, it was clear that Lend-Lease must be backed by
machinery to get the material to the United Kingdom. On April
3, Ernest Gibson broadcast on NBC's America's Town Meeting
of the Air an address entitled: "Should Our Ships Convoy Arms
to Britain?" I quote the first two paragraphs:

America has adopted a policy of defending America by furnishing
material aid to the Allies. That today is the policy of our country. If that
policy means anything, it means that America must immediately place
itself on a war-time production basis in a time of peace; that it must
start every idle wheel and piece of machinery to work in one great
comprehensive effort to produce the materials necessary for Great
Britain and her Allies to defeat, once and for all, Hitler and his gang
of brigands.

But it also means, that when this material and machinery is produced, it must be delivered to Great Britain and her Allies, at a place
where it can be used to defeat him who seeks to reduce all but the
German peoples to literal slavery. It means that if it becomes necessary, American ships must convoy materials and machinery and guns
to Great Britain. There can be no doubt but that is what our policy
means.

Mr. Gibson gave some startling figures to back this position.
At the outset of the war the British Empire owned or had

available to her 25 million tons of oceangoing shipping. After the collapse of her allies and the neutral countries, Britain had available to her about 22 million tons, but "at the present rate of sinking" by the "end of this year [1941] Britain will have lost 36% of the original ocean-going tonnage owned or available to her at the outset of the war." Gibson concluded by saying:

I have repeatedly said that the time might come when it would be necessary to use American naval vessels to insure deliveries to England. *That time is here!* This country's course is clear—we must see to it now that these sinkings stop. There are several ways in which American naval units can participate in this task.

We can, as has been advocated, lease additional destroyers and naval units to the British, or we can use American naval vessels under American command to keep these sea lanes open. It has been suggested that the American neutrality zone be extended, possibly to Iceland. The delivery is the main thing—the means are a matter of tactics. I am satisfied to leave these tactics to the Administration.

We must be honest with ourselves. We recognize that the use of the American Navy for convoy purposes involves risk. I believe that the American people are prepared to take those risks because they believe the risks are far less than those we would face if we permitted the British Isles, our advance base, to fall into the hands of the man who has boasted he is going to conquer the world.

April 1941 was one of the darkest moments in the fortunes of the democracies since the evacuation of Dunkirk in May–June 1940. The German army continued to advance in Yugoslavia and Greece; German mechanized columns swept across Libya into Egypt to menace the Suez Canal; British shipping losses continued at a frightful rate. An agreement had just been signed between Russia and Japan which could not help but be at the expense of China and probably a further menace to Britain and the United States in the Far East.

It was the job of the Committee to Defend America to tell the public the truth, no matter how dark it might be or how vast were the implications of American support necessary to avert catastrophe. I concluded a letter to the chapters on April 18 by stating: "each day reinforces the conviction that the time for the use of American naval vessels in some way to guarantee delivery has arrived. This is the issue which I believe, along with industrial mobilization, should now be the subject of your meetings, your publicity, your literature and your general discussions."

Suddenly, on June 22, 1941, when a peaceful Sunday was expected on the diplomatic front and with the fighting continuing its usual pattern, the theater of war was greatly enlarged: Germany attacked the Soviet Union.

Mrs. Eichelberger and I were the guests of Mrs. Kermit Roosevelt that Sunday at Oyster Bay. A vigorous member of the Committee to Defend America, Mrs. Roosevelt had wanted us to have a quiet day of rest at her home. Without warning the message was flashed over the radio. As the July issue of *Changing World* told it:

... suddenly, dramatically, at dawn on June 22, Hitler struck. His blow was preceded by no declaration of war, not even by an ultimatum. The Fuehrer stated that Germany was tired of border incidents provoked by the Russians, was determined to end Soviet intrigue in Europe and was, therefore, launching an attack on a heroic scale towards the east. And at once the Panzer division and the Stukas began to operate in accordance with their dreaded and familiar patterns of attack. . . .

Another nation was now allied to Great Britain against the Nazi forces, and several hundred million people added to allied numbers.[1]

The attack brought a demand for vast material, and the convoying of American vessels by the United States navy became more important than ever, expanding as the theater of war was extended. At first, American convoys had operated for only

1. For some days prior to the German attack pickets had been marching in front of the White House protesting American aid to the allies in the "imperialistic war." Suddenly, with characteristic lack of humor, the pickets began demanding material for the British to help them fight the "people's war."

short distances, then as far as the Caribbean, finally across the Atlantic. The authority of U.S. naval vessels was correspondingly increased. Starting out as mere escorts, when losses to shipping became greater, they were armed and allowed to defend themselves if attacked by submarines. Finally, on September 11, 1941, President Roosevelt announced that American naval vessels would no longer wait for an attack; they would protect all merchant vessels, "not only American ships but ships of any flag engaged in commerce in our defensive waters. They will protect them from submarines; they will protect them from surface raiders." This "shoot on sight" policy had been advocated for some weeks by the Committee to Defend America in its campaign to "deliver the goods" and "clear the Atlantic."

Although 1941 had been a year of tragedy and suffering, unexpectedly, toward the end of the summer, the peoples of the beleaguered nations were given a glimpse of a vision of a better world. In August a group of British and American warships met secretly off the coast of Newfoundland where Prime Minister Churchill and President Roosevelt, together with their aides, had a historic meeting. They signed the Atlantic Pact, which further solidified the unity of the two countries and opened the door to a long period of planning for the postwar period.

The Atlantic Charter not only proclaimed the opposition of the United States and Britain to aggrandizement, territorial or other; it looked forward to bringing about "the fullest collaboration between all nations in the economic field with the object of securing, for all, improved labor standards, economic advancement and social security." It called for a régime "which will afford to all nations the means of dwelling in safety within their own boundaries, and which will afford assurance that all the men in all the lands may live out their lives in freedom from fear and want."

In a radio address over the Columbia Broadcasting System on August 16, I said:

Somehow millions of people in the world tonight hearing of the Roosevelt-Churchill Conference feel that they have been snatched from the brink of disaster and their feet put upon the road to victory and world organization. It will be a long road, entailing many hardships—even, as Mr. Churchill predicted for his country—blood, sweat, toil and tears. But it is the only road that will lead to victory and permanent peace. It is the road that the American people, with other brave nations, must travel.

The signing of the Atlantic Pact stimulated my desire to visit the United Kingdom. I wanted to meet with the British Research Sub-Committee on International Organization which, like the Commission to Study the Organization of Peace, had been set up to plan for the postwar world. I wanted to visit my friends in the British League of Nations Union and in the American Outpost in Great Britain, which was made up of Americans in London who had organized a branch of the Committee to Defend America there.

Fortunately, the opportunity came in an invitation from the British government for me to fly without expenses on a Pan American clipper that had been secured through Lend-Lease. The plane was brought periodically to the Glenn Martin plant for servicing; since the British could not carry a payload on the plane, they gave passages on the return flight from Baltimore to people they wanted as guests in the United Kingdom. I was invited, I presume, because I was director of the Committee to Defend America by Aiding the Allies.

The flying boat took off from Baltimore on September 12, 1941. The flight was considered safe because the British and the Germans had agreed that on certain flights on neutral runs planes from either country would not be shot down. Thus British flights to and from Lisbon and to and from New York were considered perfectly safe. On this particular trip, after we had been aloft for some time, a German plane did hover in the distance to look us over, but our pilot lost him in the fog. Most of us on the plane were not aware of the incident, but our folks at home were informed because a newspaperman on board had sensed it and his story was published in the American press.

Finally we landed at Foynes in Ireland and after some little time there we took a bus to Dublin. I had heard of the rocky road to Dublin and this seemed to be it! After one night in Dublin, where my fellow passengers and I enjoyed a visit with Ambassador David Gray,[2] we flew in a blacked-out plane to Bristol, then continued to London by train. My arrival occasioned a bit of confusion at the embassy, the full story of which I never learned. I had cabled John Winant, the U.S. ambassador and an old friend, the time of my arrival signing my first name, Clark, as I always did. Apparently the embassy staff were expecting a visit from General Mark Clark and the two Clarks must have gotten mixed up. As a result I found myself in a first-class room at the Savoy Hotel!

After I had checked into the Savoy and had had something to eat, I decided to go to a drugstore to get some medicine for a cold. I went through the door and several blackout curtains and when I reached the street I was in inky blackness. I had never before experienced such blackness. I was afraid of getting lost, but suddenly I felt a hand on my arm, and a young lady made the usual proposition. I explained, no, but I would pay her adequately if she would take me to a drugstore. She took my arm and, learning that I had just arrived in London, told me a

2. I had forgotten that David Gray was a relative of the Roosevelts, but years later when Mrs. Eichelberger and I were guests of Eleanor Roosevelt at Val-kil Cottage in Hyde Park, I found this friendly ambassador sitting on her porch. By then he was approaching ninety. He was writing a history of Ireland, and each year when we met him at Hyde Park he would be a little further along. Mrs. Roosevelt used to say she hoped he would never finish it because if he did he would have no objective in life and would not last very long.

few things she thought I would like to know. (I was able to make my own way from the drugstore back to the hotel.)

The respect which the British paid to the blackout regulations was amazing. I saw only one violation in several weeks. On a night train from London to Liverpool I saw a light shining brightly in a farmhouse. Because everything else was so black that light shone as a beacon. I have always wondered whether it was a violation or a signal of some kind.

There were three friends that I was especially anxious to see in London—Ambassador Winant, and Edward and Janet Murrow. During my stay I frequently had dinner at the Murrow flat, most informally, and would report on my interviews of the day. Ed Murrow would tell, laughingly, of the tenacity of the British. They don't have enough sense to know when they're licked, he would say. If a group of men were in a pub and someone came in to report that the Germans had just made a landing, they would say, "The barstards will never make it," and go on drinking. Ed and Janet Murrow had an understanding and admiration of the British people that was evident in his nightly CBS broadcast program, "This Is London."

As for Ambassador Winant, I had known him for a long time, first as governor of New Hampshire and then as director of the ILO. I felt free to go over to the embassy, sometimes fairly late in the evening, after he had eaten and had kept some late appointments. We would sit relaxed and talk over many things. We could not possibly have had another ambassador in London in whom the British people had so much confidence because of his understanding and sympathy. He shared their experiences. He would stand on the embassy roof as the bombs fell and fires raged around him.

While I was in London, Mr. Frank Darval and his associates at the British Ministry of Information arranged a wide variety of individual appointments for me. The Ministry was quite sympathetic and not only arranged meetings at my request but suggested some people who might have helpful information to impart.

In my interviews I was in a difficult position. The United States was not in the war. Even though the Committee to Defend America by Aiding the Allies had been saying that to all intents and purposes we were in the war, we were not yet shooting or suffering loss of life. And I was aware of the fact that many Britons wanted to know when we were coming in. I did not want to extend any false hope; neither did I want to deemphasize how close we were to the war. I believe my opening statement to members of the British Research Sub-Committee on International Organization sums up what I tried to say to all the British people who wanted to know the stand of our committee. I said, "I don't want to say things people want to hear, just to be popular. I don't know when—if—the U.S.A. will declare war. Nor do I know if an actual declaration would matter much. But I hope we in our Committee have contributed to the formation of a public opinion favorable to all aid to Britain."

One of the most absorbing subjects for me in London was the future of the refugee governments. Ambassador Anthony J. Drexel Biddle was accredited to the governments-in-exile in London, and I saw a great deal of him and his wife Margaret. I remember going to their place in the country for a weekend by train. The British had destroyed all station signs, street signs, and road signs to make it more difficult for the Germans to get around if they should make a landing. To find one's way to some place in the country on an unfamiliar route when all the marks on the stations had been obliterated was difficult indeed. However, with the help of other passengers I was able to get off the train at the right station.

Through interviews I had with Ambassador Biddle, Pierre Comert, Adrian Pelt, and others whom I knew in London, I think I was given a good account of the problem of the refugee governments. I quote from my notes:

Governments-in-exile represent difficult personality and human problems which Biddle is trying to meet with the very greatest amount of tact. For illustration, the Poles and the Czechs agreed upon a customs union. Benes made a speech in which he referred to economic cooperation with the other central European countries but did not refer to the Poles, whereupon the Poles called Biddle at midnight to ask if he had heard the terrible thing that had happened, that Benes had not referred to the Polish-Czech customs union in his speech. Biddle had to straighten this out.

Weeks after the agreement was reached, every few days one of the Poles would come to Biddle and ask what he thought of the agreement, as though they wanted constantly to be congratulated on it.

Of the governments-in-exile, the Norwegians and the Dutch function most like normal governments, and least on the defensive. It is probably because these two governments come nearest to being going concerns. Holland has a large empire that Germany does not control, has a navy and air force which is reckoned as a factor for stability in the Far East. It could easily move its government to its own territory if it wanted to. The Norwegians contributed their merchant marine to the British. This merchant marine carries fifty per cent of the oil and fifteen to twenty per cent of all other products that Britain imports for war purposes. Thus, they play an important part in the winning of the battle of the Atlantic. The Dutch can take the hardest facts and the more bluntly they are told, the better they like it; whereas the Slavs are the other way, any truth must be sugarcoated with considerable flattery.

I think all of us working with people in exile, planning for the future, must always take into consideration the fact that there is a growing breach between the people who are taking it and the people in exile, and that the people in exile may not necessarily be accepted by the people back home when it comes time to organize the governments.[3]

3. The question of whether or not the governments-in-exile could go home and give leadership to the people who had had to stay and take it was to come up again in my discussions with Jan Masaryk, Czech foreign minister-in-exile, at the San Francisco Conference in 1945.

The monarchies are the most stable. The Norwegian King and the Dutch Queen will continue easily, but in the republican form of governments such as Czechoslovakia and France and Belgium (because of the cloudy status of the King) a very different group may wish to take control. I am not sure that this is so. At least the Czechs in exile seem to know pretty well what they are doing. They are giving instructions to the people in Prague all the time. France will offer the greatest problem of finding new leaders. Here the republican leaders, because of their weakness, are almost as much disliked as the men of Vichy.

The governments-in-exile agreed to the Atlantic Charter and I understand that four of them made private reservations which Mr. Eden hoped they would not make publicly.

The problem of dealing with these governments is a difficult one. In the first place, one does not wish to make them feel unequal because they are in exile and also because they are making an important military contribution to the common victory.

On the other hand, their governments are in London through the tolerance of the British, their embassies are open and their money frozen for their protection in Washington by the good will of the American Government. The British particularly are in a position to tell these small states that they can't make objections or reservations to any agreement and that they shall be restored on the terms which the United States and Britain dictate.

The rapidity with which nationalism can grow after its suppression is an interesting phenomenon. And plans must be laid now by which these governments agree privately to whatever customs union will be up or to whatever international procedure will be necessary so that within a few weeks after these countries are restored they will not set up nationalistic governments too deeply rooted for Britain and the United States to do anything about it.

Pelt spoke of the difficulty of the Dutch in developing an aggressive policy. They had been educated so long to a neutrality point of view and even now think to a considerable extent in League of Nations terms.

The Dutch wondered about our negotiations with Japan—at whose expense is the agreement to be concluded? I explained why I did not believe that our government would reach any appeasement arrangement with Japan at the expense of China, that the most our negotiations were was to try to get Japan to freeze at a certain point so that temporarily we could avoid a two-front war and that the most I thought we would do was to let up a little on our economic sanctions against Japan if Japan would promise not to expand southward or attack Russia, but I certainly did not believe we would reach any agreement at the expense of China or the Dutch East Indies, nor did I believe we would lift our embargo on raw materials to Japan. He (Pelt) said there was irritation because the Dutch and the small states had not been let in on what our negotiations with Japan were about.

How little either the British or ourselves knew the Japanese intentions!

One of the people I was most anxious to see in London was Pierre Comert. He had left the League of Nations shortly before the 1938 Assembly in order to serve his country in any way possible in the Ministry of Information. He had suffered a great deal since I had last seen him briefly in Paris in 1938. His wife had died in a concentration camp, and he himself had finally made his way to London only with great difficulty.

Because Comert did not like de Gaulle's lack of democratic ideas, he kept de Gaulle at arm's length. At the same time, he was very active with the Free French and edited a magazine for them. Possibly I can do best by quoting from the notes of my interview with him:

[Comert] said as a man who had been away from his country for almost twenty-five years, as a newspaperman in Germany and as Director of the Information Section of the League of Nations Secretariat, he sensed that there was something wrong with his country when he returned to take a post in the French Foreign Office and that this feeling grew upon him, that he found himself exiled to insignificant posts after his objection to Munich, and it was only in the very last days that he was made head of the French press service. He blamed the fall of France to a very great extent upon the fascist tendencies in the Army officers. I asked him why it was then that France went through the last war as a democracy with officers apparently giving good leadership to their men. He replied that the reason the French officers were fairly democratic in the last war was due to the Dreyfus trial and the fact that reactionary military men, who could have been called fascists had the word prevailed, were purged from the French Army at the time of the Dreyfus trial in 1907 and that these fascist-minded officers crept back in after the last war.

Ambassador Biddle arranged an appointment for me with General de Gaulle. The substance of this interview was considered quite significant by Ambassador Winant and Pierre Comert. I quote the full text of my notes, and should like to add that I know that Ambassador Winant cabled the substance of General de Gaulle's statement on democracy to the Department of State.

Appointment was arranged by Ambassador Biddle and the General apparently made a special effort to see me. He had just concluded a speech at an important gathering at which Brendan Brackett, Director of the Ministry of Information, was on one side of him, and Ambassador Biddle, accredited to the governments-in-exile, on the other. In this speech he had made a pretty strong plea for democracy. In the slang phrase of newspapermen, the General had been on ice for some time and the British brought him off the ice-box and showed that he was again accepted. What had apparently happened was that when he came to London he was in disfavor with Churchill. The British were angry because he had given out a statement that he had offered the United States and Great Britain bases in Africa without consulting them first as to the wisdom of such an announcement and he was generally suspected of being undemocratic and anti-British. Churchill had a hot session with him in which he told the General that he found a trail of Anglophobia following the General wherever he went and that he had learned that he had to get along with men whether he liked it or not. Things went from bad to worse until the Admiral commanding de Gaulle's fleet told him if he did not correct certain bad odors, the French fleet would function for the cause of liberty independent of de Gaulle. Whereupon de Gaulle said that if the Admiral did not apologize by three in the afternoon he would put him under arrest.

This caused considerable comment and amusement because how de Gaulle, a Frenchman in London, could arrest another Frenchman, was not quite clear. Apparently de Gaulle was given pretty severe treatment all around and then the British deliberately set up a very important luncheon to show that de Gaulle was again in good favor.

Everyone agreed that de Gaulle made a very good speech at the luncheon, a well-organized speech which he wrote entirely himself and he came through very well. I saw him that afternoon at four o'clock. I opened the discussion by saying that the American people had great admiration for him because they felt that he had saved French honor. I read to him the statement of policy of the Committee to Defend America which came out for recognition of de Gaulle as the *de facto* government in charge of the areas which he controlled and for Lend-Lease aid to de Gaulle. I also told him that I was privileged to be one of the two or three Americans who were members of the Board of France Forever. I told him that propaganda in the United States tried to make it appear that the de Gaulle forces were not sufficiently democratic and thus worked against our program of increased aid to de Gaulle and that I should like something that I could take back and give to our people. He said (which was exactly what Comert told me he would say, practically word for word) that he had said it was Vichy not himself that had violated the laws of France and that the laws of the French Republic were still in force and that when it was possible he would consult the French people.

Having been warned that this would be his reply I then went on to ask him if I might assure our people in the United States (I told him that I would have to report to France Forever and our Committee) that General de Gaulle anticipated the restoration of France as a democracy and he said, "You most certainly can." Ambassador Winant said that this was the strongest commitment that anyone had gotten from de Gaulle and that we should publicize it as widely as possible, making him the prisoner of his own words. De Gaulle went on to say that France was becoming more democratic, that the people were reacting against Germany and against Pétain's effort to establish a "new order." De Gaulle's repudiation of the "new order" was quite pleasing to Comert, who felt that de Gaulle himself was using authoritarian methods. I asked de Gaulle if it would help him to have a *de facto* recognition and he said it would. I asked him if it would help him to have Lend-Lease material and he said it would. He said that they had secured a good many arms from the defeated Vichy people in Syria and that what was needed above everything else were anti-aircraft guns and transport planes so that he could move officers and his government officials from place to place.

De Gaulle never understood or appreciated the objectives of the British or the Americans. The fact that Churchill offered the French unity with Britain in the closing days of French resistance meant nothing to the general. He was a man of sublime conceit with no sense of humor, as far as I could tell. Possibly the fact that he was not told until the last moment that the British and the Americans were going to make a landing on the French coast caused the greatest resentment. Apparently he was not told for two reasons: first, because he would immediately insist on putting himself at the head of all the forces and, second, because the secret of the landing had to be kept. The depth of his resentment toward the British and the Americans was revealed years later when, as head of the French state, he worked against them, even to the extent of trying to wreck their currencies. Indeed, had he been a different person, one who could work with the British and the Americans, the history of the postwar period might have been quite different.

The British maintained the normal democratic processes during the war. They never thought of any other thing to do but to carry on in the parliamentary system. I attended a session of the House of Commons in which the Opposition was criticizing the prime minister. One of the leaders criticized him for not having his ear to the ground. Mr. Churchill was in rare form. He said several of the Opposition seemed to criticize him because he did not have both ears to the ground. He wondered how dignified it would be for His Majesty's prime minister to be on his knees placing both ears to the ground. There was some laughter at the thought of the prime minister, chubby and with a large *derrière,* in such a position.

Many of my interviews were with members of the government and government officials. I would like to summarize two of them. One was with Arthur Greenwood, a British Labour leader. I found him in good form and more willing to talk leisurely than any other cabinet member I had met. He described two scenes in the House of Parliament. One had occurred just before war was declared, following the German invasion of Poland. The British were waiting for the French to declare war first. A member of the Labour Party arose and said, "Speak for England." Greenwood told of how he tried to pacify the Labour Party until the government could make its decision on when to declare war. He went to Chamberlain and said he could not hold the Opposition in line much longer. Chamberlain must make a decision and war must be declared.

The second scene was in the House of Commons at the time of the evacuation of Dunkirk. Some of the members of Parliament were nervous, but there was no defeatism, no sentiment for giving up, no thought of doing anything but resisting. However, some members were jittery. One of the leaders of Parliament went to Greenwood and said that he should come over and talk to them. What he said was so characteristically British: "What are you fellows kicking about anyway? At last this has become a first-class war. We haven't any allies to betray us, we are off the Continent, we stand on our shores to defend Britain alone, we know exactly what we have to do, and if we go on bravely and do our job we will find new friends and allies."

The second interview that I should like to outline was with Lord Catto, who at one time had been a partner of Thomas W. Lamont. I talked with Lord Catto alone at the Treasury; then he invited in Maynard Keynes and finally we met with other guests at lunch. My notes on this occasion follow:

I tried to get from them a comparison of the British war effort with the American. Of 6 billion pounds (30 billion dollars at normal exchange rates) more than 3 billion pounds is being taken by the government for war effort. Directly or indirectly, over fifty per cent of the energies, production capacity and wealth of the British people is concentrated in the war effort. They say it is the last ten per cent that hurts and that anything over thirty per cent means making considerable sacrifice. They estimate that the United States in comparison is using about 17 per cent of its wealth and its productive capacity for the war effort. They gave me a schedule of income tax payments. It will be seen that it is virtually impossible, unless a man has a tremendous income, to make over fifteen thousand dollars a year, and people with five or six thousand a year income are spending about fifty per cent of it in income taxes. The table will also show that there will be a return to the individual of a portion of his tax after the war, but this return is not in the higher brackets, so in every way the rich are making the greater financial sacrifice for the war.

They told me that this was necessary and that very few men of wealth were objecting to it. Certainly Lord Catto . . . seemed to be supremely happy in the fact that he and his two daughters were working in the Treasury Department, that his car was very small and that in every way he was forced to live on a very small income. People who are maintaining substantial establishments today are living off their principal.

They called attention to the fact that Britain had been able to cut down the charges on her national debt and that if Britain were able to recoup her export trade immediately after the war she would be solvent and could pay her debts. At the close of the last war, the services on the debt were 350 million pounds. This was cut down to 212 and has now risen to 250–260.

Here one of them called attention to the feeling on the part of the British that we have driven a very hard bargain on the Lend-Lease and that we are not only asking that Lend-Lease material not be exported but we are asking the British to eliminate exports in their normal business that approaches Lend-Lease material. I talked to an Englishman on the plane who believed that if this agreement were enforced rigidly Britain would lose 90 per cent of her export trade. Of course, the government does not wish exports of anything that is necessary for war purposes, but the fact remains that it is to the advantage of the United States and the world that there be a very prosperous Britain after the war. This can only be done by permitting the British to export as much as possible now to hold their markets for the future.

Mr. Dana says that there is this danger. Around the country young British people tell him that they will stay in Britain, fight and win the war, but that they do not intend to stay during the period of depression and paying for the war afterwards, and that they hope to migrate to the United States or Canada. Britain will need her manpower after the war, and it is to the interest of the United States that we do everything possible to encourage a solvent and prosperous Britain afterwards. Otherwise, the entire burden of reconstruction will fall on us and how can we be prosperous if the rest of the world is bankrupt; how can we maintain exports if no one else does?

Before the Lend-Lease Act was passed, Britain had paid cash for five billion dollars' worth of war materials from the United States. One-and-a-half billion was in investments that the British liquidated; over two-and-a-half billion was paid in gold and the balance in commodities such as tin and rubber.

It is not easy to liquidate securities in the manner that Senator Nye thinks it might be. Suppose that a British-owned firm in the United States is developed over a period of generations and that its business is entirely dependent upon its relationship with the parent company in London. Would anyone want to buy this business at its value, cut off as it would be from the parent business in Great Britain? Would it be able to stand on its own feet?

I was anxious to meet with the British Research Sub-Committee on International Organization, which seemed to me to be the organization most comparable to our Commission to Study the Organization of Peace (CSOP). By invitation, I attended the subcommittee's twenty-ninth special meeting on September 20, 1941. There were twelve members and myself present. Professor Arnold Toynbee was the most vocal participant and his and my views seemed generally to correspond.

Before comparing the approaches of the Research Sub-Committee and the CSOP, I might call attention to the different circumstances in each country under which planning for postwar organization could be undertaken. British planning was done under intense preoccupation with the war, with little time for people to consider the future. As I have mentioned, the British were giving 50 percent of their manpower, their wealth, and their energy to winning the war. The United States, on the other hand, had more opportunity to think of the future. Several of my friends at the British League of Nations Union, for illustration, told me how much time was required of them for war duties. Mr. A. J. C. Freshwater, secretary of the League of Nations Union, said that after being in the office all day, he went home in the blackout, put on other clothes, and was out in the fields and in the villages on air raid watch until late into the night. At some time or other, he had something to eat, but he, like many others, arrived at his office the next morning tired and sleepy. One might say that the British were too close to the war to engage in postwar planning, whereas the Americans were too far removed from it to have a sense of reality about it.

One subject that came up in my discussion with the subcommittee was the question of the timing of peace settlements. The British said that the idea of postponing the peace settlements while passions cooled had been popular in England for a while. But members of the subcommittee did not believe that to delay until passions cooled made much sense. One could not deal first with one problem and then with another—"they are all interrelated, and thinking must be done about all of them from the start." There was general agreement that "the nucleus of an international system should be set up from the first." I pointed out that one of the weaknesses of the League was that it had not started that way; it had come after the Treaty of Versailles was signed. One of the dangers of delay, I said, was that allies tend to fall out and that "one of the hardest things will be to make a settlement between Great Britain and the U.S.A. The German propaganda is exploiting possibilities of friction already." I added that I thought the United States and Britain would need close economic agreement, "even a kind of customs union."

There was unanimous agreement that the complete disarmament of Germany must be enforced from the beginning, but that the restoration of Germany as a prosperous economic unit was essential.

We talked on many subjects. It seemed that there had been no thinking about the colonies. I asked if there had been some consideration given to the idea of placing colonies under international administration. Apparently there had not. I was queried about Japan and asked if the United States would appease Japan at China's expense. It seems unthinkable now that neither the British nor the Americans anticipated Pearl Harbor. After all, it was Japan that finally brought the United States into the war as a full participant. People will always wonder why Japan did it and why the United States did not anticipate the move.

The basic question asked in the discussion was whether or not the United States would join in a new League system or something like it. Frank Walters said he thought the technical services of the League would start up again almost at once, "but, on the political side, when we try to go further, we are up against the great question-mark in Washington." To which Arnold Toynbee added, "If the U.S. does not come in, we stick in the hegemony stage—which would be fatal."

After the adjournment of the meeting, I visited the home of Mr. and Mrs. Maxwell Garnett. Garnett, for years the secretary of the British League of Nations Union, was rather an imperious fellow, but I had to admit that his drive and spirit had made the LNU a strong association. He and his wife were living in retirement in Oxford, and I was taken there to have supper with them. It was a warm, friendly, nostalgic session. We talked about the LNU and the LNA.

It had been arranged for me to spend the night at the home of a man who had an official position and therefore gas for his car, which he could legitimately use to drive me to the railroad station in the morning. Just as I was leaving Garnett's home, he gave me an egg for my breakfast. It was a brown egg, I remember. I carried the egg in my pocket and guarded it all the way with one hand as Garnett guided me through the blacked-out street to the home of his friend. I remember with what reverence the maid of my host received this egg and served it to me the next morning at breakfast.

As planned, I also met during my stay with the American Outpost in Great Britain. It was logical that Americans living in London should organize a committee to be affiliated with the William Allen White Committee. We had an interesting discussion about closer liaison between the two groups and what material the national office in New York could send them that would be helpful. A week later, I was the guest of the Outpost at a luncheon at the Dorchester. Professor Arthur V. Hill, member of Parliament, and a colleague of his liked my speech and asked me if I would meet with some members of Parliament the next afternoon.

It was not easy to talk to members of Parliament about the British and American war efforts, because America was not fully engaged. I analyzed the change in American public opinion since the rejection of the League of Nations Covenant, and related the successive steps from the revision of the Neutrality Act to "shooting on sight." They were surprised at the number of steps the United States had taken. I said I believed that if we could move from neutrality to naval belligerency in two years, the momentum would carry us much farther.

Most important to me was the opportunity to meet with my friends of the British League of Nations Union, which, since its founding shortly after the First World War had grown to a membership of about 750,000. One of the most remarkable efforts ever undertaken by any organization promoting the League was the Union's plebiscite in the early months of 1935. A ballot was distributed on which five questions were asked concerning collective security and the League of Nations. Workers were assigned to various districts under a plan to cover the whole nation. Eleven and one-half million Britons marked the ballots. The results were 31 to 1 in favor of the League of Nations.

Some of Britain's leading statesmen were members of the Union. The leaders of the three political parties—Conservative, Labour, and Liberal—were honorary presidents. However, the Union did nothing—pulled no punches—in order to please these men. On the contrary, the support of the Union was important to them.

I had visits with Major Freshwater and with Charles W. Judd, assistant secretary, as well as with Kathleen Courtney and Lord Cecil. Philip Noel-Baker attended my speech before the members of Parliament and I saw him again before I left, at an impromptu dinner at his home.

During an LNU executive meeting I was asked by Lord Cecil and others if we in the United States found it necessary to suppress the phrase "League of Nations." I explained that while there had been some agitation for us to change our name, that agitation had lessened. I repeated my analysis of why American public opinion had drawn away from the League after the First World War, adding that opinion was changing as we moved into the present war. It was not as hard to use the phrase "League of Nations" now as it had been five years earlier. According to my notes of this meeting, I found that other members of the Union were critical of Cecil, that he was too afraid to use the phrase "League of Nations." The Union seemed to be quite on the defensive. But it seemed to me that any organization with a paid-up membership of 100,000 people even during wartime could not be lightly dismissed.[4] Sir Geoffrey Mander and several members of Parliament attended the executive meeting at which I spoke, among them Eleanor Rathbone and J. R. Leslie, Labour Union leader, as well as Lytton and Cecil, Conservative lords.

The Union had a long history and many contacts abroad. It was logical therefore that it should organize the International Assembly, which was composed of many exiles in Britain, such as Professor René Cassin, member of the Council of the Free French Forces, and Jan Masaryk, foreign minister of Czechoslovakia. My notes about the International Assembly include the following:

The governments-in-exile meet in London in the Inter-Allied Council. It is natural that there be an association of private and prominent citizens of these countries meeting in exile—such men as Comert, Pelt and others, although some of them are connected with their governments. . . . The International Assembly is an organization of private citizens paralleling the Inter-Allied Council. Since their governments are taking decisions, it is natural that the International Assembly be a body in which the representatives express their views and exchange ideas for the meeting of the war situation and the peace, but that they not take militant resolutions for the winning of the war. . . .

Probably the most interesting trip arranged for me outside London was a visit to a bomber command, where I had dinner with some of the pilots before they got ready for their evening mission to bomb Frankfurt. I stood in a safe place on the sidelines to watch the parade of planes take off. One of the men with whom I had had dinner did not return.

I remember that on our way back from the bomber command

4. During the war the national office of the Union sent out instructions to their local branches to have meetings at the time of the light of the moon, so members could go to and return from these meetings without violating blackout regulations.

the next morning as we were going down the road we met a tank detachment approaching from the other direction. A British soldier—I presume one would call him an M.P.—was on a motorcycle going along beside the tank detachment. Suddenly something went wrong with his motorcycle and he fell to the road. We had a choice of running over him, hitting the tank detachment, or taking to the ditch. In a split-second decision, our driver, Corporal Brodie, chose the ditch. We were able to get the car out by its own power, but Corporal Brodie was pretty well shaken up. Squadron Leader Berridge, who was with us, pointed to a pub on the corner and suggested that we go in and have something to drink. Corporal Brodie explained that she was on duty and could not think of it. But he reminded her that he was her commander for the day and ordered her to take the drink, which she badly needed. When we returned to London, I immediately wrote a letter to the appropriate Ministry explaining how the accident happened and how intelligent Corporal Brodie had been in the handling of it. I did not want her blamed in some way for putting a guest of the government in the ditch. Never since that episode have I been able to tolerate jokes about women drivers.

The Ministry of Information had arranged for me to visit the city of Liverpool. By an act of Parliament, three men ran the city as far as air raid precautions, relief, and reconstruction were concerned. A man could not spend as much as a pound on the rebuilding of his house without the consent of these men; there was not much use rebuilding if other air attacks were expected and plans had been drawn up for a new city. Excerpts from my notes read as follows:

The city had been hit very badly. As one stepped out of the railroad station . . . and looked to the left where a monstrous department store, occupying an excellent corner, had overlooked the town, one saw that all of the store had been burned or blasted out. The back part of the store had not been destroyed completely and business was going on. . . . The libraries and most of the buildings housing the cultural life of the city had been destroyed. Thirty-three thousand homes had been hit, twenty thousand of which were capable of being rebuilt or repaired and thirteen thousand literally destroyed.

In the morning I visited a new tank factory. It was located in a district called Spek. . . . It was a factory that had been devoted to making steel filing cabinets, safes, etc., and was one of the last factories to be converted from peacetime to wartime activities because these fireproof cabinets and safes were needed for the army and the government. But now they had started making tanks. They had a model of the first tank, the machine tools were ready, steel plates were ready and it was expected that very shortly they could be able to produce thirty tanks a week. These would be what we called medium tanks and what the British call light tanks. One wondered how many tanks Germany could destroy in a day and how many such factories there must be throughout Britain producing the number of tanks necessary for military success.

They also made shells which were being turned out at a very rapid rate. There were many women working in the factory. It was on Saturday and they stopped for twenty minutes, which they do on Saturday, for cleaning the machinery. The plant is running practically night and day seven days a week. . . .

I was offered the chance to see every one of the docks for eight miles long if I wanted to. Some of the docks were undamaged. Ships were being unloaded rapidly. Some of the docks were slightly damaged but with the pillars standing and the tracks unaffected. In another case the docks were almost demolished because a munitions boat blew up in a bombardment. Just a few twisted pieces of iron protruded from the water to indicate a munitions boat had been there. The docks were functioning well. Liverpool is considered Hitler's #1 military objective, even more important than London itself because it is here that so much of the Lend-Lease material will be received.

Paralleling the docks for many miles are the warehouses and they were quite badly hit. Back of these were the workers' houses; the poor workers lived there to avoid transportation and at a cheap rent. They were miserable slums which the people of Liverpool were rather glad had been destroyed. After returning from the docks the Ministry of Information man introduced me to a Labour politician who drove me around the poorer districts. He arranged for a few people whose homes had been destroyed in a blitz to meet me. I met an interesting woman who was working in a munitions factory and doing air raid precaution work. The Labour man had helped get her son to Canada for the Royal Air Force and he was now stationed in Liverpool. They took me into her home which had been very badly damaged and I climbed around the inside to see what bombs can do. Quite a number of people in the block came over for a while. The thing that impressed me about them is the matter of fact, unemotional way in which the people have faced the bombing and will face it next winter. I am told that there was a morale problem in the beginning in Manchester and Birmingham. The authorities did not know what to do. They had no adequate preparation. Specialists in air raid precautions had to come from London to organize the work in those two towns.

On the day before I was to leave London to return to New York, I spent some time at the embassy talking informally with John Winant and Tony Biddle. Ambassador Winant suddenly said, "At three o'clock this afternoon you will receive a telephone call from the Prime Minister's secretary inviting you to have luncheon with the Prime Minister at 10 Downing Street tomorrow noon." I replied, "Well, you know I have been hoping to see the Prime Minister ever since I have been here but I am leaving London tomorrow." He then asked whether I would give up the opportunity to see Prime Minister Churchill. I said, of course not, but would change my travel plans, assuming that since he, the ambassador, controlled the priorities anyway, he could get me on another plane.

The next noon I went to 10 Downing Street and was ushered into a sitting room. I did not need to be a detective to tell there would be three people at the luncheon table because a servant pointed out a decanter of sherry with three glasses. I had thought of course that the luncheon would be a large affair to express appreciation to any Americans who happened to be in London who had been of some help to the cause of Britain. But instead there were only Winston Churchill, Malcolm Mac-Donald, Secretary of State for Colonies, and myself. After a few drinks, the prime minister was as eloquent in private conversation as in an address to Parliament. He spoke with that measured cadence which he always used to overcome a speech defect. He was very easy to talk to and we roamed over many subjects that I had not thought I would dare discuss with him. Finally, I said to the prime minister that there was one question I should like to ask him. I felt it took a lot of nerve for a person from a country that had not entered the war to ask it, but I would do so anyway. I wanted to know his thoughts on postwar organization. What would take the place of the League of Nations? The prime minister replied that he was too old to have anything to do with postwar planning; that would be the job of Franklin Roosevelt. I came away from the luncheon with that same feeling of warmth and inspiration that I always had when I read the prime minister's speeches or listened to him speak.

I can best conclude the account of my visit to Britain by quoting from an address I delivered from London over the Columbia Broadcasting System on September 21, 1941:

Almost three years ago to the day I had the privilege of broadcasting over the Columbia network from Geneva at the time of the crisis which led to the ill-fated Munich agreement. I said then that war could be avoided if the nations that wished peace indicated that they would be willing to fight. At that time the nations would not indicate that they would fight to preserve peace. The United States clung to its fictitious neutrality policy. Today we have war.

At this moment dusk is falling over this city and curtains have been drawn for the blackout. This is the beginning of the third year of the greatest war in history. In this two-year period there has been but one single, constant and consistent factor upon which the world could count—British determination. France fell, Russia changed sides, the United States hesitated. But since the war British courage has never faltered, and British policy has not wavered. Through the dark days of Flanders and Dunkirk, through the air battles of Britain last year, and now as the fortunes of war change somewhat, the one single consistent fact that the world has had to hold on to has been the courage and the determination of these British people. Here alone have men consistently fought to destroy Hitler's plan. Had their courage faltered, civilization would have been thrown back hundreds of years. The threat of Hitler to democratic civilization is so great that it defies the imagination.

I doubt if all the British people themselves understand the magnitude of what they are fighting against. Certainly many Americans do not. This is more than a struggle to protect the British Empire or the Western Hemisphere from invasion. The Hitler war is an assault on the minds as well as the bodies of men; on their civilization as well as their land.

There can be three outcomes to this war. One, Hitler can win. That result would turn a large part of the world back to an age of darkness, lighted here and there by the sporadic fires of revolution. The instruments of modern science and applied psychology would be used to make resistance impossible. Generations might pass before an opportunity would come for a reawakening of mankind to throw off tyranny.

Second, the war could be a stalemate with Hitler appeased. There is danger that if Hitler is able to seize the Ukraine and the industrial regions of Russia, he will announce the stabilization of the European continent under his authority, and tell Britain and the United States that they can have peace if they will leave him alone in Europe and part of the French Empire. It would mean a little food for people on the continent if they would adjust their economies to Germany and be willing that their people become agricultural serfs to maintain a German industrial system. It would relieve temporarily the strain through which Britain is passing and the United States is approaching. But it would be very little better than a Hitler victory. The war of nerves would continue. Our life in the democracies would be regimented to manufacture more and more armaments, and to drill more millions of men for the inevitable day when the clash between the two systems would resume. It would be a system of prolonged agony in which the souls of the democracies would starve as they prepared to meet the aggressor, who would be growing stronger in the consolidation of what he has already conquered.

The third outcome of the war and the only one that free people can contemplate is a complete victory over aggression. It alone offers the possibility for the continuance of civilization. It alone would relieve the world of the strain of militarism and aggression and permit men to turn to peace and an uninterrupted period of reconstruction.

Only a military expert could assess adequately the factors making for victory and defeat today. On the side of the moral imponderables the most important factor for victory is the courage of these British people who believe in their institutions, in human decency and the right of a people to be free. I wish many Americans could see the British people in action; could understand a people who enjoy their fatigue at night because they have spent a full day working for victory; could see a people to whom life is sweeter because they are not afraid to face death. Another imponderable is the resentment in the occupied countries. It is one thing to browbeat one's allies. It is one thing to regiment one's own people. But it is another thing to maintain such a system of tyranny. This is the question that Germany is now facing. Daily Europe is more restless. On the side of the potentials is the strength and power of the United States which, if finally committed, would assure every person in the world, allies as well as enemies, that the allies would win the war. . . .

What are the factors working against the common victory? First, 40 million people on these islands cannot be expected to mobilize the industries and manpower to save the world alone. Germany has more divisions that she can throw into the battle than the total population of these islands. From the enforced labor of the conquered countries Hitler can man his industries and farms and relieve most of his manpower for his Panzer divisions. He already has three million such slaves. It is true that the population of the British Empire exceeds the population of Germany and the conquered peoples, but the Empire is widely scattered, and many ships are necessary to maintain communi-

cations between its component parts. Just as the potential strength of
the United States is one of the imponderables on the side of victory,
so the uncertainty as to whether the United States will use this strength
to the full is one of the uncertainties that might mitigate against final
victory. . . .

There is appreciation here of the cooperation the United States is
now giving on the seas. There is appreciation for the industrial effort
our country is making. But the one thing that the forces of right must
know, and the one thing that could break down German morale, would
be that the American people will set no limits on what they will do for
a quick and complete victory, and that the United States is in the war
to the end. It is no indication of a lessening of British courage and
determination to say that the people are tired. Two years of bombing,
blackouts, preparation, the consciousness that their island is standing
against an assault on civilization that means warfare throughout the
world, cannot help but make the people tired.

I complimented a young woman who was helping me arrange my
papers on the smoothness and efficiency and good nature with which
everything was carried out. She smiled and said, "We've been carrying
on for two years this way and will continue to carry on. We're a bit
tired, that's all." Such fatigue can be endured indefinitely by a people
who continue to believe as the British people do, that full victory is
theirs. . . .

It would be a disaster if the war were so prolonged that at its close
the victorious nations would be too tired to build or guarantee an
adequate peace. Consequently, it is very important that the war be
won as quickly as possible, and that the American contribution to the
war should be geared to this objective. Yesterday I met two groups of
prominent Englishmen who are already formulating plans for world
reorganization to follow the war. Their views are very far-reaching,
and I was pleased that they agree with many of the recommendations
of the report of our Commission to Study the Organization of Peace.
The task confronting the nations at the close of this war will be very
much greater than the last. Rebuilding the structure of civilization will
be a task involving strength and wisdom and patience. Winning the
war should be a job of a few years; winning the peace will require the

best efforts of our generation. Here again the United States must finally indicate that it has no reservations. Victory in this war will be assured when the American people indicate that they have no further reservations as to the contribution they are willing to make for a speedy victory. Victory in the peace necessitates that the American people make up their minds that they will have no reservations as to the part they will play in formulating and guaranteeing peace.

The barrier to the sweep of world barbarism today is in the hearts and minds of the English-speaking people. The key to final victory must be in the hearts and minds of the American people.

12

Pearl Harbor—The Declaration
by the United Nations

On Sunday, December 7, 1941, a small drafting committee of
the Commission to Study the Organization of Peace—Quincy
Wright, Charles Fenwick, Clyde Eagleton, and myself, with
Margaret Olson acting as secretary—was meeting in the Commission's office at 8 West 40th Street. The second Commission
report, "The Transitional Period," was nearly complete, but
some revisions had been suggested at the meeting of the full
Commission on November 30.

When the group recessed for lunch, Miss Olson went home.
While she was having lunch there, the news flashed on the radio
that the Japanese had attacked Pearl Harbor. She telephoned
the office to tell us what she had heard and then hurried back
to join us. In disbelief and shock Quincy Wright, Clyde Eagleton, and I rushed to my apartment a few blocks away to follow
the radio reports there. Charles Fenwick decided to continue
work at the office. The day before he had returned from Washington where he had had a talk with Secretary of State Cordell
Hull, and where for some days a Japanese delegation had been
conferring with the Secretary of State. Although the situation
between the two countries was near the breaking point, no one
expected an overt move to be made while these discussions

were going on. Consequently, Mr. Fenwick did not believe the news.

When what seemed to be confirmation of the reports came over the radio at my apartment, we telephoned Fenwick. He and Miss Olson joined us. All across the country similar groups were huddled around radios listening to the grim reports from the Pacific.

According to Robert Sherwood:

Both Winant and Harriman were at dinner with Churchill at Chequers on Sunday evening, December 7, 1941. The fifteen-dollar American radio that Hopkins had given the Prime Minister was on the dining table and from it came the measured, emotionless tones of the B.B.C. newscaster announcing that the Japanese had attacked Pearl Harbor. Winant has told how Churchill was immediately on his feet, about to call the Foreign Office to give instructions that a declaration of war on Japan should be put through at once—"within the minute," as he had promised. He was talked out of this on the ground that one could not declare war on the strength of a news broadcast, even from the B.B.C. Winant suggested that perhaps the Prime Minister should telephone the White House for confirmation. . . .[1]

Sumner Welles says of President Roosevelt on December 7, 1941:

I had many occasions to see the President during the hours between the time the announcement of the attack on Pearl Harbor was made and the early hours of the following morning. Sitting calmly at this desk in the study of the White House, receiving constantly the reports of what was one of the blackest and most tragic episodes in all of American history he demonstrated that ultimate capacity to dominate and to control a supreme emergency which is perhaps the rarest and most valuable characteristic of any statesman. . . .[2]

1. Robert E. Sherwood, *Roosevelt and Hopkins: An Intimate History* (New York: Harper and Brothers, 1948), p. 439.
2. Sumner Welles, *The Time for Decision* (New York: Harper and Brothers, 1948), pp. 295–296.

Thus the United States entered perhaps the most difficult period of its national existence since the Civil War. In every capital in the world there was speculation as to the immediate effect of Pearl Harbor. It was generally assumed that the United States would now be a full belligerent. No longer would the British be in the position of having to ask for material; they could now plan grand strategy with the United States as an equal.

It was necessary for Winston Churchill and Franklin Roosevelt to meet as quickly as possible. Churchill came to Washington by cruiser, arriving December 22, 1941. He brought with him his military men, primarily to plan strategy.

The President and the prime minister agreed that the first business was the formation of a grand alliance. Each had a draft of a declaration forming such an alliance; the two drafts were quickly merged into what was to be called the Declaration by the United Nations, which became a joint Declaration signed by twenty-six allies. It had been less than five months since Churchill and Roosevelt had met off the coast of Newfoundland to prepare the Atlantic Charter. Now their two countries had become military as well as spiritual and economic allies.

The Declaration was announced in Washington on January 1, 1942. It read:

The Governments signatory hereto:

Having subscribed to a common program of purposes and principles embodied in the Joint Declaration of the President of the United States of America and the Prime Minister of the United Kingdom of Great Britain and Northern Ireland dated August 14, 1941, known as the Atlantic Charter,

Being convinced that complete victory over their enemies is essential to defend life, liberty, independence and religious freedom, and to preserve human rights and justice in their own lands as well as in other lands, and that they are now engaged in a common struggle against savage and brutal forces seeking to subjugate the world, declare:

(1) Each Government pledges itself to employ its full resources,

military or economic, against those members of the Tripartite Pact and its adherents with which such Government is at war.

(2) Each Government pledges itself to cooperate with the Governments signatory hereto and not to make a separate armistice or peace with the enemies.

The foregoing declaration may be adhered to by other nations which are, or which may be, rendering material assistance and contributions in the struggle for victory over Hitlerism.

It was the twenty-six original signers of the Declaration, and subsequent signers, who were to become the participants in the San Francisco Conference and the original members of the United Nations.

The British and the Americans had several other problems to consider while Churchill was in Washington. One was the question of high command, which involved quite a number of different theaters of war; another was the clarification of military objectives. There were some important issues of military strategy to be determined. It is understandable that the British were afraid the United States would concentrate its military efforts on Japan, leaving the United Kingdom and the Soviet Union to battle Germany: the remaining American isolationists wanted the United States to do just that. The British were reassured at the beginning of the conference, however, when the chiefs of staff, General George C. Marshall and Admiral Harold R. Stark, presented the two paragraphs that formed the basis for all plans:

1. At the A-B [American-British] Staff Conversations in February, 1941, it was agreed that Germany was the predominant member of the Axis Powers, and consequently the Atlantic and European area was considered to be the decisive theater.

2. Much has happened since February last, but notwithstanding the entry of Japan into the war, our view remains that Germany is still the prime enemy and her defeat is the key to victory. Once Germany is defeated, the collapse of Italy and the defeat of Japan must follow.[3]

3. Sherwood, *op. cit.,* p. 445.

Mr. Churchill addressed a joint session of Congress on December 26, 1941. It was a most remarkable speech, given with exuberance and humor, and included the words, "If we had kept together after the last war, if we had taken common measures for our safety, this renewal of the curse need never have fallen upon us."[4] This sentence brought forth prolonged applause, which boded well for the future, when international efforts to organize the peace would be made again.

The accomplishments of Roosevelt and Churchill during the fourteen days the prime minister spent in Washington were among the most important in history. In two weeks the British and American governments had determined grand strategy and brought the allies together in a grand alliance. Now they had to give attention to the military situation, which had turned against the allies in almost every theater of the war.

For some weeks our League of Nations Association had been planning a conference to commemorate the twenty-second anniversary of the coming into being of the League of Nations. It was to be held in Washington on January 10, 1942. Now, after the visit of Churchill and the announcements of the future plans of the allied leaders, there were those who thought the Association was, in a sense, attempting to turn the clock back by having such a celebration. It was very clear, however, that the members of the board of the Association and its guests at the meeting in Washington had no desire to return to the past. The spirit of the conference was typified by a cable that Frank G. Boudreau and I sent to the British League of Nations Union:

The League of Nations Association is having Board meeting and public dinner in Washington this evening to commemorate the twenty-second anniversary of the coming into being of the League of Nations. The National Board sends you greetings and expresses its admiration

4. Winston S. Churchill, *The Unrelenting Struggle* (Boston: Little, Brown and Co., 1942), p. 360.

for the faith that the Union has had for two decades. All of us believe that out of the tragedy of the Second World War will come the opportunity to rebuild the structure of international peace on an even firmer foundation, upon the experience of the past twenty-two years and the ideals of the Atlantic Charter. We look forward to working with you in the future as in the past.

Messages were received by the conference from the two surviving members of Woodrow Wilson's war cabinet, Senator Carter Glass and the Honorable Josephus Daniels, former Secretary of the Navy. Thanks to Philip Noel-Baker of the British League of Nations Union, overseas greetings were received from Lord Robert Cecil, who had been one of the authors of the League of Nations Covenant; Dr. Eduard Beneš, former president of the League Assembly; and Dr. V. K. Wellington Koo, who opened the first League of Nations Assembly in 1920 and had been a frequent Chinese delegate. Among the speakers for the evening were Dr. Boudreau, Senator Claude Pepper, Senator Elbert D. Thomas, and myself.

The theme was "It Must Not Happen Again, This Time We Stay." It might well have been taken from President Roosevelt's Address to Congress on the State of the Union on January 6, 1942, in which he said: "I know that I speak for the American people—and I have good reason to believe that I speak also for all the other peoples who fight with us—when I say that this time we are determined not only to win the war but also to maintain the security of the peace that will follow."[5]

On February 11, I delivered an address before the Canadian Club of Ottawa in which I pointed out the grim situation confronting the British and American forces throughout the world:

It is not necessary to remind ourselves today that this is a very dark moment in this war. You have listened to your noon radio reports of the assault on Singapore; of the danger to the Dutch East Indies; of the

5. *The Public Papers and Addresses of Franklin D. Roosevelt: 1942 Volume —Humanity of the Defensive,* compiled and collated by Samuel I. Rosenman (New York: Harper and Brothers, 1950), p. 7.

stringent regulations adopted in Australia yesterday as the great Commonwealth prepares itself for an attack upon its very existence; of MacArthur's brave men in the Philippines fighting an heroic but of course simply delaying and losing action; and the statement of President Roosevelt yesterday that the most the United Nations could hope for was to prevent a break-through while in the year 1942 we prepared and prepared and prepared for the time when we should have equality, and then for the time when we should take an aggressive position in the war. And so 1942 will undoubtedly be a year of withdrawals, of defeats, of losses and humiliations, because for many years our enemies planned deliberately to destroy the kind of world that you and I believe in.

. . . It is not enough to know what we are fighting against; we must know at the same time what we are fighting for. Therefore, I say that winning the war and winning the peace are parts of the same problem; that they cannot be separated, and that if you talk about the kind of world that we can have if we want, it will hearten the morale of our people.

. . . If Prime Minister Churchill and President Roosevelt can meet in the Atlantic and write the Atlantic Charter, and if twenty-six nations can form the United Nations of the World and base their agreement on the Atlantic Charter, we are not altogether wrong to follow the leadership of Churchill and Roosevelt in talking about the ideals of the Atlantic Charter and the formation of the United Nations of the World. . . .

Working hand in hand with the League of Nations Association, the Commission to Study the Organization of Peace called a meeting at the Hotel Biltmore in New York City on February 14, 1942. Its purpose was to present the Second Report of the Commission, "The Transitional Period."

On February 15 the studies committee of the Commission met to consider its future program. I was pleased that a memorandum which I had drafted on the subject, "Third Phase of the Work of the Commission," was adopted by the committee as the plan for future work. It led to the Third Report of the

Commission, which was entitled, "The United Nations and the Organization of Peace." The memorandum read:

The third phase of the work of the Commission is to be devoted to the final blueprint of the future peace. We have approached this third task with hesitancy because of its very magnitude and because of the difficulty of having a starting point. It did not seem adequate to start with a revision of the present League of Nations Covenant, nor could we start with some purely imaginary situation. Not only for reasons of convenience but because of practical necessity I believe we should work on the final blueprint of the future on the basis of the Atlantic Charter and the United Nations. I am convinced that President Roosevelt fully intends that the phrase "United Nations of the World" be the name of the organization of nations to follow the war. I am convinced that the Atlantic Charter will be its basic principles. Therefore, it is practical and also gives us our starting point, to let our future studies be directed to a discussion of how the Atlantic Charter can be implemented and the organization of the United Nations expanded into the universal society of nations which the Commission has demanded as the basis of the future structure of peace.

A very cursory examination will indicate the wide field for discussion. The eight points of the Atlantic Charter provide a rich field of exploration in the economic, social, political and juridical fields.

The acceptance of the Atlantic Charter by most of the South American States, even those that are non-belligerent, means that the Charter is something more than a principle of the belligerents. The United Nations comprise twenty-six countries. What procedure can be found in the period of transition by which the twenty-six expand to become practically universal? How can the machinery which the United Nations have created to win the war, particularly in the field of economics, such as the purchase of raw materials, be continued to win the peace?

Had the Allied Nations been called the League of Nations in 1917 and had the League of Nations been established and functioning in winning the war and been carried over into the peace as a going concern, the United States might have been a member of the League of Nations and the present war avoided. The very opposite occurred;

the League was created after the war. It grew out of the peace treaties and was nurtured in the inevitable reaction of the postwar period. It was new to the American people, giving the isolationists the chance to say that it was contrary to American historical experience.

If the phrase United Nations now becomes a household word and the organization of the United Nations wins the war and is carried over into the reconstruction without the formal break of armistice and peace treaties, the United States will continue to be a member of it.

13

The First Working Draft
of a United Nations Charter

A personal problem that I had to settle after Pearl Harbor was whether at my age I should enlist again in the United States army or whether I should continue my work with the Commission to Study the Organization of Peace, the Committee to Defend America, and the League of Nations Association. Senator Ernest Gibson, who had followed William Allen White as chairman of the Committee to Defend America, had enlisted in the army reserves and had been called into military service. Did I also have an obligation to enlist?

Shortly after Pearl Harbor I sought out two people in Washington. One was Robert Patterson, Assistant Secretary of War, to whom I explained my mental and moral dilemma. He said that if I felt I wanted to enter military service, a commission could be found for me. Then I called upon Sumner Welles, Under-Secretary of State, who had told me some months before that postwar planning would soon be getting under way. Welles was a bit caustic in our talk. He asked me if I had not been in the First World War. When I replied yes, he remarked that I wouldn't be a particularly important soldier in the Second. But if I did not enlist I would be invited to participate in the planning of the postwar world organization, where I might be able to make a more important contribution. I did not enlist.

In another interview with Sumner Welles, on January 8, 1942, just before he left on a diplomatic trip to the Argentine, I told him I felt there was evidence that the appeasement crowd would strike at this strategic moment, while he was out of the country. I cited the recent conversion of the Keep America Out of War Committee to the Committee for a Democratic Peace.

Welles replied that he had already accomplished what he had set out to do—create a State Department committee for the study of the future peace. Cordell Hull would be its chairman; Welles vice-chairman. Welles said he would also chair one of the subcommittees, probably the one on political organization—the subcommittee on which I had anticipated serving. I remarked that I presumed Mr. Hull would concentrate on the economic side of postwar planning. Mr. Welles replied that Mr. Hull would be chairman of the entire effort.

Welles said that the hardest task in his nine years in Washington had been making these preparations for the proper organization of the future peace. I asked him if this was because of the President's disinclination to delegate authority. No, Welles replied, it was because so many people in Washington wanted to be involved in this work. I said I thought the State Department must avoid any Colonel House situation developing.[1] He agreed that planning the peace must ultimately be in State Department hands, but pointed out that, of course, the State Department was not omnipotent and wanted the cooperation of all agencies in Washington. I mentioned that Bill Donovan, then coordinator of the Office of Information, had started out on a course which indicated that he was going to do some planning.

1. It seemed to me vital that the State Department make every effort to prevent the development of situations such as that which had arisen during the ratification of the League of Nations Covenant, when policy was made under the influence of advisers outside the Department, especially Colonel Edward House.

Whereupon Welles said that the President had already put a stop to that.

Mr. Welles said that he would get in touch with me upon his return from South America and that when the State Department committee began functioning, he wanted me to work in the closest, most intimate relationship to it. I would be able to guide the combined educational programs of the organizations with which I was affiliated along the lines of State Department policy. I asked him with whom I should communicate in the Department while he was away, and was delighted when he named Cordell Hull himself. I asked if he would tell Mr. Hull about our conversation so that I could talk to the Secretary without reserve, and Welles said he would.

I was pleased with the interview. Three points had particularly impressed me: the planning would not be in the hands of Colonel Donovan or of any potential Colonel House, but in the hands of the State Department; the planning would not be in the hands of minor officials, some of whom were thought to be appeasers, but would clearly be under the direction of Cordell Hull and Sumner Welles; and finally I was impressed that the teamwork between Mr. Hull and Mr. Welles was evidently very good, despite rumors in the press to the contrary.

In early March, I took "to the field." Between March 9 and July 15, when I was called to Washington to participate as a member of the "Welles Committee," I visited some twenty cities, covering an area from Boston to Seattle. This was not unusual for me. From the early days of the League of Nations Association it had been my custom to spend a considerable portion of my time visiting its local chapters. I gained inspiration and conviction from meeting people in many different parts of the country and discussing the direction our programs should take.

Hundreds of chapters of the William Allen White Committee were flourishing throughout the country—some former chapters of the League of Nations Association, some chapters of other organizations. It would be tragic if these committees, united in a program of aid to the allies, were dissolved now that the United States had entered the war. There was still much for them to do in supporting the war effort and planning the peace. In fact, now that the United States was a belligerent, it was for the first time in a position to plan for the peace as an equal with its allies.

In one of my first stops in the tour I spoke at Winter Park, Florida, where I told my audience that the phrase, Committee to Defend America, was not quite adequate since the United States was now in the war. Consequently, the Committee to Defend America, the League of Nations Association, the Commission to Study the Organization of Peace, and the Council for Democracy were uniting in a common program entitled Citizens for Victory—victory in the war, victory in the peace, and victory in the preservation of democracy—these terms representing our three aims. I was not surprised to find that the country was quite united in its war aims following Pearl Harbor, but I also found that isolationism was less than ever before. There was an increasing belief that the nation this time must be part of the effort to organize world peace.

At last the moment arrived when Secretary Hull and Under-Secretary Welles, under the direction of President Roosevelt, formally set up the machinery to plan the future peace. The three men were a remarkable combination—Cordell Hull with his nation-wide popularity and wide contact with members of the Congress; Sumner Welles, with his very considerable knowledge of the subject and his contact with foreign diplomats; and above all the President, who brought the group wise supervision and inspiration. These men could draw upon the years of experience with the League of Nations; when the League was being planned, there was no one with any similar experience.

The overall committee was called the Advisory Committee. As Mr. Welles had told me would be the case, Secretary Hull was chairman and Welles was vice-chairman. The Advisory Committee went through various phases during the course of its existence, its members gradually increasing to a number somewhat over forty. It was composed of experts in the international relations field, members of the Senate and House of Representatives, and members of the various subcommittees that were set up under its inspiration. In the year 1943 it became known as the Political Committee rather than the Advisory Committee. Under both names it received much of the material from the subcommittees on postwar planning. Occasionally the committee was virtually a seminar to which Professor Shotwell and some of its other members lectured.

Out of the overall committee grew a series of subcommittees, each with its own chairman: the political subcommittee—Hull and Welles; the security subcommittee—Norman Davis; the subcommittee on territorial problems—Isaiah Bowman, president of Johns Hopkins University; two economic subcommittees, later consolidating into one under Myron Taylor; the international organization subcommittee—Sumner Welles; the legal subcommittee—Green Hackworth; and a subcommittee on the problems of possible European federation—Hamilton Fish Armstrong.

The subcommittee on international organization first met in late summer of 1942. Besides Sumner Welles as chairman, the members were Professor Shotwell, Benjamin V. Cohen, Isaiah Bowman, and myself. Several members of the State Department were attached to the committee. One of them, Green Hackworth, later became a judge on the World Court. Another was Breckenridge Long, Assistant Secretary of State. Although he had the reputation of being a conservative, I found Mr. Long to be one of the most liberal and sympathetic people with whom I talked during our meetings in 1942 and 1943.

Professor Shotwell was the best informed member of our committee because his life had been spent in the field of international organization. Ben Cohen was not only well informed but knew the political intricacies of the Congress and governments represented in Washington better than anyone else. Isaiah Bowman was not as well versed in the details of international organization and sometimes bluffed a bit. However, when it came to discussing geographical areas, as a geographer he was very helpful. As a matter of fact, he later became chairman of the subcommittee on geography.

As I remember the committee now, it was a rather warm and friendly body. Its small size made it possible for us to discuss and reach conclusions quickly. All the committees contributed much that was helpful to the State Department and those who drafted material for Dumbarton Oaks. I think, however, that the Welles Committee was one of the most important because it actually drafted a plan for an international organization.

The first task assigned to our committee was to draft a plan for "trusteeship." The term was used by those who were planning the future world organization to describe what they hoped would be an improvement over the mandates system of the League of Nations; the concept was later incorporated in the United Nations Charter. All of us had a part in the drafting process, but I was asked to draft the final version. I confess to feeling rather proud when Professor Shotwell informed me that my draft had been adopted by the Political Committee with very few suggestions for revision, Senator Austin even remarking that the document was "a work of genius."

Drafting the plan for an international organization occupied our committee for the remainder of 1942 and on into 1943. We had a preliminary draft by March. During that period we had several joint meetings with the security subcommittee, with Sumner Welles and Norman Davis, head of the security subcommittee, serving as alternate chairmen. We were pleased when we could resume our own meetings.

A vast number of memoranda and documents was written by various committee members, including myself. Since together this material would fill hundreds of pages, it quite obviously cannot be included here, and I must content myself with outlining a few of the major questions of world organization that came before the Welles Committee. For example: what should be the relationship between the autonomous economic and social (non-political) agencies and the world organization? Mr. Welles pointed out that those agencies that had been taken over from the League of Nations, such as the International Labor Organization, and the Food and Argiculture Organization now being set up, would antedate the political organization whose plan we were currently drafting. Consequently, the political organization would never have the ability to coordinate, nor the authority to control such agencies that it would have had if it had been created first. It was recognized, however, that many new agencies would be created after the war which, while autonomous, would be more closely related to the new organization. Others would be under its direct control.

One of the most important questions before our committee was that of membership in the world organization. The members of the committee felt that one of the weaknesses of the League had been that in a sense it was a club to which a nation could be admitted or denied admission and from which it could be expelled. We took the position that the United Nations should be identical with the family of nations. Among the various notes I have before me is a memorandum I drafted which begins:

The United Nations who are making terrible sacrifices to save civilization from international lawlessness, together with their associates, proclaim that henceforth the regime of law, justice and security be binding upon all people. To that end, they proclaim that all people should be bound by international law and morality whose first tenets are that the use of force for the settlement of international disputes is prohibited and that all disputes must be settled through the peaceful processes of the international community. Consequently, all duly recognized independent states and dominions shall be recognized as members of the international organization.

I argued, of course, that a nation that was in violation of the law could not very well enjoy the privileges of the world community, but nevertheless, it should remain a member.

This concept of automatic membership was gradually accepted by our committee, but when later the terms of membership to be stated in the Charter were being debated, Isaiah Bowman, off the top his head, gave the following definition of "universal membership":

All qualified states and dominions shall be members of the international organization. The Council should decide as to the nature of the qualifications.

Ben Cohen had a much better definition, for truly automatic membership:

All self-governing states shall be recognized as members of the international organization and shall be recognized as entitled to exercise the rights of members as provided in the instrument.

Unfortunately, Isaiah Bowman's definition was finally adopted by the committee.

Although few foresaw then the danger that would arise from giving the Security Council the authority to determine "the nature of the qualifications," the phrase was to haunt us. Because of the lack of provision for truly automatic membership in the United Nations Charter, as late as the beginning of 1955 almost half of the states of Europe were not members of the United Nations, kept out either by the United States or the Soviet Union. The Soviet Union used its veto in the Security

Council against those states it did not wish to be members, while the United States was able to persuade a majority of the Security Council to vote against the admission of states it did not want to see admitted. If the principle of automatic membership had been adhered to, if the Cohen definition had prevailed, years of confusion as to who should be members of the United Nations would have been avoided.

Another problem confronting the committee was the composition of the Security Council. Membership in the League's Council had been one of the insoluble difficulties of the League of Nations. Many nations had wanted to be members, but since seats were rotated some states had a chance at membership once every three years while others had virtually no chance at all. In reply to the insistent demands of Brazil, Spain, and others, a system was finally agreed to whereby the League's Council would include permanent members, non-permanent members, and a special class of members who, though not holding permanent seats, nevertheless could be reelected indefinitely for a non-permanent seat. This resulted in the latter class becoming in fact permanent members, and was a situation our committee wished to avoid.

The members of the Security Council, we argued, should be representative of the entire world community or some region of it and not simply representative of themselves. I suggested at the beginning of the committee's discussion that the members of the Security Council be elected as individuals, somewhat in the way that judges of the World Court were elected. This proposal was rejected on the grounds that the Security Council, because of its importance, must be composed of states. However, as time went on the views of the other members of the committee changed, until they approached mine. It was finally agreed that the world should be divided into regions and the states in each region should elect members to the Security Council, presumably individuals.

It was also agreed that at least initially there should be four permanent seats on the Security Council, which would compose the Executive Committee. In addition, there should be seven non-permanent seats, which would be assigned to the various parts of the world as follows: two for the group of the European states; two for the group of American states; one for the group of Far Eastern states; one for the group of Near and Middle East states; and one elected by the British dominions. I felt that in the long run the regions—say eight or ten—limited to one or two seats in the Security Council would select to be members of the Council the very best and most distinguished person or persons in the area. In the long run these people might have the distinction and detachment of the members of the World Court, and the element of national sovereignty in the Security Council would be reduced.

Obviously we had many discussions which would not become part of the draft constitution of the international organization. One of the most interesting involved whether a new organization whould be created at all, or whether the old League structure should be retained. Many factors dictated the creation of something new, but there was at the same time a growing appreciation of the work of the League of Nations and concern with how it could and should be fitted into the new organization. We spent a few moments at one session of the committee trying to think of synonyms for words in the League of Nations lexicon. No new word could be substituted for Secretariat, we decided; the Assembly could become the General Assembly; there would be very little difference in the wording of the titles of the first and second World Courts. The League of Nations Council, of course, would be expanded into the Security Council, the Economic and Social Council, and the Trusteeship Council.

Unfortunately, by the end of 1942, differences had begun to surface between Secretary Hull and Under-Secretary Welles on the question of how much information on postwar planning should be given to Congress and the public. According to my notes of December 22:

I talked with Professor Shotwell over the phone after returning to New York. Apparently the President has consulted the Congressional leaders about speaking to Congress on postwar plans. McCormick urged him to do it. Rayburn was opposed and Barkley, as usual, was neutral. Apparently [Vice President] Wallace and McCormick won out. How far he [the President] will go is another question. Welles wants him to take a strong position all along the line; Secretary Hull holds back. Myron Taylor told Shotwell that it was Hull who was holding back and he thought Sumner Welles was broken-hearted because there was not more leadership.

There are two tragedies in this situation. One is that Secretary Hull altogether overlooks the fact or cannot see the fact that the only way to beat the isolationists at their game is an all-out offensive; that, when in doubt about public opinion, present the boldest plan. This is what the public wants. If the peace is lost it will be because of timidity. It will be, to use the old expression in another form, "too little and too late."

The other tragedy is that because of Secretary Hull's timidity and fear that the public and the Congress will be alarmed, the magnificent planning that the State Department is doing is not known by the public and particularly those liberals who are criticizing the State Department for everything. I do not mean that the details of the plans could possibly be given publicity at this time. Such matters as international trusteeship are questions for considerable diplomatic negotiation. However, the knowledge that the plans are being formulated and that they are liberal and far-reaching would silence much of the criticism of the Department. The liberals do not think the Department is doing anything, and the isolationists think the plans are being formulated in deep, dark secrecy. Neither, of course, is correct.

This difference between Hull and Welles did not immediately affect the work of the Welles Committee, which by March 26, 1943, had before it the rough draft of the constitution of a world organization. All of it had been worked out in the international organization subcommittee and its drafting committee, except for the article on police powers, which had been submitted to us by the security subcommittee, and the article on the Bill of Rights, which had been submitted by the legal subcommittee.

Discussions went on until June 20 about refinements in the draft. I quote from my notes of June 20, 1943:

Mr. Welles then interrupted to say in confidence, and asked the Secretary not to take notes, that he had kept President Roosevelt informed of our work and the President was in agreement with our draft for a Four Power Pact, a Provisional United Nations agreement, and the Security Draft. But that President Roosevelt had called attention to the length of these drafts, how impossible it would be to have the public read and understand them. And because they were so long and would be so difficult to understand, therein lay the great danger of confusion and Congressional debate, a situation which would give the opposition the opportunity to prejudice the public against these documents. Mr. Welles pointed out how very long our documents were in comparison to the League of Nations Covenant which was very brief and quite understandable. . . .

At another point in the discussion Mr. Welles said he felt the time had come to be as specific as possible and a little bit later, when he was queried as to why there was emphasis on principles rather than on special drafts, Mr. Welles replied that that was the wish of the Secretary of State.

The bitterness between Hull and Welles became more evident as the days wore on. Possibly Mr. Hull's resentment of Mr. Welles's access to the White House contributed to the rift between them: although a small drafting committee had been set up in the Department of State to coordinate the drafts from all the subcommittees before they went to the President, it was clear that Mr. Welles had contact with the President and was taking material directly to him. At any rate, by spring 1943, whenever the Political Committee, which had by then superseded the Advisory Committee, met with Secretary Hull, he would go around the room asking the opinion of each person about the matter at hand—except for Mr. Welles. He alone was not called upon.

In Mr. Hull's book describing the work of the committees, he refers to the draft produced by the international organization subcommittee thus:

This work began on October 23, 1942, and resulted in the preparation by March 26, 1943, of a draft of a proposed charter for an international organization.

While this draft contained many good features it leaned rather strongly in the direction of regionalism by providing that the Executive Council of the proposed organization would consist of eleven members, of whom only the four major powers, as permanent members, would be represented as individual nations. The other seven members would each represent a region of the world rather than any individual nations. In this respect the draft reflected Welles' influence since he was a convinced advocate of regional organization.

When these plans were brought to my attention in the Political Subcommittee, I could not go along with the regional feature; hence I started the subcommittee upon a detailed consideration of international organization in the spring of 1943 on the basis of fundamental issues rather than on the special subcommittee's draft.[2]

I beg to differ with Secretary Hull's assessment. In none of our discussions did I notice Mr. Welles leaning toward regionalism as Mr. Hull indicates he did. In fact, the only reference to regionalism in the draft was the plan for the Security Council, and I must say that I share a large portion of the responsibility for that part of the draft—and am proud of it.

I do not think any of us realized at the meeting of June 19, 1943, that this would be our last. I received letters from the Department of State on July 5, 13, 27, and August 2 saying that

2. *The Memoirs of Cordell Hull,* Vol. II (New York: The Macmillan Company, 1948), pp. 1,639–1,640.

no meeting of the international organization subcommittee was planned for "this week." I had a conference with Mr. Welles on August 10, when he said that he hoped our committee would resume meeting in September. But by the end of August, Mr. Welles had resigned from the State Department.

It was tragic indeed that Mr. Hull and Mr. Welles pulled apart in the midst of planning for the future peace and the world organization. With the rupture between them the Advisory Committee and subcommittees, which had been formed with so much imagination in 1942, faded into history. One of the most remarkable things about the committees was that official participation in them had been reduced to a minimum and instead private citizens had contributed their ideas. Now the planning reverted to the State Department bureaucracy, and took place without the systematic infusion of ideas from the public.

Fortunately, the committees had already gone far to outline the framework of a world organization and the principles of future peace. However, I should like to conclude by saying that if Secretary Hull and Under-Secretary Welles could have continued their collaboration, more liberal ideas might have found their way into American plans for the Dumbarton Oaks and San Francisco agreements. I cannot help but refer to the principle of automatic membership and the idea for a Security Council whose members would represent the entire world instead of particular states.

14

⊷❦⊷

Mobilizing Public Opinion

The year 1943 saw a remarkable mobilization of public opinion in support of the future organization of peace. It began with the introduction of resolutions in Congress expressing support for the idea of a world organization. It concluded with the Moscow Declaration, in which the United States, the United Kingdom, the Soviet Union, and China agreed to the establishment of a general international organization.

Gradually in 1942 the military situation had begun to improve. The bombing attack on Japan by James H. Doolittle and the battle of the Coral Sea in May 1942 promised progress in the Far East. On November 7 came the invasion of French North Africa by U.S. forces under General Eisenhower, which placed 500 miles of coastline under allied control. On February 24, 1943, round-the-clock bombing of Germany began. On July 25, Mussolini was deposed. A spirit of optimism and confidence was growing in the United States and in Great Britain.

In the early summer of 1943 the following memorandum was widely distributed by the United Nations Association:[1]

1. The term "United Nations" was then being used to designate the fighting forces of the allied nations, but it was assumed by many that the new world organization to ensure peace would also be called the United Nations. So popular had the term become by 1942 that it had seemed necessary to protect it from commercialization. Consequently, the president of the League of Nations Asso-

Because it was felt that there is a pressing need, at this time, for widespread democratic discussion on the problems of the peace, the United Nations Association prepared a countrywide itinerary for speakers on this subject. The speakers are members of the Senate and House of Representatives traveling in "teams," to all sections of the country. Each team is composed of one Democrat and one Republican, and will speak for one to two weeks in the regions outlined for them.

Meetings have been arranged in key cities and towns throughout each area. Not only mass meetings, but luncheons of business men's groups, women's clubs and service clubs, are scheduled. The United Nations Association, in cooperation with Citizens for Victory and the Church Peace Union, and with local organizations, have arranged the itineraries for the speakers.

There is an urgent need for immediate Congressional action to in-sure American participation in a world organization now, and after the war. The United Nations Association feels, that by sending these "teams" of Senators and Congressmen to discuss this need with the people, they are accomplishing what has not been attempted before; namely, they are helping to present the question to the people in their homes, factories, clubs and town meetings.

The plan of the congressional speaking tours—eight tours were arranged to cover communities in twenty-six states—was unique. Congressmen who had been faced during the legislative session with pressing matters pertaining to the war were willing to spend some of their brief weeks of summer vacation touring certain areas and talking to the public about the need of joining a world organization to prevent a third world war.

The tours focused on passage of two congressional resolutions. The first had been introduced by a freshman congressman, J. William Fulbright of Arkansas. It read:

Resolved by the House of Representatives (the Senate concurring): That the Congress hereby expresses itself as favoring the creation of

---

ciation chapter in Washington, D.C., one of his associates and myself that year incorporated the United Nations Association in Washington.

appropriate international machinery with power adequate to establish and to maintain a just and lasting peace, among the nations of the world, and as favoring participation by the United States therein through its constitutional processes.[2]

The second resolution, and the most vital, had been introduced in the Senate by Joseph H. Ball of Minnesota and Harold H. Burton of Ohio, Republicans, and Carl A. Hatch of New Mexico and Lister Hill of Alabama, Democrats. Commonly known as the B_2H_2 Resolution after its sponsors, the proposal read:

Resolved: That the Senate advises that the United States take the initiative in calling meetings of representatives of the United Nations for the purpose of forming an organization of the United Nations with specific and limited authority.

(1) To assist in coordinating and fully utilizing the military and economic resources of all member nations in the prosecution of the war against the Axis.

(2) To establish temporary administrations for Axis-controlled areas of the world as these are occupied by United Nations forces, until such time as permanent governments can be established.

(3) To administer relief and assistance in economic rehabilitation in territories of member nations needing such aid and in Axis territory occupied by United Nations forces.

(4) To establish procedures and machinery for peaceful settlement of disputes and disagreements between nations.

(5) To provide for the assembly and maintenance of a United Nations military force and to suppress by immediate use of such force any future attempt at military aggression by any nation.

That the Senate further advises that any establishment of such United Nations organization provide machinery for its modification, for the delegation of additional specific and limited functions to such organization, and for admission of other nations to membership, and

2.*In Quest of Peace and Security, Selected Documents in American Foreign Policy, 1941–1951* (Washington, D.C.: GPO, Department of State Publication 4245, 1951), p. 5.

that member nations should commit themselves to seek no territorial aggrandizement.

There was no longer any doubt that the citizens of the United States were in favor of this country's cooperation with the other United Nations after the war. A Gallup Poll in June 1943 had revealed that 74 percent of the people favored an international police force! But B_2H_2 was a specific proposal, which called on the United States to take the initiative in forming the postwar international organization. It was opposed by the chairman of the Senate Foreign Relations Committee, Tom Connally of Texas, who had pigeonholed it. The sponsors and supporters of B_2H_2 fought back through the congressional tours.

Besides B_2H_2's four sponsors, the touring congressmen included Senators Albert Gore of Tennessee, Harry Truman of Missouri, Homer Ferguson of Michigan, and Burnet R. Maybank of South Carolina; from the House, Representatives Walter Judd of Minnesota, James A. Wright of Pennsylvania, Robert Hale of Maine, Robert Ramspeck of Georgia, Mike Monroney of Oklahoma, Charles M. LaFollette of Indiana, Christian Herter of Massachusetts, and Howard McMurray of Wisconsin.[3]

The public was quick to compare these congressional tours to the Lincoln-Douglas debates, but the comparison was hardly accurate. Lincoln and Douglas had debated issues on which they disagreed, whereas the congressmen on the tours were taking the same position. Their differences were in their political complexions.

Some of the planning for the tours had taken place in the office of Senator Ball—the Minnesota senator was particularly helpful in discovering senators and congressmen who were willing to take to the road—but the effort was actually directed from the office of the United Nations Association at 8 West 40th Street in New York City.

3. These were the original sixteen participants. During the course of the summer some of them dropped out, to be replaced by others of the same party and persuasion.

Organization locally was a difficult task. Important communities had to be selected and the widest local sponsorship arranged. The members of Congress who were making sacrifices to appear had to feel that their time and energy were well invested. Fortunately it was not necessary to build a special field staff to undertake the local arrangements. They were made, to a great extent, by people on the spot who had been in charge of the program of the League of Nations Association or of the William Allen White Committee in their areas. Mr. Harry Terrell of Des Moines, Iowa, Midwest director for the Carnegie Endowment for International Peace, organized the congressional tours in Iowa and adjoining states. Mrs. Lucille Beck, who directed the office of the League of Nations Association in Denver, set up the program in the Rocky Mountain area. Miss Irene Armstrong of the League of Nations Association of Massachusetts organized part of the New England tour. Mr. E. Guy Talbott of San Francisco, director of the International Center—which served the Carnegie Endowment for International Peace, the League of Nations Association, the World Alliance for International Friendship Through the Churches, the Church Peace Union, the Commission to Study the Organization of Peace, and Citizens for Victory—arranged the Western tour.

The first meeting was in Los Angeles on July 5, 1943, with Senator Ball and Representative Gore as speakers. I quote a letter from Mr. Talbott dated July 10 which illustrates the kind of local cooperation that was secured in most communities. He wrote:

I sent you a report on Ball-Gore meetings in Los Angeles. Wednesday, July 7, they spoke at Kiwanis Club luncheon in Reno, and that evening at mass meeting in Civic Auditorium—600 present. Gov. Carville was on the platform. Very successful meeting, they report. Thursday, July 8, they addressed luncheon meeting in Sacramento, sponsored by Rotary and other civic organizations. Good interest reported. (Same sort of sponsorship in Reno, including veterans, churches, women's organizations, etc.)

July 8 we had a fine press conference here in San Francisco. All papers and press services represented. Enclosed are some samples of publicity, including one Los Angeles story. Publicity there and here was excellent.

Tomorrow morning, Sunday, at 9:15 we fly to Portland. Have an evening meeting there tomorrow night with League of Women Voters. Will send you full reports of meetings in Portland and Seattle.

OWI is making very full coverage, sending their reports on to Washington. They are also sending out the short-wave broadcasts. They are showing great interest in the tour. So far it has been a great success.

July 9, yesterday, at noon Ball and Gore addressed an overflowing crowd at the Commonwealth Club. Fine interest. Speeches were broadcast. Ball gave another broadcast last night; also two transcriptions for shortwave release to Orient and Australia-New Zealand. He also gave transcriptions for release on Citizens for Victory program tomorrow. Last night they spoke at mass meeting in Scottish Rite Auditorium. Attendance about 1100. Most enthusiastic meeting we have ever sponsored. Dr. [Monroe] Deutsch presided at that meeting. Enclosed is the resolution unanimously adopted.

Yesterday afternoon they visited one of the shipyards. This noon we are having two off-the-record political meetings. Ball with Republican leaders and Gore with the Democrats.

Most local meetings had a number of sponsors. The following is a list of some who sponsored meetings in Nebraska for Senator Harry Truman and Congressman Walter Judd:

August 1—Hastings, Nebraska. Community meeting Sunday evening 8 p.m., city auditorium. Sponsored by Ministerial Association, Rotary, Lions, Kiwanis and Civic Groups.

August 2—Grand Island, Nebraska. Sponsors: Grand Island Rotary Club, Mr. Charles C. Crawford, President; Mr. Arch W. Jerrell, Editor, *Grand Island Independent;* Mr. C. Ray Gates, Superintendent of Schools. Meeting at 12:00 noon, Yancey Hotel.

August 3—Omaha, Nebraska. Sponsors: Omaha Chamber of Commerce; Mr. John Fogarty, Secretary; Meeting at 12 noon. Social, Civic and Business groups invited.

August 4—Lincoln, Nebraska. Chamber of Commerce at noon. Evening at Student Union at University of Nebraska.

Some of the senators sent interesting letters telling how they felt the tours were progressing. Senator Truman wrote a letter to the office every night, including his expense account. Following are a few excerpts from a letter sent by Senator Burton telling about his New England trip:

Briefly, we addressed in five days eighteen audiences in Rhode Island and Connecticut; one in Rhode Island, and seventeen in four days in Connecticut. I spoke on thirteen of these occasions—eight times alone and five times in conjunction with Representative McMurray. Each of us broadcast once, and we both joined in a radio interview at Waterbury. I estimate the total attendance at all of our meetings at about forty-five hundred. The radio time totaled one and one-quarter hours.

The attendance at these meetings was in general larger and a more wide-spread interest seemed to be expressed than was the case at most of the meetings on my Indiana, Ohio, Louisville and Pittsburgh tour, although the difference was not great. In every instance, those who attended were deeply interested and generally showed familiarity with the subject. In every case our bi-partisan approach (even though one of us was not able to be present at the particular meeting in question) opened the doors of local consideration to us. Governor Raymond E. Baldwin made available to us for the entire trip two police cars in Connecticut. He welcomed us in person in New Haven. . . .

Governor J. Howard McGrath welcomed us personally to Rhode Island. Senator Theodore Francis Green entertained us at his home in Providence, Rhode Island. Congressman-at-large B. J. Mankiewicz of Connecticut attended the meeting in New Britain and introduced me to the audience there. Congressman Ranulf Compton of the Third District of Connecticut sat on the platform with us at New Haven. Congressman Joseph E. Talbot of the Fifth District of Connecticut sat with us on the platform at Waterbury. The Mayors of most of the cities welcomed us in person and generally the leaders of both political party organizations did likewise. Leading citizens in all fields, including especially business and government, took a cordial interest in our presentation of postwar policy.

The touring congressmen learned a good bit about people in other parts of the country, outside their own constituencies. Sumner Welles, for example, told me of Senator Hatch's remark to President Roosevelt that Iowa was not at *all* isolationist. The senator was surprised, but those of us familiar with the Middle West knew that while there was some isolationist sentiment in the state, there was liberalism too. The Des Moines *Register,* for example, was a liberal paper, and Iowa had had senators and congressmen who had been in favor of the League of Nations.

Some of the congressmen were surprised that the tours had such broad local sponsorship, but there were many national organizations with local chapters which had supported the League of Nations. The will of many of them had been defeated by party partisanship in the fight for the League; they would not readily be defeated again. And this time there was no senatorial plot to defeat the wishes of the people. Instead, leading senators themselves were in a crusade for some kind of world organization.

It is impossible to name some of the national organizations that expressed themselves in support of a future world organization without doing an injustice to other important ones. Hence, I shall mention very few. The Commission to Study the Bases of a Just and Durable Peace, instituted by the Federal Council of the Churches of Christ in America, had wide national influence. A number of distinguished Protestant clergy and laymen were affiliated with it; the chairman of the Commission was John Foster Dulles. I should also mention "Pattern for Peace," a declaration by Catholic, Jewish, and Protestant leaders. In addition, labor unions, educational groups, and leading women's organizations expressed their support.

Also in that summer of 1943, the National Broadcasting Company and its affiliated independent stations carried a series of twenty-six weekly radio programs entitled "For This We Fight." The first thirteen were conducted by the Commission to Study the Organization of Peace and dealt with what the allies were fighting for internationally. The second thirteen were undertaken by the Twentieth Century Fund, which presented a program of proposals for a better America to follow the war. The titles of the Commission's programs were: "Underwriting Victories"; "Science and the Future"; "The United Nations"; "Peace Through World Trade"; "Making the World Secure"; "Alternatives for War"; "Food and Health in the Future"; "World Problems of Labor"; "The World of Sight and Sound"; "Education for Freedom"; "Justice and Human Rights"; "The Role of the Americas"; and "The Role of the United States."

Some of the speakers who participated in the series at the invitation of NBC and the Commission to Study the Organization of Peace were Senators Elbert D. Thomas, Warren E. Austin, and Claude Pepper; Isaiah Bowman; Waldemar Kaempffert, science editor of *The New York Times;* David Sarnoff, president of RCA; John Foster Dulles; James T. Shotwell; Thomas Watson, president of IBM; Thomas W. Lamont; Rear Admiral Harry E. Yarnell; Matthew Woll, executive vice president of the American Federation of Labor; James Rowland Angell, president emeritus of Yale University; Justice Owen Roberts, United States Supreme Court; John W. Davis; Nelson Rockefeller; Sumner Welles; and William Allan Neilson.

One senator, Burton K. Wheeler of Montana, objected to the character of the programs. An ardent isolationist, he said that while the isolationists would support the war they did not necessarily support the plans for a new world organization, and he felt that the programs were slanted in favor of such an organization. To correct the imbalance, he suggested a number of names out of which we selected Senator Robert E. Taft to speak on the program with his friend, James T. Shotwell. Taft was rather quixotic, however, and did not always take the point of view that was expected. In this case he spoke of the need for an international police force and expressed other ideas that we would not have expected of him. Senator Wheeler's reaction was, "Hell, that man isn't an isolationist!" He wanted someone else, and we finally agreed that he should do a broadcast himself. Because I had been so involved in the negotiations, it was suggested that I absent myself from the NBC studio that night.

It was estimated by a commercial monitoring association that these broadcasts reached 25 percent of the listening audience during that radio period, an unusually high rating for an educational program.

The efforts of that summer produced significant results, although they did not achieve the passage of B_2H_2, which remained bottled up in committee and never reached a vote. The Fulbright Resolution passed the House on September 21. On October 21, Senator Tom Connally finally bowed to the increasingly roused public and, while not releasing B_2H_2, introduced his own resolution on the subject of international organization.

At the time of the adoption of the Joint Declaration by the United Nations on January 1, 1942, there had been some who had criticized the fact that the Declaration said nothing about the form a future world organization should take. However, it had seemed clear to us that President Roosevelt was then simply not yet ready to spell out a structure that might be rejected by an insufficiently prepared public. As the introduction to the Fourth Report of the Commission to Study the Organization of Peace pointed out,

The Atlantic Charter and the Declaration of the United Nations gave the first authoritative expression to these fundamental principles but announced no plans for embodying them in a working organization of which the United States would have to be a leading member. Mindful of our record in the past, our Government was very careful not to commit the country to plans which it was not ready to carry out. Meanwhile, however, American public opinion had undergone a change with reference to postwar planning which was little short of revolutionary. Isolation, symbolized by neutrality legislation which would treat all warring nations alike, has given way under the pressure supplied by the Axis governments which would use our indifference to establish a ruthless militarism upon the world.[4]

Now, by October 1943, the public was ready to go further, much further. Not only had Senator Connally introduced his resolution, but the Moscow Declaration, by which the allies openly committed themselves to a world organization, was being negotiated. On October 25, 1943, I had a conference with President Roosevelt in which he indicated how pleased he was with the efforts that were being made to gain public support for what was to become the United Nations Organization. When I went in, the President said, "Clark, what can you tell me?" I replied that I had come to see what he could tell me. He said that he had just been talking to Joe Guffey, former senator from Pennsylvania, and Guffey had asked him about the Connally Resolution and whether or not they should make an effort to strengthen it. The President said that he favored the Fulbright Resolution, the Connally Resolution, and the Ball Resolution, and that it would do no harm to make an effort to strengthen the Connally Resolution; that after all, a Senate resolution was simply an effort to put the Senate on record. I asked, "But a Senate resolution would help now, would it not, particularly our delegation in Moscow?" He replied that it certainly would. When I then commented that I did not like Tom Connally's statement that his resolution was all that the people would stand for, whereas the Gallup Poll had showed that 75 percent

4. Commission to Study the Organization of Peace, Fourth Report, *Fundamentals of the International Organization* (New York, November 1943), p. 11.

of the people wanted an international police force, the President said that he thought Senator Connally meant an international police force in his resolution.

We then discussed briefly the tours the senators had made during the summer. The President was not aware that the United Nations Association had arranged them.

On November 1, before Senator Connally's resolution could come to a final vote, the Moscow Declaration was signed by Secretary of State Cordell Hull, Foreign Minister Anthony Eden, Foreign Minister Vyacheslav Molotov, and the Chinese ambassador to Moscow, Mr. Foo Ping-sheung. The portion of the text of the Moscow Declaration which deals with a general international organization is as follows:

The Governments of the United States of America, the United Kingdom, the Soviet Union and China:

united in their determination, in accordance with the Declaration by the United Nations of January 1, 1942, and subsequent declarations, to continue hostilities against those Axis powers with which they respectively are at war until such powers have laid down their arms on the basis of unconditional surrender;

conscious of their responsibility to secure the liberation of themselves and the peoples allied with them from the menace of aggression;

recognizing the necessity of ensuring a rapid and orderly transition from war to peace and of establishing and maintaining international peace and security with the least diversion of the world's human and economic resources for armaments;

jointly declare:

1. That their united action, pledged for the prosecution of the war against their respective enemies, will be continued for the organization and maintenance of peace and security.

2. That those of them at war with a common enemy will act together in all matters relating to the surrender and disarmament of that enemy.

3. That they will take all measures deemed by them to be necessary to provide against any violation of the terms imposed upon the enemy.

4. That they recognize the necessity of establishing at the earliest practicable date a general international organization, based on the principle of the sovereign equality of all peace-loving states, and open to membership by all such states, large and small, for the maintenance of international peace and security. [5]

That part of the Declaration contemplating the "establishing at the earliest practicable date" of a general international organization was incorporated into the Connally Resolution, which was passed by the Senate on November 6, 1943. At last the Congress was on record; it would be far more difficult for them, at the war's end, to reject U.S. participation in the world organization as they had done in 1919.

Even after the signing of the Moscow Declaration and passage of the Connally Resolution, efforts to increase public support for the forthcoming world organization did not slacken. For example, in November the St. Louis *Star-Times* requested the Commission to Study the Organization of Peace to prepare a series of articles for publication in its columns. The managing editor, R. M. Blagden, received a congratulatory telegram from President Roosevelt on December 11, 1943:

I am delighted to hear that the St. Louis *Star-Times* is to begin publication of a series of articles presenting discussion of many of the pertinent questions which arise when men and women talk about "Winning the Peace." The fullest and frankest examination of the manifold issues involved is necessary if we are to have a sound public opinion. Only an informed public opinion can give us the guidance we must have in determining the issues which you are throwing open to discussion.

There were twenty-three articles in the series. Among the contributors were Philip C. Jessup, Elbert D. Thomas, John Foster Dulles, Frank G. Boudreau, and Professor Quincy Wright.

5. *In Quest of Peace and Security, op. cit.,* p. 9.

The resolutions that have been referred to, the Moscow Declaration, and my interview with the President of October 25, 1943, all dealt with the political side of the new world organization. Meanwhile, however, important steps were being taken to create United Nations machinery in the economic and social fields. The improved military situation and the anticipation of the end of the war, with victory for the allies, prompted the planning of autonomous non-political agencies of the United Nations. The first international conference with this objective was the United Nations Conference on Food and Agriculture held at Hot Springs, Virginia, in May 1943. It led to the establishment of the United Nations Food and Agriculture Organization, which has grown to become one of the most important parts of the United Nations family.

Dr. Frank G. Boudreau, president of the League of Nations Association, and director of the health program of the League of Nations for many years, was one of the leading officials of the conference. In a restricted memorandum dated June 22, 1943, Dr. Boudreau wrote:

The Governments or authorities of forty-four countries, nine of them occupied by enemy forces, took part in this Conference, which was unique in several respects. It was the first United Nations Conference in wartime dealing with postwar problems. In contrast to the last war when the issues preoccupying men's minds were mainly political: reparations, security against aggression, peaceful settlement of disputes, arbitration; this first wartime Conference on postwar issues was focused on the needs and aspirations of the common man.

June 10, 1943, was the date of another important event. On that day the representatives of the United States to the United Nations presented an agreement for the establishment of an international relief organization in which all of the United Nations would participate. On November 9, representatives of the United Nations and associated states—then forty-four in number—assembled in the White House in Washington and signed the agreement establishing the United Nations Relief and Rehabilitation Administration (UNRRA). Two days later, on November 11, the Council of UNRRA held its first session in Atlantic City, New Jersey. The former governor of New York, Herbert H. Lehman, was elected Director-General and assumed his office.

The conference at Atlantic City was attended by representatives of a number of national organizations, and was policed by international "huissiers," the forerunners of the security guards at United Nations headquarters today. The conference also had a profound effect on Atlantic City itself: it marked the first time the city let down the barriers against "colored people" being admitted to boardwalk hotels.

15

Talks with President Roosevelt

President Roosevelt was the only statesman who could call a conference to write the United Nations Charter before hostilities ceased. The choice was naturally limited to one of the Big Four. In a talk I had with the President on October 11, 1944, he said in strictest confidence that he found Churchill very meagerly prepared on the subject of postwar planning. I remarked that I was not surprised, mentioning my 1941 luncheon with Churchill in London, when the prime minister had said that he was too old to have anything to do with postwar planning, that it would be the job for Franklin Roosevelt. I asked the President if Foreign Minister Anthony Eden were not better prepared on the subject than Churchill. He said, yes, and if Eden were prime minister he would be much freer, for as foreign minister he was held down by some of the conservatives in the British Foreign Office. Stalin could not call the conference because his only concern was military arrangements between the great powers. And it would have been unthinkable for Chiang Kai-shek to call it.

In that interview I also asked the President about timing. When would the full-dress conference be held? When would he submit the matter to the Senate? He said he did not think the conference could come before early 1945. Secretary of State

Stettinius wanted it sooner, but the President did not think this was possible. First a preliminary conference of all the United Nations would have to be called. If it went well, then it would be considered the final conference. If trouble developed, the participants would be protected by having called it a preliminary conference.

The President did not think it was possible to submit the plans for the conference to the Senate before the next summer. I said I hoped it could be done much more quickly because it was necessary to avoid postwar domestic reactions that might defeat the plan in Congress. However, the war did not move as rapidly toward victory as we had anticipated in this conversation. When the conference opened in San Francisco on April 25, 1945, the war in Europe was to continue for some weeks and the war in the Pacific would go on for several months.

My first visit with President Roosevelt had taken place at Hyde Park in 1936. My final visit with him was the one to which I have just referred, at the White House in 1944. In this chapter I wish to confine my observations entirely to my talks with the President and to the memoranda I sent him during that period. Perhaps I may have caught some moods that otherwise might have been missed. In any case, our talks let me see the evolution of his views on international organization from initial doubts to his final decision to call the conference of the United Nations months before the war could end.

Unfortunately, I do not have notes on my first visit with the President. In a letter to him dated August 12, 1936, however, I refer to my conversation with him on the previous Friday, saying that I was taking advantage of his willingness to have me write a memorandum on our talk. Apparently we had discussed the extremes of fascism and communism, for my letter includes the statement, "It is true that the issue of peace and war has been crowded into the background by the struggle between two extremes—Fascim and Communism," and some discussion of this subject.

The letter goes on to say,

Now for the question of world cooperation. If war comes we want to stay out of it, but as long as there is a shred of hope that world cooperation can preserve peace we must cooperate to preserve it. When one considers the outlawry of war, through the Kellogg Pact, the rapid development of the machinery of the League, the Court and the International Labor Organization, it seems clear that in fifteen years there has been more tangible progress toward a community of nations than had been made in centuries. This is a period comparable, on a much greater scale, to the critical period of American history when one could not tell from hour to hour whether the colonists would lose the liberty that they had won or would succeed in creating a union. I am not so sure that the smaller states and some others would permit certain statesmen to let the League die. Even if for the moment the League should become a shell it must be kept alive as a symbol for us to rally people around. If it is snuffed out, the light of hope has been extinguished.

This conversation took place in the midst of the 1936 political campaign, which the President was enjoying. I recall his remarking that political figures might not stay on top very long. He referred to Wisconsin's Governor Julius Heil, an honest old fellow whom the citizens nicknamed "Julius the Just." "Two years from now," the President said, "he'll be just Julius." The President was right. By 1938 the governor had faded from the political scene.

My second visit with the President was on July 8, 1937. We began by discussing the address he had given at Chautauqua Lake, New York, on August 14, 1936.[1] The President said that

1. In that speech the President said, "No matter how well we are supported by neutrality legislation, we must remember that no laws can be provided to cover every contingency. . . ." And he concluded with the following warning: "Of all the Nations of the world today we are in many ways most singularly

the speech had been widely quoted in England, France, and other democracies, but not in Germany, Italy, Poland, and Hungary. He added that he had tried to announce the same doctrine in Buenos Aires and elsewhere.

I then remarked that the weakness of the present situation was due to the fact that the collective ideal of the League of Nations had been weakened, first by the refusal of the United States to join, with which he agreed, and next by the defection of a few member nations. Fundamentally, our problem was to reestablish the moral and physical solidarity of nations that wanted peace. I described my long-time interest in the League, to which he remarked that he too had been in favor of it and for three years after the United States refused to join had had people throughout the country agitating for it. He added that the League of Nations Association had held meetings in Poughkeepsie, New York, which he had attended, but that they were always for the converted, for a small circle, and that no effort had been made to reach the masses of the people with the truth about the League.

I told him that I was devoting all of my time to the cause of the League, but on the very broadest basis. I regarded the League as the first machinery of the collective ideal. While the Covenant should be greatly revised, while many things should be done to reorganize and strengthen the League, nevertheless it represented an ideal which must triumph. He agreed, adding that its name might even be changed.

The President then turned the conversation to the reasons for the League's failure. He thought the League failed primarily

blessed. Our closest neighbors are good neighbors. If there are remoter Nations that wish us not good but ill, they know that we are strong; they know that we can and will defend ourselves and defend our neighborhood"—*The Public Papers and Addresses of Franklin D. Roosevelt, Volume Five—The People Approve, 1936,* compiled and collated by Samuel I. Rosenman (New York: Random House, 1938), pp. 291–292.

because it dealt with situations *after* they had become *faits accomplis.* For example, he said, shortly before the Italian invasion of Ethiopia, he had been about to sail on a cruise. Before departing he had given Secretary Hull a neutrality proclamation, which was to go into effect the moment a state of war existed. When he was in Mexican waters, Secretary Hull cabled that press announcements in Rome reported that the Italian army was 15 miles inside Ethiopian territory. Whereupon the neutrality proclamation was issued. But, the President said, "What did the League do? It argued for weeks and didn't do a damn thing about it." Obviously this was an overstatement, for the President certainly knew that sanctions had been invoked by the League under Anthony Eden's leadership—unfortunately, the nations abandoned the sanctions when they were beginning to work. But throughout these interviews the President's disillusionment with the League was evident, although he repeated several times that he had supported the organization as vice presidential candidate in 1920.

In this conversation the President also gave me his definition of aggression: the aggressor was the nation whose troops were found on someone else's territory. Then, after stating that our discussion was off the record, he added that he had been doing considerable thinking on the question of armaments. In the early days man could only kill at a distance of 5 feet, slightly more than the length of his arm. Later, with crude weapons of warfare, he could kill at a distance of 50 feet. Even as late as the Civil War, only 3 percent of the people killed were killed by cannon. But though now man could kill at a distance of miles, if only tanks, gas, long-range artillery, and bombing planes were abolished, a nation could still defend itself with wire, rifles, and machine guns. Switzerland, with 100,000 men armed with machine guns, could hold off a German army of millions limited to the same weapons. In other words, if armaments were limited to what a man could carry on his back, we would have a new approach to the disarmament problem and each nation could protect itself from invasion.

I remarked that such a proposal, coupled with his definition of aggression, would go very far, and asked him when he thought he could make it publicly. His response was, "Would it be possible to acquaint the German and Italian people with the proposal?" Of course, he said, Hitler and Mussolini would know. I replied that the people in those countries couldn't know immediately, but that the overwhelming weight of the nations that did know and accept the principle would count for something. Later on in the interview he stated the same proposition, that if most of the nations agreed to a principle, only a few could hold out against it very long.

I also said that possibly the pendulum would swing back to the moral consciousness of the collective system, in which case men and nations would be ready to accept its ideals. He added that the increasing economic difficulties of the dictator states, particularly Germany, might have their effect. I told the President I thought he was probably the one who could give the pendulum the push in the right direction, but he said he did not want to make a speech now, that he could only do it when the right moment came.

We then discussed the question of supervision in any arms limitation agreement. The United States, the President said, could say to Great Britain: You don't trust Germany's respecting this agreement; the United States is neutral, so let the United States inspect British and German arms and be perfectly willing that one of them inspect American arms to see how the United States is living up to the agreement. I asked him whether he would object to the League doing the inspecting, to which he replied that he didn't give a damn who did it, quite all right if the League wanted to.

I noted that military disarmament and economic disarmament must be approached together, and he agreed heartily. He added that Paul Van Zeeland, prime minister of Belgium, insisted that the nations could go ahead with economic agreements now, but that he had replied that it was absolutely wrong to think we could go very far along economic lines unless there was military disarmament at the same time. What would be the use of finding raw materials for Germany, as we seemed fairly willing to do through British and French colonies, through South America, and through the United States, if they were simply to be used for arms to make war?

The nations should apply his simple definition of aggression, the President continued. Then, if one nation was bent on making war, we would not use sanctions against it but a blockade. The possibilities of blockades had not been thoroughly thought out, he believed. For example, if Japan made war, we could blockade her from certain points in the Pacific and the French from certain other points.

I said that despite the agitation for neutrality, I thought that the American people would support strong action if they knew it would work, and agreed that the most important sanction was to prevent a nation from trading. In conclusion, the President said that anything I could do along this line (meaning, I presumed, the development of public opinion) would be helpful.

I have given practically this entire interview with President Roosevelt because it represents a good example of how he thought his way through international problems: he liked to talk them out with visitors whom he trusted. Before leaving I asked the President if I could submit a memorandum, and whether he would see it. He said, certainly, he would be delighted, he wished I would. The memorandum, dated July 17, 1937, is included here in its entirety:

My dear Mr. President:

Despite growing threats of war I maintain my confidence in the future because the ills of the world come not so much from human pathology as from a tremendous concentration of problems. Within the past four hundred years there has been greater development of science and industry than in all previous centuries and within the past hundred years the world population has doubled. We are challenged to develop the social techniques to meet the human problems resulting from this sudden development.

I am much impressed by the similarity between your program for the United States and the planning necessary for a peaceful world. The United States reached the end of the pioneer period at the same time that the world reached the end of the colonial period. Someone said that modern history began with the Spanish discovery of precious metals in the new world and ended with oil gushers of Texas and Mesopotamia. In that brief time most of the land of the world was settled and its existing sources of raw materials made known.

Your administration was the first to recognize that the American pioneer period had passed, that the great fortunes made upon our natural resources were not to be duplicated and that if we are to enjoy our heritage and democracy we must conserve these resources, provide for social welfare, and plan our future.

May I express my observation that one of the most effective addresses you could make on the subject of world peace would be to demonstrate that the same problems exist for the world—that the time has come to organize and plan international life, particularly in the economic field. Naturally, it is not going to be easy for Americans, British and French to recognize the internationalization of economic life that will be necessary to provide social justice for others. It is difficult for Japanese, Germans and Italians to realize that the period of colonial expansion has passed and consequently they must look . . . to cooperation [for their raw materials,] rather than to conquest.

Another reason for optimism, despite threats of war, is to be found in the fact that within the past few years, possibly months, there has been more realization of the truth of the world situation and efforts to face it than in previous history. I cite as evidence the pronouncements of yourself and Secretary Hull which link economic and world peace, the successful work of the International Labor Organization, the present Conference on Peaceful Change, the League Committee on Raw

Materials whose work though as yet inconclusive is significant itself, and the speeches of other statesmen such as that of M. Blum on January 14th. Truth will prevail once it has been pronounced and understood by enough people. If so, the present threats to peace by war lords and dictators need not be fatal.

I should like to make another observation which I know is in harmony with your thinking. The phenomenon of the postwar period is the feeling of world consciousness which grew out of the sudden realization that problems had become worldwide. Consequently nations outlawed war and established machinery for the adjustment of difficulties in practically every phase of human life from economics to opium. They even went so far as to believe they could coerce aggressors. International helpfulness and idealism began to appear, a by-product of community life.

The fundamental difficulty of the present moment is that the collective ideal has been dimmed. Nations are returning to a piecemeal and nationalistic solution of their problems. The refusal of the United States to join the League of Nations was the first blow. Dictators have not respected it. The statesmen of other democracies have been cowardly.

I presume that the task of all of us is to say and do everything possible to revive the faith in the collective ideal. In many instances your administration has lifted its voice in support of this concept. The Buenos Aires treaties added that moral solidarity for the new world without lessening the allegiance of the part of the whole. The reciprocal trade program which insists on equality of treatment, our membership in the International Labor Organization, and participation in the financial work of the League, all add to the collective ideal in the economic sense. You have spoken out in support of world democracy.

The situation is terribly confused today but I hope as you have intimated the time will come when a dramatic statement on your part to the world will not have the effect of "simply another speech" but will lead the world on the upward path. It may be that the Chinese-Japanese situation, if it does not result in world war, will return to cooperation for the solution of the world's problems.

As you have frequently pointed out the danger comes from surprisingly few dictators and war lords who do not rule more than fifteen per

cent of the people. The Latin American countries, the British dominions, the northern European states, as well as the liberal government
of France, await leadership. I see hope in the unity that has been
developed among the smaller northern European countries so that
they present a bloc with power as well as ideals.

When the moment comes the challenge must of necessity be stated
as simply and as comprehensively as possible. May I be so bold as to
suggest that the following points, most of which you have mentioned,
would be comprehensive.

1. Acceptance of your definition of aggressor, as the nation whose
   troops are found on the territory of another.

2. The principle of consultation under the Pact of Paris, agreed to
   at Buenos Aires, extended to all of the nations of the world.

3. Military disarmament by accepting the principle of reduction to
   the point of arms for defense only, arms limited to what a man
   "may carry on his back." Inspection as a corollary to the arms
   agreements.

4. Securing of world economic and social justice by providing equality of access to raw materials, reduction of barriers to trade and
   solution of currency problems so nations may have the means of
   exchange to purchase raw materials.

5. The above point involves fulfilling obligations under the International Labor Organization and creating boards of planning and
   strategy.

As a matter of fact, inspection, commissions on economics, the
I.L.O., etc., are or would be to a great extent activities of the League
of Nations. These, plus consultation, would lend the moral force of the
United States to an evolving League and would make unnecessary the
facing of the problem of ratification of the Covenant, at the moment.

The American people accepted the principle of consultation under
the Pact of Paris at Buenos Aires without hesitation. There would be
little objection to its extension to the rest of the world. Once the world
had accepted your principles, the denial of trade to the aggressor
would be accepted by the American people. Instead of sanctions being

voted piecemeal, they would take the form of a denial of the economic benefits of the more nearly just international society to the nation that would make war.

I am as certain as anything in the world that before your administration is over, barring an international catastrophe, the opportunity will come for you to give a clear and comprehensive pronouncement which all the world will be ready to follow.

There is at least one way in which I think some of us shall be able to develop helpful public opinion now. Certainly the American people want peace overwhelmingly, but the trouble is that they have not thought through the policies necessary to have it. They are still reluctant to believe that peace must be upon an international basis. The organizations of the National Peace Conference, whose director is Walter Van Kirk, have accepted my suggestion that from October 1st of this year to January 1st, 1939, irrespective of other emphases, they will concentrate upon a joint program of world economic cooperation. I enclose a brief statement of principles for this campaign which I shall direct. We mean to carry it on through the press, radio, local communities, and through such occupational groups as business, labor and farmers. We hope to talk less to the small informed circle but to reach many people.

I should like, later on, to make more detailed comment on some of the specific points contained in this memorandum and to indicate other ways in which some of us might be helpful in the development of public opinion.

On July 28 I received a note from the President, saying:

I am grateful for your comprehensive memorandum, enclosed with your letter of July seventeenth, which analyzes in so interesting a light the present complex international situation. I shall welcome an elaboration of the points which you have set forth in your notes.

My next visit with the President, on June 9, 1938, on the eve of my departure for Europe to attend the annual meeting of the International Federation of League of Nations Societies, is largely recounted in Chapter 6. As noted there, I told him why

I was going to Europe and we discussed the merits of automatic membership in the League. More or less off the top of his head, the President then speculated on what other revisions could be made in the League's Charter. He said that he believed the Council should be abolished. "Does that mean you would simply have one body?" I asked. His answer was, yes, the interim business could be handled by commissions. The Assembly should meet four times a year; one time, as now, when decisions were taken, and three times for conferences and discussions without decisions.

The President said he would also initiate the secret ballot, pointing out that just because Chile and the Argentine were close together in the Western Hemisphere, there was no reason why they must vote together in Geneva. I had seen small states put unmercifully on the spot by the open ballot in League votes, and remarked that, with the secret ballot, fifty or fifty-five states would probably vote for sanctions against aggressors, and public opinion would thereby be mobilized.

After some further discussion our conversation was interrupted (see Chapter 6) and, as it turned out, I did not see the President again for more than a year. Although he had asked me to report to him on my trip to Copenhagen, he was unable to see me before I returned once more to Europe on September 1.

I next saw the President on Thursday, September 7, 1939. The White House seemed to be a different sort of place, with a new alertness now that war had broken out, even though the United States was not a belligerent. This interview was largely consumed by a discussion of the Neutrality Act, and has therefore been reported virtually in full in Chapter 8. However, just before it was time for me to leave—indeed, long past time: the President was by then an hour behind his schedule; Henry Wallace had come in for lunch, and there were many other people waiting—the President speculated a little bit on the nature of peace if the right side won. He would like to see a Europe, he said, in which every fragment of nationality, every portion of Germany, had its political independence, with trade barriers abolished and with a European police system. Without saying so he was proposing, more or less, the idea of an economic united states of Europe with police protection, but with political independence for every portion, even Austria, and the small German states, if they wished to assume such a status.

Although I met with the President several times in the intervening months, my next extensive interview was on November 13, 1942, after a meeting of the Welles Committee.

I had never seen the President in such good form. Everyone around seemed to be in good humor. My appointment was for twelve o'clock, but it was 12:35 when I was ushered into the President's office. Admiral William Standley's appointment had preceded mine and I heard him and the President laughing heartily. After the usual pleasantries, I told the President that there were many things I would like to say about the great victories he had won but they were too great to describe. The President replied, "Well, things do seem to be going rather well, don't they?" He went on to say that what he had to put up with in the world situation at the moment, even on the civilian side, was very difficult, and it was a good thing he had a sense of humor—negotiating with the Free French was particularly taxing.

The President then turned to the subject of the United Nations, telling me his general plan for the future. He said he was going to be tough and that the approach had to be that of a dictator. He did not mean himself or an individual, and quickly explained that he meant that the four great powers, the United States, Great Britain, the USSR, and China, were going to police and disarm the world. Without being able to quote his exact language, I gathered he meant there would not be time for a great deal of sentiment in the immediate postwar world, that disarmament and the reorganization of the world would be a tough job. Germany must be thoroughly disarmed; we must destroy every gun, with inspectors everywhere to see it done. Factories must also stop making the machine tools and the materials of war. Inspectors must see to it. Secretary of the Treasury Henry Morgenthau had told him that one of these days we would have to give Germany some economic help, with raw materials and so on. The President said that he agreed with this view and felt that German factories, denied the right to make material for rearmament, could turn to peacetime activities and keep the Germans at work.

The President also indicated that he favored complete disarmament for the rest of the world, including the French. Striking a pose, he imitated a Frenchman saying, "Do you mean that we must disarm? How are we going to protect our empire?" Our reply would be that if Germany was disarmed, France did not need arms, and as for the empire, we (the four great powers) would protect it for them. The President said that Churchill kept asking, But can we trust Russia? To which the President would answer, We have got to trust someone and, realistically, who else is going to disarm Germany anyway? The President then made a statement that he had made to me on another occasion, that during the depression the national deficit had been equal to the sum of expenditure on armaments in each country. It is clear that he anticipated thorough disarmament for all nations except the big four, whom he referred to as the four big policemen.

He then went on to talk about the League of Nations. He started out by saying he didn't know just how to break up the old League of Nations. I didn't know just what he meant—was he considering abolishing the League? Fortunately, an interruption occurred—his secretary came in with a letter for him to sign—which gave me time to catch my breath. "You were saying, Mr. President, how you were going to decentralize the League," I said after the secretary had left. I had correctly sensed his meaning. The President thought the various autonomous organizations of the League might well be scattered throughout the world. The ILO, which had done and was doing a very good job, could return to Geneva, but the health organization might be located in some high land north of Panama. There were excellent doctors in Latin America, but very few hospitals or training facilities, and doctors could be trained at the League health center. With air transportation it would be no harder to get there than any place else. The department of agriculture in Rome had been no good. I noted that it had been simply a place where some stuffed aristocracy could be placed on Mussolini's payroll. When the President suggested the agriculture organization might be located in the United States, I jokingly proposed we put it in Des Moines to please Henry (Wallace).

The President said he had not thought through what to do with the machinery for the adjustment of disputes—that it might well go to The Hague, to make use of the old buildings there, although of course under different conditions. This gave me a chance to say that if the four policemen were going to compel disarmament they would also have to have the authority to settle disputes, that there could be no choice; the nations must be forced to renounce war and to settle their disputes peacefully. I saw this as an opportunity to drive home the point that disarmament must be linked with international justice.

At this point I brought up my belief that there must be universal membership in the international organization. I made my usual speech to the effect that the mistake of the League had been that it was a club to which a nation could be admitted, in which it could be blackballed, or from which it could withdraw. The very idea that a nation could withdraw from its obligations to the world community seemed to me fantastic. The President, however, was not interested in pursuing the subject, and the discussion veered to his own idea, first enunciated in 1937, for quarantining aggressors. He maintained that if any nations objected he would say it was just too bad, that we could make a quarantine very effective. He added that he didn't mind the Association sending up some trial balloons, providing they were never pinned to him. I said this was what we wanted to do.

I then made the observation that his four big policemen and the various pieces of machinery that he had in mind must be set up before hostilities ceased. Nations cooperate only when cooperation is absolutely necessary, when it is fatal if they do not. By getting the organizing done while the situation was still desperate enough, we could avoid the tragedy of Woodrow Wilson. The President agreed.

He then surprised me by saying he had made two mistakes in the international field. One was not supporting the Spanish Loyalists with arms, material, and so on. He had been dissuaded by Neville Chamberlain, the French, and the League itself. The second was not supporting the Ethiopians against the Italians. Here again, he had been dissuaded by the same forces. The President emphasized these two mistakes several times, saying that he should have gone through with his support of the Spanish Loyalists and the Ethiopians despite the British, the French, and the League. I replied, "But don't you see, Mr. President, that because the United States did not belong to the League you were not in a position to take the leadership and force others to follow you?" He concurred readily.

My time was running short, and I still wanted the President to tell me how we could help. Not only was it necessary for the agencies of the new League to be set up while the war was going on, but the peace could be lost in the minds of the people before the war was won. I was assuming that the war might be over in a year or a year and a half and we would have just a year

in which to do a job ten times greater than that of the old
League to Enforce Peace.[2] I had had an understanding with the
President's secretary when I went in that I would not look at
the clock. I did not want to be worried about the length of time
I was taking; I wanted to take advantage of every minute. Unless the President dismissed me, I would stay until the secretary
interrupted. The secretary assured me that if the President
wanted me to stay, he would so indicate. This he now did,
waving his hand and saying, "Two minutes more," when the
secretary interrupted us. I saw that I would have to talk fast if
I were to make the most important points I wanted to make. It
was a common legend in Washington that if the President did
not want to answer your questions he talked so well and so
charmingly you didn't get a word in unless you interrupted, and
that was difficult. He was telling me so many important things;
he was revealing so clearly his thinking on the future world
organization, that I felt it was important to get as much as I
could.

I said I wanted to ask him a question about organization. I told
him I had assumed when he had brought the nations together
in the signing of the Declaration of the United Nations on January 1, 1942, that he had intended, when the time came, to
proclaim the United Nations of the World. He did not demur,
and thus encouraged, I went on to say that I did not think we
could rouse public opinion adequately under the name
"League of Nations Association." Instead I was tempted to suggest that we use the machinery of the League of Nations Association and the Commission to Study the Organization of Peace,
which together had twenty-five offices and a considerable out-

2. The League to Enforce Peace had been organized in 1915 by a group of
notable men, including Hamilton Holt, A. Lawrence Lowell, and William Howard Taft. Following the presidential election of 1920, its income declined to the
zero point and it became inactive in April 1922. The League of Nations Non-
Partisan Association, organized in 1923, was in a sense a successor to the League
to Enforce Peace.

reach throughout the country, under the name "United Nations Association." He said he thought this a good idea and agreed that I should recommend it to our board meeting on Saturday.[3]

On rising, I said that I hoped he liked to travel. He paused for a moment, startled perhaps, and asked me why. I said, because as President of the United Nations of the World, he was going to have to do a devil of a lot of traveling, visiting those autonomous organizations that he was going to set up in decentralizing the League. He laughed. He would be too old, he said, and he was going back to Hyde Park to raise Christmas trees. I told him I thought he was the only person in the world who could hold the United Nations together to do the police job required and to organize the future. His mood suddenly changed. He said something like, well, perhaps for two years. It was rather an aside, and completely up in the air, but his remark left me with the impression that he might be willing to devote two years or so to the great world job.

During this interview an incident occurred which, while disturbing, was for me an illustration of the President's extraordinary determination. When I came in, the President had given me a cigarette and lighted it for me. His own he put in the famous holder. As he was waving his arm to make a point, the cigarette fell out of the holder and onto the rug between his feet. I wanted to pick it up for him, but he would not permit it, and reached down to pick it up himself. This meant reaching over those matchstick legs, and the braces. It was a slow and painful exercise for him and a painful one for me to watch, although as his secretary pointed out afterwards, I could have done nothing else.

3. Despite the President's support for the idea, the name of the League of Nations Association was not changed at this time, although, as indicated in Chapter 14, the name "United Nations Association" was incorporated by a few of us in Washington to preserve the name "United Nations" from exploiters. The name of the League of Nations Association was changed in 1945 (see Chapter 17).

As always, I was struck by the original and unorthodox way the President had of arriving at sound conclusions. He had thought through the question of disarmament quite thoroughly. He had also grasped the necessity of autonomous international organizations, although he had not considered the relationship between the League and the Court, between the settlement of disputes and the rendering of juridical decisions.

I could see from this interview that the thinking of our international organization subcommittee (the Welles Committee) was not too different from the President's own views, and that a compromise might well be worked out. Later, I gave Professor Shotwell a full account of this talk, and he was highly pleased. His draft of an international organization was the draft which was being used as the basis of discussion in the committee, and it included a series of highly autonomous international organizations. Many of the members of the committee, including Sumner Welles, had felt that he was planning on too high a degree of autonomy. Thus Professor Shotwell was gratified that his plan was in keeping with the President's thinking, that in fact the President was thinking of even more autonomy than he was.

I had another visit with the President on October 25, 1943, the first part of which, a discussion of the congressional resolutions on international organization, I have referred to in Chapter 14. The discussion then turned to the future world organization. I mentioned a series of ads that had been run by David Lawrence, editor of *U.S. News and World Report,* a few weeks earlier promoting a return to the League of Nations. The President had not seen them. I said that a few LNA board members would probably say that I had let others such as Lawrence do what the Association should be doing, that is, push a return to the League rather than promote formation of a new "United Nations" organization. But I felt the overwhelming majority of

LNA members would support our UN orientation. The new world organization should grow out of the United Nations alliance, although League machinery, such as the ILO and the Court, should be used very widely. After all, some 500 international treaties were tied in in some way with the League of Nations. The President agreed that the League had very important machinery that should be used, and went on to give me his current views on the world organization.

He now felt that the Assembly should meet around, in different places each year—somewhere in South America, London, Washington, and somewhere in Africa and Asia. He said he had told Sumner Welles he was not in favor of going back to Geneva. It was not the League's fault, but Geneva was associated with failure. I said I could give a better reason for not returning to Geneva—Swiss neutrality.

The President repeated his view that the Assembly should meet once a year, when there should be a full debate and authority would be given to the Executive Council. I asked him if he thought the four big powers should be permanent members of the Executive Council. He replied, "For a while, then others." I asked about sending up trial balloons on the idea of an international police force, but he said it would be better to refer to the "four big policemen" who could settle disputes with the help of others. This would be his procedure.

I suggested that the Executive Council should be located in a permanent place, but he was opposed. It must meet around, like the Assembly, with the delegates' affairs kept "under their hats." Later he agreed that there should be a small permanent Secretariat for the Council somewhere, as I pointed out, if the delegates were to keep their affairs under their hats, they would need a large staff for technical work.

Clearly, the President disliked the idea of headquarters. On January 7, 1944, I sent him an outline prepared by the Commission to Study the Organization of Peace, giving details of our views on the structure of the international organization. Part of our plan struck the President as wrong. He wrote, on January 11,

That is an interesting outline of a general international organization.

I don't like the idea of a central headquarters for the United Nations. They could and should meet in a different place—possibly a different continent each year. All they need is a storage warehouse for records —most of them obsolete.

I would not say anything at this moment about a United Nations' air force made up of voluntary enlistments. Such a thing might come later on—especially if everybody spoke basic English!

Otherwise, I think you are moving distinctly along the right lines.

Nevertheless, there are hints in our interview of October 1943 that he recognized the necessity for a United Nations headquarters—for example, in his statement that there should be no "return to Geneva"—even if the Assembly meetings were to be held in different places. For my part, having seen the paper work at the United Nations grow—having seen the documentation submitted in 5 languages by representatives of close to 150 states pile up—I can now sympathize with one sentence of his memorandum: "All they need is a storage warehouse for records—most of them obsolete."

On October 11, 1944, the President and I met again. This was in the midst of the election campaign. The Dumbarton Oaks Proposals had been announced on October 7, and the San Francisco Conference was soon to be announced in Yalta. It was only a few months before his death.

When I went in to see him I was warned to take only five minutes because a delegation of Poles was waiting. The President said that he thought he already had some knowledge of the Polish-Russian situation, but I said that the delegation was waiting for him and he was going to have to listen to some Poles whether he wanted to or not. He said he could not tell on which side of a frontier some little village would be, but he believed that part of East Poland would go to the Soviet Union and part of East Germany to Poland. I reminded him that the Curzon Line had been accepted as a just line twenty years ago; he countered by saying a Pole had remarked to him recently that if the Poles had control of any area for two generations, they would make it Polish because of their high birth rate. He said he believed that Stalin wanted a strong Poland; that it was to Stalin's interest to have a strong Poland.

Despite the presence of the waiting delegation, the President gave me thirty minutes. No matter how pressed he was, he had the time to think of our organizations and how we were getting along financially. I explained that for tax reasons we had kept two organizations. The political action work was being undertaken by Americans United for World Organization, which had been recently created for that particular purpose, and the educational work by the League of Nations Association and the Commission, which now of course would use the United Nations name.

The President then talked about his forthcoming Foreign Policy Association speech, to be given on October 21. He said he was going to speak on ideals. I was glad to hear this, for in order to avoid Woodrow Wilson's mistake of giving the issue of world organization too rarefied an air of idealism, we had gone to the other extreme and had put discussion of the subject in the most realistic terms. Now that we were assured of the success of the Dumbarton Oaks Conference, the President could make a speech that would elevate the discussion halfway up the scale of Wilson's idealism.

We then took up the subject of Dumbarton Oaks, whose Proposals were better than the League Covenant, in my opinion. He agreed with this, and went on to state that the Russians were adamant on the point of having a veto when they were party to a dispute. Someone had given him pause the other day, he said, by asking whether, if Mexico acted up, we would be willing to have the dispute settled without our having anything to say about it. I asked him if he had a solution or if that was too much to expect. He replied that he would like to put in the Charter of Dumbarton Oaks an agreement that no nation would attempt to change its frontiers at the expense of another. He thought that might reduce the Russian fear of invasion. I realized he would have to compromise, but I hoped the compromise could maintain the moral position that the four large states were not above the law which they expected others to respect.

He said of course Stalin might show up one of these days with sixteen ambassadors to Washington. I asked if Stalin was asking for sixteen seats in the Assembly. The President grinned and nodded his head, yes, but he wasn't worried about that because he could counter with forty-eight states from the American Union and numerous states from Brazil. He said he could kid Stalin about that one.

The President next took up the election campaign, reminding me that Belle Roosevelt—the wife of Kermit Roosevelt, the only one of Theodore Roosevelt's sons to support him—had made a speech for him a few days earlier and had organized the Servicemen's Wives for Roosevelt. I told him that I had suggested to Clochette Roosevelt Palfrey, Belle Roosevelt's daughter, that after they had reelected Roosevelt they should keep their organization together to call on senators and insist that they vote right to win the peace. He said that was good. But, he said, "I may not be the next President." He thought the race would be very close; I told him I thought that nevertheless he would win by a large majority of the electoral vote, although his popular majority might be small. (As it turned out, of course, we were both too pessimistic.)

By this time "Pa" Watson, the President's secretary, was popping in and out of the door trying to indicate that my time was up. But as long as the President leaned back in his chair and continued to talk, I paid no attention to Watson.

I said I feared there would be an imperialist race after the end of the war. I knew we had to have control of the Japanese mandated islands, but how could we get control without starting a race for strategic bases? The President said that when he had signed the Atlantic Charter, he had said we did not want more territory and that he was fool enough to mean it and would stand by it in the future. So far there had been no non-national sovereignty, but now was the time for it. The President was playing with the idea of United Nations sovereignty. Let the United States control only the military installations on the Pacific islands. Except for those, let us use the word "trusteeship." He emphasized that he was not using the word "mandate," that by "trusteeship" he meant something quite different. The United States would be a trustee on behalf of a sovereign United Nations. The President was even experimenting with ideas for a United Nations flag. He said the Russians had had a very popular play recently called *The Rainbow,* and he thought that the flag might have a rainbow on it. He had some artists working on the matter.

The subject of trusteeship was very close to me because as a member of the Welles Committee I had worked on the draft proposal. The President remembered that, and said that in fact trusteeship was one of his pet ideas. Interestingly, when I had joined the Welles Committee I had been surprised that our first task was to draft a plan for trusteeship, and only afterwards a plan for the General International Organization. I could see now that the President and Welles had been talking over the idea of trusteeship long before the Welles Committee was even formed. He said that he had actually talked to de Gaulle about this idea and the general was willing to accept the trusteeship principle for some of the Pacific islands, providing other nations did the same so the French would not be the only ones.

I told the President I hoped he would spring the idea in his speech before the Foreign Policy Association; if he was going to speak on ideals, here was a very practical application of them. He said he thought he would.[4]

There were a few more points I wanted to take up, but now the President nodded to Pa Watson. As I left, he thanked me for coming and said he hoped to see me soon, very soon.

But this proved to be my last visit.

4. He did not, however, mention the idea in his speech, much to my disappointment.

16

Dumbarton Oaks

Dumbarton Oaks is the name of a beautiful estate in the Georgetown section of Washington, D.C. As a term, it has come to stand for the Proposals, drafted and signed there, which preceded the United Nations Charter.

The negotiations leading to Dumbarton Oaks were begun in the spring of 1944, when Secretary of State Cordell Hull, after conferring with various United States senators, felt it was possible to take the next step in writing a United Nations Charter.

Mr. Hull invited the British ambassador, Lord Halifax, and the Soviet ambassador, Andrei Gromyko, to visit his office on May 30, 1944. He told the ambassadors that he was now ready to proceed with informal talks with the representatives of their governments, and asked them to request that their governments fix a date as early as convenient for the conferences. He proposed that China be permitted to take part, although she was not an ally of the Soviet Union. A plan was worked out whereby the American, British, and Soviet delegates would meet first at Dumbarton Oaks; the delegates of the United States, the United Kingdom, and China would meet immediately afterwards. The first ambassadorial meeting lasted from August 21 to September 28, the second from September 29 to October 7.

The announcement of the Dumbarton Oaks Proposals on October 7 was the signal for a vast mobilization of public opinion in their support, for it was anticipated that in the near future a conference of all the United Nations would be held to write a Charter based on the Proposals. Leaders of American public opinion were well aware of the rejection of the League of Nations Covenant by the United States Senate following the First World War. They were determined that history should not repeat itself with a Senate rejection of a United Nations Charter.

The League of Nations Covenant had not been submitted to the United States Senate or to the people until the end of the First World War. This time things would be different. The Dumbarton Oaks Proposals were thrown open to the public for wide discussion before the end of the Second World War was in sight.

Many organizations and individuals participated in the educational campaign to win support for the projected agreements. Some were devoted exclusively to international relations; some covered domestic fields as well. Some had a long history and had participated in the campaign for the League of Nations. Others were new, and some were ad hoc organizations created for this emergency. The League of Nations Association cooperated more and more with this growing number of organizations. Our long continuous effort had resulted in the existence of many local committees and knowledgeable people supporting the principles of collective security and international community life.

The campaign began even before the Dumbarton Oaks Proposals were announced. On September 28, 1944, a letter from the Commission to Study the Organization of Peace, which I signed, was sent to over fifty national and community-service organizations, inviting them to send representatives to a meeting in New York City, to "help plan a tremendous coordinated campaign of popular education on the purport of the

Dumbarton Oaks agreements. . . . We should devise a general plan, map our strategy, and determine what each of us can best contribute to the common effort." If it seems strange that the letter from the Commission was sent on September 28, whereas the Dumbarton Oaks Proposals were not announced until October 7, it should be noted that much news about them had appeared from many sources, including James Reston in *The New York Times.*

The first meeting of delegates from more than forty national organizations was convened on October 6, 1944, in the Woodrow Wilson Library.

Most of the representatives expressed their favorable interest in a cooperative campaign. Robert Norton, speaking for the American Legion, indicated that the Legion "program was hospitable to this action campaign," and quoted the Legion's recent statement on international cooperation. John Conners of the American Federation of Labor said he could promise his organization would distribute literature and reach the labor press, but that he could make no commitments for the CIO. Walter Van Kirk, Federal Council of Churches of Christ in America, believed that the more than seventy-five religious publications throughout the country would welcome material on Dumbarton Oaks. He promised that World Order Sunday on November 11 would stress the Proposals. Father Edward A. Conway of the Catholic Association for International Peace recommended the preparing of canned sermons for the busy clergy. Mrs. William Dick Sporborg of the General Federation of Women's Clubs guaranteed to reach two and one-half million women. . . .[1]

Many different means of popular education were discussed, from simple pamphlets and broadsides, and materials for school use, to radio, comic books, and commercial advertisements. There was no formal organization of the group, but an informal committee was designated to plan a cooperative campaign, and

1. Dorothy B. Robins, *Experiment in Democracy* (New York: The Parkside Press, 1971), p. 41.

the full group agreed to meet again on October 20. Thus we proceeded on an ad hoc basis without being hampered by formal organization.[2]

If the Commission's letter of September 28 was the opening gun in the campaign for the Dumbarton Oaks Proposals, two documents published earlier in 1944 contributed much to the public's thinking about the subject. The first, published in August by the Commission, was entitled *The General International Organization, Its Framework and Functions.* One of its most important features was the statement that "All States abiding by these obligations should have the right to participate in the General International Organization established for security and for economic and social betterment. The General International Organization should be set up immediately by the United Nations with provision for eventual participation in it by all other nations."

The second document bore the title *Design for a Charter of the General International Organization,* and had been published, also in August, by a group of Americans of which Manley O. Hudson, a judge on the World Court, was chairman. Louis B. Sohn, who succeeded him as Bemis professor of international law at Harvard University, was secretary of the group. The *Design* contemplated automatic membership in the future organization, suggesting that it "shall at all times comprise all existing States, and hence no provision should be made for the expulsion or withdrawal of any State."

The Dumbarton Oaks Proposals outlined the framework of the international organization whose final structure was to be determined by representatives of all the United Nations at the

2. Another contribution to the education of the public on this issue was begun by Ernest Minor Hopkins, president of Dartmouth College and chairman of Americans United for World Organization. His and similar efforts reinforced ours.

yet-to-be-announced conference in San Francisco. The Proposals set forth the purposes and principles of the new organization, stating that membership should be open to all "peace-loving" states, and presenting a general structure for the organization, which was to include a General Assembly, a Security Council, and International Court of Justice, and a Secretariat. The Proposals also included specific arrangements for the maintenance of international peace and security, including the prevention and suppression of aggression, and arrangements for international and social cooperation.

In my pamphlet entitled *Proposals for the United Nations Charter—What Was Done at Dumbarton Oaks,*[3] which was issued immediately after the Proposals were made public, there is a section entitled "What Was Postponed for Later Decision." Among those subjects were: the method by which the Security Council would vote, the problems of trusteeship and of strategic bases, the question of a headquarters, the procedure by which the property assets of the League of Nations would be transferred to the United Nations and, finally, the matter of the budget. The Commission to Study the Organization of Peace, along with other organizations, lost no time considering how some of the gaps could be closed. For example, a committee on human rights was set up by the Commission almost immediately after the Dumbarton Oaks Proposals were announced. Their efforts resulted in a statement read over CBS on February 4, 1945, by John W. Davis, advocating, among other things, the creation of a Commission on Human Rights as part of the structure of the world organization.

Also, a number of Commission members engaged in war work in Washington set up a committee on trusteeship and produced a report on both trusteeship and strategic bases. The

3. Clark M. Eichelberger, *Proposals for the United Nations Charter—What Was Done at Dumbarton Oaks,* Commission to Study the Organization of Peace (New York, October 1944).

Commission made a distinction between dependent peoples, who should be the charge of the trusteeship council, and strategic bases in areas where there were few dependent peoples. The latter would come under the purview of the Security Council. This distinction between the two kinds of trusteeship was to find its way into the United Nations Charter.

While these efforts were under way, an attempt was made by a few people and organizations to limit the obligation of the United States to supply troops to the United Nations to put down aggression. These people felt that, without a declaration of war, United States troops should be used only in the Western Hemisphere. To counter this argument, a letter to the editor of *The New York Times* was published November 5, 1944. Signed by John W. Davis, W. W. Grant of Denver, Philip C. Jessup, George Rublee, James T. Shotwell, and Quincy Wright, members of the Commission, it asserted that an American President had the power or could be given the power by ratification of a treaty or an act of Congress to use the armed forces of the United States under the direction of the proposed world Security Council anywhere in the world without a declaration of war. It was supported by an editorial in the *Times*.

The year 1944 was, of course, a presidential election one, but this time the two parties were not divided on the issue of world organization. Both party platforms in general supported the creation of such an organization and United States membership in it. A few isolationists, Gerald L. K. Smith for one, did appear before the platform committees of both parties, but they could find nothing in the platforms of either that could be cited as opposing the creation of the United Nations.

The almost unanimous desire of statesmen and politicians to consider the creation of an international organization including the United States among its principal members was encouraging indeed. Mr. Willkie, Governor Dewey, John Foster Dulles, and other Republican statesmen were actually anxious to register their support, in welcome contrast to the situation in 1918. There were, of course, some questions among Republicans about the State Department's plan for the organization, especially before the publication of the Dumbarton Oaks Proposals. Of particular concern was whether the small states would be adequately protected. As a member of the State Department committee that had prepared the first working draft of the United Nations Charter, I was able to reassure Mr. Willkie, and through him Mr. Dulles and Governor Dewey, on this point, at least.

I appreciated Mr. Willkie's confidence, and we had talked about many things at various times over the years. A few days before his death, I had a telephone call from one of his secretaries, who said that he wanted to see me, but if I went to the information desk at the hospital where he was a patient, I would be turned away. Consequently, I was instructed to come directly to his room, where I was expected. A few hours later, the secretary phoned again to tell me that our previous conversation had been overheard and that therefore I had better postpone my visit for a few days. Unfortunately Mr. Willkie passed away before new arrangements could be made. Many people had been speculating about the possible rivalry or collaboration between President Roosevelt and Wendell Willkie in the postwar world. It was a tragedy indeed that neither man lived to see it, both passing even before the San Francisco Conference and the setting up of the United Nations Organization.

The educational program on behalf of the Dumbarton Oaks Proposals was overshadowed in December 1944 by the military news from the Western front. As Robert Sherwood wrote,

This was certainly a fateful Christmas. The American and British people had been given cause to forget all about political or ideological disputes by the shocking and bewildering news of the German break-through in the Ardennes and the resultant Battle of the Bulge. Three months before it had seemed that Germany might quit at any moment. Now, it seemed that a large part of the triumphant American and British forces in Holland, Belgium and Northern France might be pushed into another Dunkirk. . . .[4]

Furthermore, political crises involving Belgium, Italy, and Greece had resulted in misunderstandings between the United Kingdom and the United States. Consequently Professor Shot-well, together with a few others, including myself, sent a tele-gram to a list of distinguished Americans:

Public reaction to political and diplomatic difficulties may endanger unity for war and peace. A statement of fifty words from you saying steady America, don't play into German hands, back up our fighting men, stressing the need of early creation of the United Nations organi-zation to prevent disintegration would help. Could we have this state-ment within twenty-four hours? Statement will be released as part of symposium leaders of public unity by United Nations Educational Campaign Committee.

Strong replies were received, urging the closest possible unity among the allies and the early creation of the United Nations Organization, and were released to the press.

The President journeyed to Yalta the day after Inauguration Day in January. He returned February 28, 1945. At Yalta the San Francisco Conference was at last announced and the invita-tion issued:

The Government of the United States of America, on behalf of itself and of the Governments of the United Kingdom of Great Britain and Northern Ireland, the Union of Soviet Socialist Republics, and the Republic of China, invites the Government of [name of government] to send representatives to a Conference of the United Nations to be

4. Robert E. Sherwood, *Roosevelt and Hopkins: An Intimate History* (New York: Harper and Brothers, 1948), p. 843.

held on April 25, 1945, at San Francisco in the United States of America to prepare a charter for a general international organization for the maintenance of international peace and security.

The above-named Governments suggest that the Conference consider as affording a basis for such a charter the proposals for the establishment of a general international organization which were made public last October as a result of the Dumbarton Oaks Conference. . . .[5]

Usually, when the President returned from a trip, he took several days to rest and test the climate of opinion before addressing a joint session of Congress. This time, against the advice of some of his official family, he insisted on discussing the Yalta Conference before a joint session of Congress almost immediately upon his return. He spoke on March 1, 1945.

Members of Congress were shocked at the President's appearance. He apologized for sitting down during his speech, referring to the weight of the braces he carried on his legs. His voice lacked the customary ring, and he interrupted his speech to extemporize more than in any other speech he had delivered to Congress. Senator Elbert Thomas of Utah told me that after the President's address, he sought out Vice President Harry Truman and said, "Harry, you better say your prayers."

Shortly after his speech, the President went to Hyde Park for a few days, and then returned to Washington for a grueling round of sessions on international and domestic concerns. He journeyed to Hyde Park again for a few days, and left Washington for Warm Springs, Georgia, on March 29.

Many people have speculated as to what passed through President Roosevelt's mind in those brief days at Warm Springs. That he was preoccupied with the San Francisco Conference, where he hoped to appear on the opening day, April 25, we

5. *The United Nations Conference on International Organization* (Washington, D.C.: Selected Documents, GPO, Department of State Publication 2490, Conference Series 83, 1946), p. 3.

know. He asked officials to give him a railroad itinerary for San Francisco, and worked on plans for some of the logistics of the conference, such as the seating of the delegations.

I believe there may have been moments at Warm Springs when the President had peace of mind. The allies had resumed the offensive in the Western theater of the war. At Yalta the statesmen had agreed on the date of the San Francisco Conference and that the Dumbarton Oaks Proposals would be the basis of the deliberations. The President had often urged that if peace were to be maintained there should be four big policemen, the United States, the United Kingdom, the Soviet Union, and China. While the Dumbarton Oaks Proposals did not speak of these four policemen, they provided that the Security Council, to be composed of eleven states, would give permanent seats and the right of veto to the four great powers and, in due course, to France. Trusteeship, which meant much to the President, as the notes of my conversations with him indicate, was missing from the Dumbarton Oaks draft, but it could be inserted in the Charter at San Francisco.

Possibly the President's mind went back over the years of his presidency, beginning with his first inaugural address when he said, "The only thing we have to fear is fear itself": on March 11 he had prepared a draft of a speech for delivery on Jefferson Day, April 13. He had concluded with the words, "The only limit to our realization of tomorrow will be our doubts of today. Let us move forward with strong and active faith."[6] Whether the President realized that his strength was ebbing rapidly, and that he would not be able to play a role at San Francisco, was never revealed, so far as I know, by anything he said. He died thirteen days before the conference was to open.

One of the first questions asked of the new President after he had taken the oath of office was if the San Francisco Conference

6. *Documents of American History,* edited by Henry Steele Commager, Vol. II (7th ed., New York: Appleton-Century-Crofts, 1963), p. 500.

would open on the date that had been agreed upon. With characteristic directness, President Truman replied that the conference would meet on the date on which Franklin Roosevelt had called it, April 25, 1945.

It was important that President Roosevelt's death not cause a drop in the spirit of anticipation of the opening of the San Francisco Conference. On April 13, the day after the President died, I wrote to the organizations which had cooperated in the Dumbarton Oaks campaign as follows:

The only tribute we can pay worthy of him is to see to it that the world organization is created with American membership just as quickly as possible.

With our great leader gone, there devolves upon all of us a greater responsibility to work harder to compensate somewhat for his loss. Therefore, we will redouble our efforts. We urge that all of the meetings arranged for Dumbarton Oaks Week and after go forward just as planned. Our meetings should be in the nature of a memorial to President Roosevelt and should mark our determination to carry forward his ideals in the structure of permanent peace.

The week of April 16 to 22 was known as Dumbarton Oaks Week. Twenty-eight governors issued proclamations calling on citizens to observe the occasion. One of the last messages of support we had received for the educational campaign during Dumbarton Oaks Week had come from President Roosevelt. He had concluded his note to me, written on March 14, as follows:

I hope that the whole country will observe this week by studying the Dumbarton Oaks Proposals and by joining in prayers for the success of the United Nations Conference and for the firm establishment of a world organization for permanent peace.

17

San Francisco—The Signing of the United Nations Charter

The conference to draft the United Nations Charter opened in San Francisco on April 25, 1945. It was the largest diplomatic conference in history up to that time. Delegates from fifty countries represented four-fifths of the world's population.

The statesmen had agreed at Yalta that the conference would not deal with peace terms. Although the delegates in San Francisco could not help but think about their relationships with their enemies and how they would face their postwar problems at home, it was wise that these preoccupations were barred from the agenda of the conference, whose sole purpose was to write the Charter.

As I have already indicated, President Roosevelt had come to believe that the United Nations Charter should be drafted, and the organization set up before the war ended, if possible. Like other statesmen, he feared a reaction against the idea at the end of the war if the organization was not already established. With all the overwhelming problems there would be, it was imperative that people be aware of the United Nations as the one solid universal institution to which they could turn. Had the statesmen waited until after the final days of the war to write the Charter, it is doubtful if they could have recaptured the spirit of San Francisco. Probably they could not have done more than create a military alliance of the superpowers. There would not have been time or patience to write the finest part of the Charter dealing with economic recovery, human rights, and a régime of law.

A few days before April 25, 1945, delegates and experts from the fifty participating governments began arriving in San Francisco. They entered the United States by many ports. According to the San Francisco *Chronicle,* the main transportation offices were set up in Washington and San Francisco, and key men were placed at every entry point. In one week's time, 300 notables were shunted across the country. Nine special trains traveled 27,000 miles, carrying over 1,850 persons. Foreign aircraft, the Air Transport Command, and commercial planes brought 1,250 more. Some delegates came by way of the Pacific, and others from Latin America. Even after the start of the conference, planes were constantly flying back and forth across the country on conference business.

San Francisco received the conference in a manner not short of amazing. The city was a very important military port. From its hills could be seen warships and convoys headed for military theaters in the Pacific, and the conference was treated as part of the total war effort. It obviously added to already crowded conditions in the city, taking over major hotels and clubs for over sixty days. Yet I cannot remember a single criticism from any of the delegates of their treatment in San Francisco. Many years later, I look back on the days of the conference with a certain sense of exhilaration. I think that if the delegates had had their way, San Francisco would have become the permanent seat of the United Nations instead of New York City.[1]

1. General Carlos Romulo, head of the Philippine delegation, who had seen some rough fighting in the Pacific, told me this story. He had landed at San Francisco wearing a G.I. fatigue uniform with an old army slicker thrown over his shoulder. After checking into his hotel, he went in search of a few things of which he had long been deprived. In a drugstore, he asked for his favorite

The delegates to the San Francisco Conference ranged from statesmen in exile whose countries were occupied by the enemy to delegates from the Latin American countries which, although contributing much materially to the war, had not suffered invasion or loss of life. Some of the delegates had lived in a blackout for months and suddenly found they could walk in the light without fear. I think particularly of the representatives of the governments-in-exile whom I had met in London in 1941, some of whom I saw again at San Francisco.

President Roosevelt had selected the American delegation to the San Francisco Conference before his death. It was beautifully balanced between both political parties and among the various sections of the country—the President had learned a great deal from the political reaction to President Wilson's delegation to the Paris Peace Conference, which included only one Republican and contained no representatives of Congress. The delegates President Roosevelt appointed included his Secretary of State, Edward R. Stettinius, Jr., as chairman of the delegation; the chairman of the Senate Foreign Relations Committee, Tom Connally; the ranking minority member of the Senate Foreign Relations Committee, Arthur H. Vandenberg; the chairman of the House Foreign Affairs Committee, Sol Bloom; and the ranking minority member of the House Foreign Affairs Committee, Charles A. Eaton. Also appointed were Harold E. Stassen, former governor of Minnesota, and Virginia C. Gildersleeve, dean of Barnard College. Former Secretary of State Cordell Hull did not feel physically able to be a delegate, but agreed to be named as senior adviser.

---

shaving cream. The clerk said that they didn't have that brand and, anyway, where was his empty tube to exchange? "Buddy, don't you know there's a war on?" That afternoon the newspapers carried the names of some of the distinguished delegates who had arrived that day. General Romulo's name was near the top of the list. The next morning there was a rap on the general's door. He opened it, and recognized the druggist's clerk. The young man apologized and presented General Romulo with a box containing various brands of shaving cream.

The delegation was accompanied by a large staff, including consultants and advisers. Among the latter were the president of Johns Hopkins University, Isaiah Bowman; Adlai E. Stevenson; and John Foster Dulles. Forty-seven members of the Commission to Study the Organization of Peace, including myself, were attached to the United States delegation or the conference in some capacity—as delegates, advisers, consultants, or members of the international Secretariat.

When Commander Stassen's appointment was announced, he came to Washington to meet with other members of the delegation. He told Professor Shotwell and me how very much impressed he was with the reports of the Commission to Study the Organization of Peace that had been sent to him in the Pacific, and asked us to work with him at San Francisco. As a result, there were periods of time when we called at his office at 8:30 every morning. He would tell us about deliberations of the delegates on the previous day, and frequently asked us to draft memoranda for him.

One of my close friends among the delegates in San Francisco was Jan Masaryk, the foreign minister of the Czechoslovak government-in-exile. He was much impressed with Stassen and asked me to arrange a private meeting with him. This took place in my hotel room. Masaryk said that many of the heads of governments-in-exile were not sure what their reception would be when they returned home. He and Eduard Beneš, prime minister of the Czech government-in-exile, lived a comfortable life in London. Would they be welcomed at home by the people who had stayed and had had to "take it"? He wanted Stassen to know that if he and Beneš remained at the head of the Czechoslovak state, although it might appear that they were making compromises, they would always be loyal to democracy.

Delegates to the conference wondered what the Russian attitude would be toward Czechoslovakia and other countries on the Soviet border. Masaryk's relationship with Molotov, head of the Soviet delegation, was rather sensitive. He told me that every few days Molotov would ask him to take an automobile ride with him. He could not command Masaryk to join him, but Masaryk felt it would not be good policy to refuse. Apparently no threats were made in the conversations, but the invitation to take the automobile ride was a subtle pressure that could not be lightly denied.[2]

The problem of rebuilding democracy in the liberated nations was a particularly difficult one. As I wrote in the May 1945 issue of *Changing World:*

A representative of one of the liberated countries . . . outlined most forcibly [to me] the problem in his own country. He will return to a people enslaved by the Germans for four years. His people kept the faith and carried on active resistance throughout these years. But it is understandable that their information on what has happened in the world or is happening in San Francisco is very meager. Their schools are closed, in many cases desecrated or destroyed. Many of their teachers have been executed or driven into slavery in the German plan to destroy the leaders so this country could never rise again. His government has ordered some thousands of dollars worth of textbooks in the United States, but because of shipping problems may not be able to secure delivery for many months.

Pamphlets describing the San Francisco Conference cannot be printed in Europe because of the shortage of paper and destruction of presses. It is agreed that there be printed in the United States or Great Britain one-page flyers summarizing the results of the San Francisco Conference that could be easily carried by these men personally when they return to their ravaged homelands. It is difficult for an American who sees hundreds of comic strips and pulp magazines daily on the

2. As it turned out, when they returned home, Masaryk and Beneš were well received and reorganized the Czechoslovak state. Masaryk led the Czech delegation to the first sessions of the UN General Assembly. The two statesmen struggled to maintain the very delicate balance between Western and Communist influence. However, it was only a matter of time before the Communists gained the ascendancy. As is well known, Masaryk was killed. Beneš went into exile.

news stands to understand a people trying to rebuild the democratic processes without newsprint or presses. And yet the process must go on—it must go on quickly if public opinion is to support and make a living reality of the United Nations Charter. The problem will be equally serious when vast areas of Asia are liberated from the Japanese, who have tried with equal ingenuity to destroy the cultural processes and leadership of vast populations in Asia.

The major crisis of the conference was the disagreement between the Soviet Union and literally all the rest of the delegates as to how the vote should be taken in the Security Council. This problem had not been solved by the "Big Three" at Yalta nor at Dumbarton Oaks. It was generally agreed that for the Security Council to take action against an aggressor, the four great powers must be in unanimous agreement. The negative vote of one of them would constitute a veto and prevent action from being taken. Most of us favored the veto up to that point. For example, Senator Tom Connally stated that the American people would not stand for a pledge to use American troops without the consent of the American government.

Mr. Molotov wanted to go farther, however, and ensure that the negative vote of a great power against placing an item on the agenda of the Security Council could prevent the item from being discussed. Most of the other states felt that the right of discussion in the Security Council should not be limited. Both sides were adamant and the conference was deadlocked. Finally President Truman sent Harry Hopkins to Moscow to talk to Stalin, and Stalin gave in. Molotov was instructed to withdraw the Soviet insistence that the veto should apply to placing items on the agenda.

There were additional crises involving the Soviet Union, although none was as serious as the question of the veto. The Soviets wished, for example, to delay the admission of the Argentine delegates to the conference. The other nations replied that in that case, they would vote to delay the admission of the delegates from the Ukraine and from Byelorussia. There was also constant disagreement between the USSR and other delegates as to the acceptance of the Polish government.

The United Nations Charter was drafted in sixty-two days. As a guide the statesmen had, of course, the Covenant of the League of Nations, which could not help but be the pattern that the United Nations would follow. They had in addition the Dumbarton Oaks Proposals, which were the basis of their deliberations. For all its flaws, the finished product, the work of hundreds of delegates and experts from fifty countries, will be considered by history as one of mankind's greatest achievements.

One of the best analyses of the San Francisco Conference was made by Vera Micheles Dean, in a Foreign Policy Report dated July 15, 1945. In her article, Mrs. Dean writes of the major achievements of the small and middle nations in their unremitting efforts to liberalize the Dumbarton Oaks Proposals.

The Proposals had no preamble. The preparation of the Charter's preamble was entrusted to a committee headed by Marshal Jan Smuts, Prime Minister of the Union of South Africa, and the sole survivor of the group of statesmen who had drafted the League of Nations Covenant in 1919.

As Mrs. Dean points out:

The preamble, the work of many hands, as finally adopted, lists matters that had been left out of the Dumbarton Oaks Proposals—human rights, the dignity and worth of the human person, the equal rights of men and women and of nations large and small, justice and respect for obligations arising from treaties and other sources of international law, and the promotion of social progress and better standards of living in "larger freedom." To achieve these ends the member nations undertake "to practice tolerance and live together in peace with one another as good neighbors"; to unite their strength to maintain international peace and security; to ensure "that armed force shall not be used, save in the common interest"; and "to employ international machinery for the promotion of the economic and social advancement of all peoples."

This preamble reflects the concern of many delegates, and of the fighting and suffering men and women they represented, that the human values cruelly and systematically debased by the Nazis and Fascists should become the cornerstone of the new Organization.[3]

Senator Vandenberg, referring to the preamble and the first chapter of the Charter, said: "Dumbarton Oaks has been given a new soul—the Charter names justice as the prime criterion of peace."

As I wrote in an editorial in *Changing World,* in May 1945:

While not disturbing the delicate balance of the major bodies of the projected organization as outlined at Dumbarton Oaks, the Conference will have democratized the plan in many respects in favor of the small states. In addition, the provision on Human Rights has been strengthened; a trusteeship plan will probably be agreed to; the Act of Chapultepec has been clearly brought within the framework of the world organization with a dangerous temptation to regionalism avoided.

In her article, after noting the efforts to "liberalize" the Dumbarton Oaks Proposals, Mrs. Dean goes on to discuss the work of the consultants in San Francisco. She writes of their determined pressure to "humanize" the Charter. The presence of the consultants in San Francisco, where they were in a position to bring pressure to bear on the United States delegation, was the result of a remarkable change in the attitude of the Department of State toward private organizations. In early 1944, the Department had announced the establishment of the Division of Public Liaison in a paragraph of 2 sentences, one containing 150 words. The gist was to make the Department an instrument

3. Foreign Policy Association, Inc., *Foreign Policy Reports,* Vol. XXI, No. 9 (New York, July 15, 1945), pp. 117–118.

of the people, and it resulted in informal consultations between officials of the State Department and representatives of various organizations, particularly in connection with the Dumbarton Oaks Proposals. The climax had been reached when the Department invited forty-two national organizations each to name a consultant and two alternates to attend the San Francisco Conference. The process of selection had been a difficult one, but the forty-two organizations were well balanced among professional, religious, labor, business, and women's groups. The Association had been one of the organizations selected. I was its consultant, with Philip C. Nash, president of the University of Toledo, and Margaret Olson as my alternates. The United States government reserved plane or train travel space for each consultant, as well as a room in a leading hotel. On the plane ride to San Francisco, I wondered what our role actually would be. Were we simply to observe, with the expectation that we would support the Charter upon our return, or would the term "consultant" mean that we would be consulted by the delegation? The latter proved to be true.

Secretary of State Stettinius in his Report to the President on the Results of the San Francisco Conference, wrote:

The purpose of inviting these Consultants was to inform them of the work of the Conference and of the United States Delegation and to secure their opinions and advice. Regular meetings were held with the Chairman and members of the United States Delegation, and a liaison staff kept the Consultants in continuing contact with the documentation of the conference and with information about it. As subsequent Chapters of this Report will indicate, the Consultants were largely instrumental in the introduction into the final Charter of certain important provisions. Their presence in San Francisco meant that a very large body of American opinion which had been applying itself to the problems of international organization played a direct and material part in drafting the constitution of the United Nations.[4]

4. *Report to the President on the Results of the San Francisco Conference* by the Chairman of the United States Delegation, the Secretary of State (Washing-

The consultants were concerned particularly with human rights; with cooperation between private organizations and the United Nations; with formation of an interim committee to function as soon as the Charter was adopted; and with the strengthening of the economic and social provisions of the Charter. In San Francisco, I remember, I was first informed by Dean Gildersleeve, a member of the Commission to Study the Organization of Peace, that the delegates, in order to shorten the Charter, would omit many details. Instead of providing specifically for a Commission on Human Rights, the Economic and Social Council would be empowered to appoint whatever commissions would be necessary. Some of us were afraid that, with the reaction that would inevitably set in after the war, the nations would never get around to appointing a Commission on Human Rights. Prompt action was required. On the evening of May 1, a group met to discuss the possibilities. It included Professor Shotwell; Judge Joseph Proskauer, consultant of the American Jewish Committee; Jacob Blaustein, president of the American Jewish Committee; Margaret Olson; Dr. O. Frederick Nolde, consultant of the Federal Council of Churches; and myself. We drew up in a brief document the salient points, and, before five o'clock the next afternoon—the deadline for submitting proposed Charter changes—had obtained the signatures of twenty-one of the consultants. It was clear that many more signatures could have been obtained had there been more time.

Arrangements were made for the consultants to speak to the Secretary of State at five o'clock on May 2. Dramatic speeches were made, particularly by Judge Proskauer, Professor Shotwell (who attended the conference as the consultant of the Carnegie Endowment for International Peace), and Philip Murray, consultant of the CIO.

Finally, Secretary Stettinius left to present our document to

ton, D.C.: GPO, Department of State Publication 2349, June 26, 1945), pp. 27–28.

the U.S. delegation. As Dr. Nolde said in a speech on the subject delivered in 1955 at a tenth anniversary reunion of the consultants in San Francisco,

Final decision revealed that the promotion of respect for and observance of human rights and fundamental freedoms for all had been added to the major purposes of the U.N., and that the objective had been appropriately assigned to various organs. Perhaps the most significant accomplishment lies in the provision that the Economic and Social Council is required to set up among various commissions a Commission on Human Rights.

The text of the letter that the consultants handed to Mr. Stettinius on May 2, 1945, appears below. I have omitted the signatures.

The undersigned consultants to the Delegation of the United States of America earnestly urge upon the Delegation that it sponsor the following amendments to the Dumbarton Oaks Proposals:

1. New purpose to be added to Chapter I of the Dumbarton Oaks Proposals:
   "To promote respect for human rights and fundamental freedoms."

2. New principle to be added to Chapter II of the Dumbarton Oaks Proposals:
   "All members of the Organization, accepting as a matter of international concern the obligation to defend life, liberty, independence and religious freedom, and to preserve human rights and justice in their own lands, shall progressively secure for their inhabitants without discrimination such fundamental rights as freedom of religion, speech, assembly and communication, and to a fair trial under just laws."

3. Addition to Chapter V, Section B, 6, after "economic and social fields":
   "of developing and safeguarding human rights and fundamental freedoms."

4. Addition to Chapter IX, Section D, 1, after "social commission":
"a human rights commission."

Principles Involved

The ultimate inclusion of the equivalent of an International Bill of
Rights in the functioning of the Organization is deemed of the essence
of what is necessary to preserve the peace of the world.

a. The dignity and inviolability of the individual must be the cornerstone of civilization. The assurance to every human being of the fundamental rights of life, liberty and the pursuit of happiness is essential not only to domestic but also to international peace.

b. The conscience of the world demands an end to persecution, and Hitlerism has demonstrated that persecution by a barbarous nation throws upon the peace-loving nations the burden of relief and redress.

c. It is thus a matter of international concern to stamp out infractions of basic human rights.

d. Therefore in the language of Judge Manley O. Hudson of the Permanent Court of International Justice: "Each state has a legal duty . . . to treat its own population in a way which will not violate the dictates of humanity and justice or shock the conscience of mankind."

Relevancy to the Conference

a. It is fully realized that the primary objective of this Conference is to devise the structure of the new world organization.

b. Nonetheless, it would come as a grievous shock if the constitutional framework of the Organization would fail to make adequate provision for the ultimate achievement of human rights and fundamental freedoms.

c. The Atlantic Charter, the Four Freedoms, the Declaration of the United Nations and subsequent declarations have given mankind the right to expect that the area of international law would be expanded to meet this advance toward freedom and peace.

d. Sponsorship of this project by the American Delegation would win the enthusiastic support of the American people, and speaking particularly for the organizations we represent, would command their hearty approval.

Conclusion

We therefore urge upon the American Delegation that in this vital field it take a position of leadership.

Another important contribution of the consultants at San Francisco was the steps taken by the delegates to bridge the gap between private organizations and official bodies. The conference itself was the first time in modern political history that private organizations were given the right to appear before official bodies on matters in which they were competent. The consultants felt that they should try to work out some formula by which representatives of private organizations would continue to have direct contact with official bodies of the United Nations. Secretary of State Stettinius, in his Report to the President, said:

The close and fruitful cooperation between the United States Delegation and its consultants, representing private American organizations, pointed to the desirability of some orderly channel through which national and international organizations of a non-governmental character, having interests in international problems falling within the competence of the Economic and Social Council, could bring their views to the attention of the Organization. In an unprecedented example of cooperation and unanimity, a recommendation was addressed to the United States Delegation by consultants representing major organizations in the fields of agriculture, business, education and labor in the United States suggesting that there be added to the Charter a paragraph providing for consultation and cooperation between non-governmental organizations, national and international, and the Economic and Social Council.

Article 71 is the answer of the Conference to this proposal: "The Economic and Social Council may make suitable arrangements for consultation with non-governmental organizations which are concerned with matters within its competence. Such arrangements may be made with international organizations and, where appropriate, with national organizations after consultation with the Member of the United Nations concerned."[5]

When the conference was still in the planning stage, a large number of non-governmental organizations had decided to have representatives in San Francisco. It was agreed that a core committee of nine individuals would function as an information center for the various organizations. In spite of the fact that the State Department later named forty-two organizations to have consultants at San Francisco, the core committee functioned as planned, with less official supervision than the consultants had.

The League of Nations Association, the Church Peace Union, and a number of other organizations had joint headquarters in San Francisco, in a convenient building at 68 Post Street. This also became the headquarters of the core committee, providing offices for Professor Shotwell, myself, and others, and was, in a sense, the headquarters of non-governmental organization activities in San Francisco. Representatives of many organizations visited this office. Bulletins were sent from it to New York to be processed and distributed to various organizations. Many of them were of a confidential nature and asked for expressions of public opinion on burning issues before the conference.

5. *Report to the President,* pp. 120–121.
The consultants who attended the tenth anniversary of the signing of the United Nations Charter in 1955 put a plaque on the wall of the room in the Fairmont Hotel where they met. The plaque reads:

25-April–26-June 1945

In this room met the Consultants of forty-two national organizations assigned to the United States Delegation at the Conference on International Organization in which the United Nations Charter was drafted. Their contribution is particularly reflected in the Charter provisions for human rights and United Nations consultation with private organizations.

The American Association for the United Nations and the Commission to Study the Organization of Peace were well equipped to play a role of leadership at San Francisco. We were able to consult with many individuals, members of the Commission, who were at San Francisco in some official capacity, and were back-stopped in New York by a well-trained staff. Miss Estelle Linzer had the task of dealing with our national board and the chapters, and responsibility for operations in New York, while Miss Olson and I had charge in San Francisco.

One of the most important subjects on the agenda of the San Francisco Conference was the question of trusteeship.

As noted in Chapter 16, shortly before the San Francisco Conference, the Commission to Study the Organization of Peace had put forth a plan for two kinds of trusteeship, one type to advance the well-being of dependent peoples, the other primarily concerned with seeing to it that strategic bases were part of the United Nations security system. President Roosevelt, as I related in Chapter 15, had told me that he looked forward to a form of international sovereignty. I am not sure that the trusteeship system as actually worked out at San Francisco approached his conception of international sovereignty as nearly as he would have liked, but it was closer to it than anything ever seen before. Thanks largely to the emphasis given to trusteeship by the Welles Committee, the American view on the issue was already refined before the delegation reached San Francisco.

In San Francisco, the subject was first referred to a committee of five, of which Commander Harold Stassen was a member. It is rather interesting to note that while the details of the plans for trusteeship over dependent peoples and strategic bases were primarily of American origin, Article 73 of the Charter, establishing the principles of a new day for dependent peoples, is of British drafting.

Chapter XII of the Charter, as finally agreed upon, deals with the international trusteeship system. Three classes of territories are named:

1. Territories held under a League of Nations mandate. It was presumed that most states would be willing to change their Mandates to Trusteeships. The Union of South Africa was the one exception.
2. Territories which would be detached from enemy states as the result of the Second World War.
3. Territories voluntarily placed under the system by States responsible for their administration.

There is also a provision for a Trusteeship Council, to consist of the trust powers and an equal number of states without trusteeships. The Trusteeship Council has the right of visitation, and the right of petition is provided for.

The framers of the Charter inserted another chapter, Chapter XI, entitled "Declaration Regarding Non-Self-Governing Territories," which imposes definite obligations upon those nations that have non-self-governing peoples who are not in trust areas. It begins by stating:

Members of the United Nations which have or assume responsibilities for the administration of territories whose peoples have not yet attained a full measure of self-government recognize the principle that the interests of the inhabitants of these territories are paramount, and accept as a sacred trust the obligation to promote to the utmost, within the system of international peace and security established by the present Charter, the well-being of the inhabitants of these territories.

The Russians and some other delegations at San Francisco wished the eventual objective of trusteeship to be independence. The British and other colonial powers wished the objective to be self-government; only the French wished to restore their ancient colonial empire without change. Finally, as recorded in Article 76(b) of the Charter, it was decided that a very basic obligation of trust powers would be to "promote the political, economic, social and educational advancement of the inhabitants of the trust territories, and their progressive development toward self-government or independence as may be appropriate to the particular circumstances . . ." Chapter XII further imposes upon the trust powers the obligation to maintain equality without distinction as to race, sex, language, or religion.

Twenty-five years after the Charter was adopted, the principle of independence for colonial areas had been so rapidly accepted that the trusteeship system worked out in San Francisco had been practically liquidated, as trust areas attained their independence. Chapters XI and XII of the Charter alone would have given great impetus to the movement for independence of colonial peoples. However, there was also a spiritual and emotional factor that had a large influence. During the war the colonial powers were very much dependent on their colonies for manpower and materials, and the loyalty of the colonies was deeply appreciated by the hard-pressed colonial powers. The Queen of The Netherlands made definite promises of greater freedom after the war; it was unthinkable that the colonial powers would retreat to their prewar attitudes.

One decision at San Francisco with which I, by chance, was particularly concerned was the one to call the new organization the "United Nations." Some delegates preferred a name that would not be associated with the alliance of the nations that won the war. Others felt that the name should be a tribute to Franklin Roosevelt, and the organization should be called whatever he had wished. I was in a position to tell some delegates what his wishes had been. Not only had we discussed the subject in our conversation of November 13, 1942, but in 1944 I had checked again with the President through the kind offices of Mrs. Kermit Roosevelt. I had asked her to ask the President if he felt it was time for us to change the name of the League of Nations Association to "United Nations Association." If I remember rightly, the President replied that she should tell Clark that the name of the Association should be changed to include the words "United Nations." He and Winston Churchill had agreed that the name of the new organization should be the United Nations. He said that when a conference was held, many fancy names would be suggested but he and Churchill would have their way.

The League of Nations Association had announced the change of its name to American Association for the United Nations at a banquet in New York in February 1945. I left for San Francisco as a consultant for the American Association for the United Nations, even though the United Nations had not yet been created. Thus when Henri Rolin of Belgium, among others, said to me that he did not particularly like the name United Nations for the organization, but that he would be in favor of any name that President Roosevelt wanted, I was able to prove that President Roosevelt had favored the name "United Nations" by relating this story of the change in the name of our Association.

In the final discussion of the conference on the name, the delegate from Panama asked those who had proposed other names to withdraw them in favor of "a rising vote which unanimously and by acclamation" would approve the name "United Nations." It was done as a tribute to Roosevelt.

Social life in San Francisco was obviously limited. There were, however, some receptions and several mass meetings, if they can be called social. The officers of the Kaiser Company, which was launching a number of cargo ships, invited women delegates or the wives of the delegates to break the traditional bottle of champagne over the bow of each ship. I remember that Mrs. Stassen did well, but that some other women failed miserably; down below there was a well-muscled shipyard girl who never missed.

There was usually a luncheon or dinner party following these ceremonies. The food was exceptionally good—steaks such as not many of us had seen for a long time. Several times at these parties I was seated next to Mrs. Ogden Reid of the *New York Herald-Tribune,* whose beauty, delicacy, and wit made her an ideal dinner companion.

The cable cars were a fascination to everyone. One could swing on a car in front of several leading hotels and in a few minutes be at the rear entrance of the Fairmont Hotel, which was the official headquarters of many delegations. There were free taxis and limousines which an official could hail at one of the hotels or the Opera House where the plenary sessions took place. The nights were cool and sometimes the fog quietly embraced one.

Delegates, consultants, newspaper people, the thousands who were at the conference could have enjoyed life in San Francisco with more abandon had it not been for the sense of urgency felt by everyone. Americans were anxious to go home to explain the Charter and work for its ratification. Delegates from other countries wanted to approach perfection in writing the Charter, but were also eager to go home as quickly as possible to help steer their countries into the régimes of peace. My greatest fear was that there would be a gap of time between the adoption of the Charter and the setting up of the organization, because it was necessary for the five great powers and a majority of the other powers to submit the Charter for ratification before the organization could be set up. I was afraid that, in the absence of some interim machinery, the Charter drafted by the delegates might fade away before there were enough ratifications to set up the organization.

In a confidential letter to the consultants on June 1, 1945, I wrote:

Second only to the drafting of the Charter of the United Nations is the need for the creation of provisional machinery to function in the interim between the adjournment of the present conference and the establishment of a permanent United Nations Organization.

This machinery is needed both for its psychological effect and for the important tasks that need to be performed immediately. Any lessening of public enthusiasm or concentration between the conference and the setting up of the organization must be avoided. Many delegates will return from San Francisco to their homelands that have just been liberated, and all will return to pressing domestic problems of recovery. It would be of immense satisfaction to them to know that interim machinery is functioning.

There are important problems concerning future security and economic welfare whose solution cannot be delayed. The months between the adjournment of the conference and the establishment of the organization may be very critical ones in which false starts might be made without provisional machinery.

The provisional machinery could also proceed to investigate a site for the permanent headquarters, select a staff, arrange for the absorption of the League of Nations, and prepare the documents necessary for the first general assembly and the two council meetings.

An interim preparatory commission whose tasks would be limited to the latter functions would not seem to be adequate in the light of the critical problems that will face the world between the adjournment of the San Francisco Conference and the first general assembly. The provisional machinery should be given authority to promote economic and social cooperation, including initiation of such governmental conferences as may be necessary in the economic field. The machinery should also be given authority to facilitate the pacific settlement of disputes in accordance with the procedures set forth in Chapter VIII, Section A of the Charter.

The simplest procedure would be for the present conference to establish a provisional commission composed of one representative from each of the states signing the Charter. The provisional commission should create an executive committee whose membership would be composed of representatives of the same states who constitute the present executive committee.

This executive committee, it must be remembered, is composed of the five powers that will have permanent seats on the Security Council and nine representatives of smaller states. It should be in continuous session.

Toward the end of the conference, the delegates agreed that a provisional commission should be created, composed of one representative from each of the states signing the Charter. But such a commission could let weeks elapse before it had its first meeting. Consequently we were all encouraged when it was further agreed that there should be an Executive Committee composed of the five powers which would have permanent seats on the Security Council and nine representatives from the smaller states. This Executive Committee would be in continuous session after the conference adjourned.

The signing ceremony was dramatic. Each delegate was handed two documents to sign. One was the Charter of the United Nations, and the other was the Agreement on Interim Arrangements providing for the establishment of the Preparatory Commission and the Executive Committee. Each delegate signed both documents. At the close of the final session, June 26, Mr. Stettinius, who had been serving as chairman, announced: "Ladies and gentlemen, the Preparatory Commission will meet at 11 o'clock tomorrow morning in Room 223 of the Veterans Building. I now hereby declare the United Nations Conference on International Organization adjourned."[6]

Many of us from the United States left San Francisco feeling that nothing could prevent the organization's being set up quickly. This time, we were determined, nothing should prevent ratification of the Charter in the United States.

6. *The United Nations Conference on International Organization,* San Francisco, California, April 25 to June 26, 1945 (Washington, D.C.: Selected Documents, GPO, Department of State Publication 2490, 1946), p. 939.

18

The United Nations Locates in New York City

At the close of the San Francisco Conference, the representatives of the fifty countries looked forward with anxiety to the task facing them. They had no doubt that their own countries, almost all of which had been members of the League of Nations, would join the United Nations. These states had no isolationist tradition, and were waiting eagerly for the organization on which they would be so dependent and to which they wished to contribute their share to be set up.

We, the returning Americans, faced a different situation. Compared to representatives of other countries, we had no hungry people to take care of, no shattered economy to rebuild. However, there was some doubt as to whether the United States would join the United Nations, since we had rejected the League of Nations in 1920. We were the only people with an isolationist tradition.

Events proved that there was little to fear. The Charter had been well publicized throughout the country, and the nongovernmental organizations had worked vigorously not only to help shape the Charter, but to convince the American people that this time they must join. The debate in the United States Senate lasted about a week, and evoked little of the bitterness occasioned by the debate on the League of Nations Covenant twenty-five years earlier.

As I witnessed the favorable vote in the United States Senate, I experienced that sense of anticlimax which is a common experience of people who have worked long and hard for a particular achievement. But if I left the Senate Chamber with a terrible feeling of letdown, that mood soon lifted at the thought of the formidable task ahead. The realization came to me that those of us who had helped to bring into being the United Nations were surely morally responsible for helping to make the new international machinery function.

While the people overwhelmingly favored ratification of the Charter, there were two conflicting moods with which we had to contend. Some people asked, "Now that the Senate has approved the United Nations Charter, what is the reason for continuing the work of the CSOP or the AAUN or other organizations? The job is over." Another group maintained that the nations had already outgrown the Charter, that it should be scrapped for something stronger. It seemed to me that any effort on our part to get rid of the Charter would be an affront to the other nations who had helped draft it and who were now eagerly awaiting the practical results.

Then came August 7: The world saw the picture of a mushrooming cloud rising from Hiroshima into the sky. The atomic explosion was repeated at Nagasaki. People everywhere knew that the bomb had profoundly changed their lives and their fortunes. A new responsibility was thrust upon the United Nations.

As would be expected, the chairman of the Commission to Study the Organization of Peace and honorary president of the American Association for the United Nations, James T. Shotwell, called together immediately an informal group of physical and political scientists to consider the problem of atomic energy. Two days after the first bomb was dropped on Hiroshima,

I sent the President of the United States a telegram on behalf of the Association which read as follows:

It was your destiny to announce to the world a scientific achievement so overwhelming that mankind enters the atomic age. The gravity of the tone of your announcement indicates how aware you are of the responsibility that comes to the United States in this great discovery, and the implications for all mankind. Because we realize how much thought needs to be given to the problem which this great discovery presents, we put forward the following tentative suggestions in a spirit of humility.

One suggestion is that a national committee, composed of scientists, representatives of industry, farm and labor, educators, congressmen, cabinet members, and representatives of the general public, be created with proper subcommittees to study how the United States can best utilize this discovery for our own well-being and that of the world.

Two, since the effect of the discovery will be international, either in universal destruction or universal betterment, we suggest decisive action through the United Nations to prevent the former and make possible the latter. The United Nations Charter provides the framework through which adequate controls can be inaugurated. But the machinery will need to be elaborated; some of the bodies of the organization may stand out in bolder relief and the controls must be stricter. As one illustration we refer to the necessity of rigid world inspection, probably undertaken by the Military Staff Committee of the Security Council. We suggest an appeal to all of the eligible nations to ratify the Charter immediately so that the United Nations can be set up without delay.

Following its establishment, might it not be worthwhile to suggest the appointment of two committees of the United Nations? One committee appointed by the Security Council would have as its purpose the working out of the controls necessary to maintain universal peace and prevent universal destruction. The second committee could be appointed by the Economic and Social Council. Its purpose would be to consider how the industrial and social benefits of the discovery may be developed and made available to all the peoples of the earth.

The extent to which the United States, Britain and Canada share their secret with the rest of the world can be determined by the cooperation that the members of the United Nations give in such a problem.

The Charter provided that the organization would come into being upon the deposit of the ratifications of China, France, the Soviet Union, Great Britain, the United States, and a majority of the other signatory states. The last of the required signatures were deposited on October 24. Because the Preparatory Commission and its interim committee, which had been appointed by the San Francisco Conference, had been preparing the machinery of the United Nations in the months of waiting for the ratifications to be deposited, the organization started functioning almost immediately. The decision was made at the first part of the first session of the General Assembly in London in February 1946 that the permanent headquarters of the organization should be in the Westchester-Fairfield area near New York City. A site committee was set up to study and visit possible locations in that area and report to the Assembly at its fall session. Interim headquarters were to be located in New York City.

Many people, particularly in Europe, were disappointed that the headquarters of the United Nations could not be in the League of Nations buildings at Geneva. But there were important reasons for rejection of Geneva as the United Nations headquarters. The League of Nations site suggested failure. Besides, the League buildings, although comparatively new, would not be large enough for the greatly expanded activities of the United Nations. Another reason was Swiss neutrality. The Swiss took the position that all non-political activities of the United Nations could function from Swiss soil without difficulty. However, if any military sanctions were to be voted against an aggressor, such action could never be directed from Switzerland.

President Roosevelt had thought that the Azores might make

a truly independent center for the United Nations, but he saw the practical impossibility of such a move. The nations settled on the United States for the headquarters because only in this country was there the verve, the building material, the labor, and the will to put up the necessary buildings quickly.

Nevertheless, members of various United Nations associations were upset over the moving of the United Nations from Geneva. Europe had carried much of the burden of the League of Nations. It lost millions of lives in the war. Europeans felt very deeply that the world lost its center of gravity when Geneva was abandoned—it had passed from Europe to the New World.[1]

Invitations to the United Nations came from many communities in the New York area. The site committee visited suburban areas surrounding New York, looking over such areas as Hyde Park, Westchester County, and going as far afield as Philadelphia. Hyde Park had some emotional attraction, but the Hudson Valley is very warm in the summertime; moreover, the delegates to the United Nations did not wish to locate in Hyde Park or any suburban area outside greater New York. They did not wish to build a District of Columbia or to be segregated in a specified area. They wanted access to a metropolitan area, to cultural life, to art galleries and restaurants similar to what could be found in their own countries. It was clear that they preferred New York City.

As an observer, I attended a meeting of the site commission with Mayor O'Dwyer, Robert Moses, and a few others. Members of the site commission asked the mayor what his group had to offer; he replied, the old World's Fair site in Flushing Mead-

1. It would have been logical since the headquarters of the United Nations would be in New York City to move the headquarters of the International Federation of League of Nations Societies, now changing its name to World Federation of United Nations Associations, to Manhattan. However, the sentiment against such a move prevailed, and the international body's headquarters remains to this day in Geneva.

ows. But no one wanted that location. The United Nations Secretary-General then asked if New York had anything else to propose, whereupon Bob Moses replied in his rather curt manner that that was all there was. The meeting shortly adjourned and I returned to mid-Manhattan. Shortly after I arrived in my apartment, I had a phone call from Stoyan Gavrilovic, a Yugoslav and member of the site commission, saying that, after the mayor and Moses had withdrawn, the UN site commission had voted to reject the offer of the City of New York.

It seemed that an impasse had been reached. The Assembly session was drawing to a close. The suggestion was even made that the decision be put off until the following year, but no one wanted that. Evidently the United Nations would have to accept an offer outside the New York vicinity, such as Fairmount Park, Philadelphia. But if the organization could not be in San Francisco, I saw no reason for it to be anywhere else but in the New York City area. I think most of the delegates would have agreed with me.

I phoned Frank Jamieson, who was one of Nelson Rockefeller's assistants, and told him that I understood Nelson was in Texas. Could I have his telephone number? He asked me what I wanted to call him about. I told him. He said, "Well, I'm going to call him in a few minutes and I'll relay your message to save you the telephone charges."

I know none of the details of what happened after that. Perhaps many people got the same message to Nelson. But whoever was responsible, Nelson flew home on December 9, 1946, to make a last-ditch effort on behalf of New York as the UN site. I understand the Rockefeller family offered the United Nations their combined estates at Tarrytown or a parcel of land on the East River in New York City. When the United Nations selected the latter, John D. Rockefeller, Jr., gave the organization $8.5 million for the purchase of the property. Most people looking at the beautiful United Nations buildings today do not remember, if they ever knew, what the area was like in 1945—it contained slum housing, a brewery, and a slaughterhouse.

While the United Nations was waiting for the buildings to be erected on the East River, temporary headquarters had to be found. The organization rented a large portion of the Sperry Plant at Lake Success as a working headquarters. The Security Council, however, met originally in quarters provided for it at Hunter College in the Bronx. The United Nations also temporarily took over a building left standing on the World's Fair site for the General Assembly. There was a feeling of friendliness and gaiety as we moved back and forth among these various locations, and considerable informality existed among the statesmen who were helping set up the headquarters. I remember being asked by Andrei Gromyko to sit down with him and Dmitro Manuilsky one morning. The latter was a tough old fellow from the Ukraine, who for some reason or other was rather friendly to me, and asked me to visit the Ukraine. This kind of informal chat with these two men would have been impossible a year or two later.

It had been considered very important in 1945 for President Roosevelt to appoint among the delegates to the San Francisco Conference the majority and minority members from the House Foreign Affairs Committee and the majority and minority leaders from the Senate Foreign Relations Committee. Their actions had much to do with ensuring the success of the conference.

At the first General Assembly session in New York City, the majority Democratic and minority Republican members of the Senate Foreign Relations Committee were invited to be delegates. One noon in the temporary lounge during the second part of the first session of the General Assembly, Senators Vandenberg and Connally were discussing the wisdom of having senatorial representatives on future delegations. They did not mind my presence and comments, a fact which illustrates the

informality of the early days. Senator Vandenberg, while granting the importance of having congressional members on the
United States Delegation at San Francisco, said that in the long
run he doubted the wisdom of having such representation on
succeeding delegations. He argued that the U.S. Senate must
eventually ratify or reject agreements concerning the United
States reached at the General Assembly. Was it wise then to
have senators sit in judgment in the Senate on decisions they
had taken in the General Assembly? Senator Connally, less con-
stitutionally minded, thought it was to the advantage of the
United States in the United Nations to have that representation.
Whatever the constitutional niceties might be, the fact remains
that each succeeding delegation to the General Assembly has
included one year two senators from the Senate Foreign Relations Committee, a Democrat and a Republican, and the next
year two representatives from the House Foreign Affairs Committee.

The feelings of initiative, adventure, and comradeship that
developed among Americans and representatives from other
countries in the early days at Lake Success helped give the
United Nations a congenial foundation. Now almost thirty years
have passed since the site for the headquarters of the United
Nations was agreed upon. It is hard to realize that whereas in
the beginning there were some 50 members in the organization, there are now close to 150. There was a time when Andrew Cordier, executive assistant to the Secretary-General,
could count the votes from his seat on the dais in the Assembly
Hall. People were used to seeing his left forefinger performing
the count. Now it is done by an electronic machine that flashes
the votes on the wall. Few of the old UN officials are here today.
Like Cordier and Ralph Bunche, who became one of the organization's early heroes, they have passed away. Even Martin Hill,
who was old enough to have served on the League of Nations
Secretariat and young enough to serve on that of the United

Nations, passed away in the spring of 1976.

Few of the United Nations officials at Lake Success believed that there would be much public interest in what went on at the meetings. There was general surprise, therefore, when many automobiles arrived on the spot with passengers who wanted to see what the organization was doing. UN officials were delighted, but how could they handle the situation? They asked the American Association for the United Nations if we would supply volunteers to help the general public find out where various meetings were being held and what was going on without getting underfoot. This the Association was glad to do, and United Nations officials so appreciated the service that they offered the Association the opportunity of supplying professional guides to take the public through the new buildings when completed. As a result, young women who were college graduates speaking several languages, outfitted in blue uniforms designed by Lily Daché, became guides. They were not simply to point out places of interest; they were, to a degree at least, to discuss substantively what each committee was considering, and were briefed every day. Suspicious delegates were constantly listening to the girls to detect any statement that might seem unfair to a particular country. After the Association had operated the guide service for several years, the United Nations took it over as part of its headquarters functions. It continues to this day, following the pattern established by the Association.

C H A P T E R

19

Afterword

In the period of twenty-five years from March 19, 1920, to July 28, 1945, the United States evolved from the mood of isolation in which it had rejected the League of Nations Covenant to that of cooperation in which it accepted the United Nations Charter. In this book I have tried to portray the main events of this evolution in American foreign policy as I saw them. My account really closes with the San Francisco Conference, the ratification of the United Nations Charter by the United States Senate, and the establishment of the headquarters of the new organization in New York. However, I cannot resist commenting here on some of the developments of the following thirty years.

The first two decades of the United Nations saw changes that marked them as one of the great revolutionary periods of history. The scientific revolution in which the atom's potentials were exploited and men successfully ventured into space was accompanied by a human revolution characterized by the revolt of colonial peoples. From the first days of the United Nations, American leadership made itself felt in various bodies of the organization. True, there were bitter debates in the cold war in which the United States played a part, and not always a constructive part. Nevertheless, this country maintained a certain moral position. Almost all nations, including the new states, had a particular respect for the United States.

To describe the multitude of political issues and other problems that came before the United Nations in the years following San Francisco would require several volumes. Another would be needed to describe the ways in which the United States exerted its moral influence in the organization. I shall cite only a few illustrations, in the areas of atomic energy, economic cooperation, human rights, and outer space.

On June 14, 1946, the United Nations Atomic Energy Commission, composed of the members of the Security Council plus Canada, sat around the horseshoe table in the temporary Security Council Room at Hunter College. Bernard Baruch was speaking. He presented the plan of the United States for the regulation and control of atomic weapons. It was an amazing plan indeed. Mr. Baruch proposed that an International Atomic Development Authority have a monopoly on the world's production of atomic energy. The Authority would have exclusive control of all atomic activities, from the mining of raw materials to the production and use of fissionable fuel. In addition to owning and managing all uranium and thorium mines, refineries, chemical separation plants, and reactors, it was to have the exclusive right to engage in atomic research. It could also punish an individual or nation for violating the atomic energy agreements without a great power veto interfering. This was the most far-reaching and dramatic proposal for supranational authority that any government had ever presented anywhere.

The Soviet representative rejected the entire plan as "thoroughly vicious and unacceptable," and adopted the line that the USSR has consistently followed ever since: Outlaw atomic weapons with a bare minimum of international control. Undoubtedly a major, basic Soviet objection to the Baruch plan, although not presented in so many words, was that under it the United States would forever be the only power knowing the secrets of nuclear weapons. The United States might scrap all its nuclear weapons, all peaceful atomic plants might be operated by the United Nations, but in the Russian mind the United States would always have the advantage of having the experience of making the bomb. Russia's growing pride demanded that she, too, must make bombs before agreeing to their renunciation. The Soviet Union also feared that the proposed International Atomic Development Authority would be dominated by Western nations.

If only the American proposal could have been accepted, modified, of course, to suit the susceptibilities of other nations, not only would the approach now to atomic energy be very different, but the example of the International Atomic Development Authority might have established a model for other UN bodies with supranational authority.

Despite this failure, the United States proposal did bear some fruit. On December 8, 1953, the United States again took the initiative, although not as drastically. President Eisenhower, addressing the eighth session of the General Assembly, proposed that governments jointly contribute normal uranium and fissionable materials to an international atomic energy agency to be set up under the aegis of the United Nations. Eisenhower said, "The United States would be more than willing to take up with others 'principally involved' the development of plans whereby the peaceful use of atomic energy could be expedited." And he went on to state that, "of those 'principally involved,' the Soviet Union must, of course, be one." After a lapse of several years, in 1957 the International Atomic Energy Agency came into existence.

General Eisenhower was an internationalist. I remember a conversation I had with him when I was in Paris attending the third General Assembly of the United Nations in 1948. The general, then commander of the Allied Forces at SHAPE (Supreme Headquarters Allied Powers of Europe), was being pressured to be the Republican candidate for President. I wanted to see him. In a telephone conversation with his secretary, I remarked half jocularly that I would probably be the only person coming to see the general who would not discuss politics. He invited me to come out.

Andrew Cordier, executive assistant to the Secretary-General, gave me a United Nations car and a driver. We started early in the morning to SHAPE. It was a chilly morning. As we drove through the French countryside, we could see the mists rising from the valley.

General Eisenhower was a great conversationalist and we covered many topics. He opened the political subject himself, by asking whether I thought the United States could go isolationist again. He said that some people who had come over to talk to him had raised this specter. He was referring, of course, without mentioning it, to the fact that some of these people had urged him to secure the Republican nomination from Robert Taft, who was thought to have some isolationist tendencies. I gave him a careful answer. I told him I did not think the country could go isolationist in the way we usually use the word, withdrawing from the world as we did in 1920. Certainly the country could go conservative, retreating from the idealism which was associated with support of the United Nations. I said, "You see what the Senate has done to your friend, Phil Jessup," referring to the fact that the Senate had refused to confirm Jessup as a member of the United States delegation to the third General Assembly.[1]

The general made no comment, but I think he was interested in my views. At that moment his aide interrupted us to say that Sir Winston Churchill was waiting to have lunch with him. I rose immediately, saying, "Won't you let me ask you what I

1. President Truman, not to be outdone, gave Philip C. Jessup an interim appointment anyway, knowing that the Assembly would be over before the Senate resumed.

came for?" We had had such a good time that I hadn't presented him with my mission. I told him that the American
Association for the United Nations was going to hold a conference in Chicago on the subject "United States Responsibility for
World Leadership." I said that we would like very much to have
a message from him. He agreed to send one, and then made a
rather amusing point. He said that when I returned to New
York, I should write him a letter and begin by saying that he had
asked me to write him requesting a statement—otherwise, he
might never see the letter. He was wise in the ways of secretaries, who sometimes keep correspondence from the boss.

The general at that moment had the snap characteristic of
him before he was taken ill. I was not an impressive corporal in
the First World War, but I felt the same exhilaration at General
Pershing's inspection of our outfit in France as I did upon meeting General Eisenhower.

At the third session of the General Assembly in Paris one of
the items on the agenda was the report of the Human Rights
Commission, of which Mrs. Eleanor Roosevelt was chairman.
The delegates to the General Assembly had before them a draft
which represented two years of discussion and deliberation in
meetings of the Commission. It was near midnight on December 10, 1948, when the General Assembly adopted the Universal Declaration of Human Rights, by 48 votes in favor, none
against, and 8 abstentions. Before its adoption, Mrs. Roosevelt
stated that it was first and foremost a declaration of basic principles to serve as a common standard for all nations. It might well
become the Magna Carta for all mankind, she said.

It is appropriate to digress at this point to refer to Mrs. Roosevelt's contribution to the United Nations, not only in the field
of human rights but to the spirit of the organization. In the early
days of the UN she invited members of various delegations and
Secretariat officials to informal receptions, usually on Sunday, at

her cottage in Hyde Park. Frequently she entertained delegates at the request of the State Department.[2]

Mrs. Roosevelt was named a delegate by President Truman to the first session of the General Assembly in London in January 1946. Informed that she would serve on Committee 3, which was concerned with social and humanitarian items, she assumed that the delegation did not want her to deal with political subjects. However, the question of refugees, which had been before Committee 3, became a sharp political issue. The United States and the USSR took opposing views. When the item came to the plenary session, Andrei Vishinsky, head of the USSR delegation, took the floor instead of the Soviet representative on Committee 3. It was unanimously agreed among the U.S. delegation, however, that only Mrs. Roosevelt, who was familiar with the question, could answer him. As she mounted the dais, Senator Vandenberg, who had wondered why she was to be on the delegation, remarked to other delegates, "There goes a great lady, and I take back everything I ever said against her, which was plenty."

With the coming of a Republican administration in 1953, Mrs. Roosevelt knew that she would no longer be appointed to the delegation or serve as a member of the Commission on Human Rights. One day she walked into the office of the American Association for the United Nations and told me that she would like to serve as a volunteer. I was, of course, both surprised and delighted. Later she asked me to take her letter of resignation

2. The State Department occasionally gave her a rigid schedule for the guests. The late Emperor Haile Selassie was her guest one time; his schedule called for a thirty-minute rest period. At a certain time, Mrs. Roosevelt reminded His Majesty that he should retire to another room for this period. But a little later she found the emperor enjoying himself watching television with the grandchildren; again she reminded him that he was supposed to rest. He assured her that he had only wanted a thirty-minute rest so that he could take off his shoes. This he had done and was enjoying himself in his stocking feet.

to John Foster Dulles, who was helping to set up the régime for the new administration. I presented her letter to Mr. Dulles and told him that Mrs. Roosevelt was going to serve the United Nations through the American Association for the United Nations. Foster said he thought we were very lucky to have her service but that we must be careful that the Association not be known as a Democratic body.

It would be impossible adequately to describe what Mrs. Roosevelt meant to the Association and to those of us who were privileged to be her colleagues in the nine years that she worked with us. Working day by day at the office, traveling through the long nights to arrive at early morning field meetings, speaking before mass audiences, Mrs. Roosevelt always translated the ideals of support for the United Nations into the need for growing chapter activities and for an increase in members.

President Truman, one of the founders of the United Nations, was particularly interested in its economic programs. In his inaugural address of January 20, 1949, he outlined four major programs for peace and freedom which his administration would emphasize. He stressed:

First. We will continue to give unfaltering support to the United Nations and related agencies, and we will continue to search for ways to strengthen their authority and increase their effectiveness. . . .

Second. We will continue our programs for world economic recovery. . . .

Third. We will strengthen freedom-loving nations against the dangers of aggression. . . .

Fourth. We must embark on a bold new program for making the benefits of our scientific advances and industrial progress available for the improvement and growth of underdeveloped areas.

More than half the people of the world are living in conditions approaching misery. Their food is inadequate. They are victims of disease. Their economic life is primitive and stagnant. Their poverty is a handicap and a threat both to them and to more prosperous areas.

For the first time in history humanity possesses the knowledge and the skill to relieve the suffering of these people.

The fourth and last point became known as the Point Four Program. It served as an inspiration for many of the programs for world economic development then being considered in the UN, and represented the moral leadership of the United States at its best.

One of the greatest speeches delivered in the United Nations General Assembly was the address which President John F. Kennedy delivered in September 1961. The Secretary-General, Dag Hammarskjold, and several of his aides, en route to the Belgian Congo, had just been killed in a mysterious plane crash. At that tragic moment President Kennedy attempted to lift the world above the current gloom and point the way to positive steps to peace. He addressed himself to outer space; he suggested that the Assembly adopt a resolution that the celestial bodies not be subject to appropriation. Following his speech the Assembly passed a resolution forbidding the annexation of celestial bodies. One year later, in the spirit of President Kennedy's speech, the Assembly resolved that no spaceship could carry atomic weapons.

President Kennedy did not close his speech with the proposal about the celestial bodies. He proposed that the nations engage in a Decade of Development for the less developed parts of the world. In other words, while man in his imagination must deal with the heavens, he must also tend to the practical things on earth. While what President Kennedy proposed could not be accomplished in a decade, it began a broad program of assistance for the developing world.

In the mid-1960s, occurred the tragedy of massive United

States involvement in Vietnam. Beginning with a few thousand advisers, the American involvement grew until this country had 550,000 troops in that country. Enormous numbers on both sides were killed and vast areas in North and South Vietnam devastated. When it was finally agreed that the United States should pull out its troops, this was not accomplished until after Cambodia, too, had been bombed. The war in Vietnam, unlike the Korean conflict, was waged without authority from the United Nations. Thus quickly can the moral position of a nation erode.

Since Vietnam, the United States has made some important contributions in some of the conferences that have been held, but has not given the consistent leadership to the world organization that it did in the past. The government has seemed to emphasize national defense above everything else. No effort has been made to check arms sales; rather, they have been encouraged. It has seemed that the United States has played an important role in particular conferences only when it suited our immediate self-interest to do so. The General Assembly, instead of evolving toward a parliament of nations, as it might have done with U.S. leadership, has become a quarrelsome body which for the moment seems satisfied to pass meaningless resolutions, many directed at the United States. There has been no vision for the future.

Disappointment in the United States as a moral leader pervades the hearts of many statesmen. I recently talked with a representative of a small state who had been in San Francisco and had taken a leading part in drafting the Charter. He has attended every General Assembly meeting and at times has made important contributions. He has had a great affection for this country and still maintains it. But now, in reviewing this country's position, he said to me in sorrow: "The American dream is fading."

The United Nations is now almost universal, and its machinery has grown so that it touches every phase of human existence. The decline of the empires and the fragmentation of the liberated colonial areas has resulted in a membership of over 140; a new parliamentary expression must evolve to accommodate the mini-states. For three years over 100 nations have attended sessions of the Law of the Sea Conference. If successful, the Conference will establish a legal régime for the 70 percent of the earth's surface which is now the high seas.

New York remains the political capital of the organization, but Geneva has become an amazing center of UN activity; it is filled with new buildings, some of them alongside the old League of Nations buildings, which are now being enlarged. The International Atomic Energy Agency has its headquarters in Vienna and the UN Environment Program has its in Nairobi. This vast, growing machinery could disintegrate unless it is held together by a renewed sense of moral unity.

The spaceships of the Soviet Union and the United States have traveled millions of miles in an effort to explore our solar system. Because of United Nations resolutions, citizens of earth need have no fear that death might be rained upon them from outer space. On Christmas Eve in 1968 astronauts Borman, Lovell, and Anders inspired millions who were listening to their conversations. All the world was aware of our own earth, so fragile in the vast emptiness of space. Borman read the story of the Creation from the King James Version of the Bible: "In the beginning, God created the heaven and the earth . . ." Countless people heard the age-old story heralded from the skies by the newest methods of transmission. Some were aware that it would be translated into many languages. Listeners to the story, retold in different lands, would be reminded of their own story of creation as handed down by their elders. Faith and confidence in human endeavor rose with the knowledge of the wonders human beings could bring about.

This is the kind of moral inspiration that is needed as we face the future. More than 140 nations have become members of the United Nations, but where can be found the statesmen with the daring and the world vision to remind these nations of their obligations under the Charter? A new sense of moral urgency is needed if peace is to be achieved. Whence it will come, no one knows. But Americans hope that once again we may see the United States occupy a position of moral leadership in the United Nations. And there are now in the new administration indications that American leadership is being renewed.

Acknowledgments

During the long years between the rejection of the League of Nations Convenant in 1920 and the entrance of the United States into the United Nations in 1945, countless people both here and abroad have had an influence on my thinking. There come to my mind the old Chapters of the League of Nations Association scattered throughout the country, and of the officials of the League of Nations at Geneva.

It is with sadness that I recall the many people who picked up the wreckage of American foreign policy in 1920 and carried it forward to 1945, and the creation of the United Nations. Unfortunately there is not space to mention them all. Neither can I mention all my contemporaries particularly in the American Association for the United Nations and the Commission to Study the Organization of Peace, through which many people campaigned for the creation of the United Nations and our entrance into it.

I will limit myself to those who actively took part in helping me with the preparation of this manuscript. Others not mentioned, some of them important and influential names, will be missing but I trust they will understand that they are included in this message of thanks and appreciation. Without their assistance and encouragement the book would not have been possible.

For reading the manuscript and for their thoughtful suggestions and encouragement, I am grateful to Clarence A. Berdahl; Benjamin V. Cohen; Norman Cousins; James Frederick Green; Donald Szantho Harrington; Arthur N. Holcombe; Estelle Linzer; Wallace McClure; Charles L. Marburg; Hugh Moore; Raymond D. Nasher; Margaret Olson; Leslie Paffrath; Louis B. Sohn; Obert C. Tanner; Richard R. Wood; Mr. and Mrs. Clarence Wynd; and, for reviewing and checking certain passages, to General Carlos Romulo, and to George W. Taylor, Jr., representing the Rockefeller family.

Index

303